Development Centre Studies



# Securing Livelihoods for All

## FORESIGHT FOR ACTION

OECD DEVELOPMENT CENTRE

**Please cite this publication as:**
OECD (2015), *Securing Livelihoods for All: Foresight for Action*, Development Centre Studies, OECD Publishing, Paris.
*http://dx.doi.org/10.1787/9789264231894-en*

ISBN 978-92-64-23174-0 (print)
ISBN 978-92-64-23189-4 (PDF)

Series: Development Centre Studies
ISSN 1563-4302 (print)
ISSN 1990-0295 (online)



**Photo credits:** Cover © OECD Development Centre.

Corrigenda to OECD publications may be found on line at: *www.oecd.org/about/publishing/corrigenda.htm*.

# Foreword

Human livelihoods face grave threats, from demographic change to financial crises to climate change. Yet, people around the world are better educated and more connected than ever, offering new opportunities to billions. This report is motivated by two daunting challenges. The first is to develop inclusive economies that allow the poorest and most vulnerable to access those opportunities. The second is to create secure livelihoods that allow individuals, families, and communities to not just survive but thrive in the face of these threats.

This work originated from a four-day workshop held at The Rockefeller Foundation's Bellagio Center in August 2014. An exceptional group of entrepreneurs, scholars, policymakers, and non-profit leaders gathered to discuss the future of livelihoods. As part of their conversation, they developed some of the creative new concepts for securing livelihoods highlighted in this report. The workshop was co-organised by the Economist Intelligence Unit and the OECD Development Centre as part of The Rockefeller Foundation's Visionaries Unbound series.

This work contributes to the central mission of the Development Centre, which is to help developing countries and emerging economies find innovative solutions that promote sustainable growth while reducing poverty and improving people's lives. The Centre brings its expertise in multi-dimensional analysis as well as its long history of tracking the trends in the global economy that have a direct or indirect impact on people's livelihoods.

In this report, which was supported by The Rockefeller Foundation, the Development Centre takes the ideas explored in the workshop in Bellagio and extends them in important, novel ways. The authors present new data on how people around the world think about their livelihoods and on the trends that will shape livelihoods in the future. They challenge us to think deeply about the future with a set of scenarios that are provocative, yet grounded in the OECD's research. Finally, they offer new ideas for the ways that innovations in diverse fields might be brought together to promote inclusive economies and more resilient livelihoods for poor and vulnerable people. This wide-ranging exploration is intended as a call to action to help individuals and organisations envision bold steps toward a future in which all people have secure livelihoods.

| Mario Pezzini | John Irons | Mamadou Biteye |
|---|---|---|
| Director | Managing Director | Managing Director |
| OECD Development Centre | The Rockefeller Foundation | The Rockefeller Foundation |

# ACKNOWLEDGEMENTS

*Securing Livelihoods for All: Foresight for Action* was written by a team of the OECD Development Centre, under the supervision of Carl Dahlman, Head of Global Research and of Thematic Division and the direction of Mario Pezzini, Director. The report was drafted by Jean-Eric Aubert, Senior Consultant, Carl Dahlman, Martin Wermelinger, Economist at the Centre, and Eriko Suzuta, Consultant.

The report is the result of a collaboration between the OECD Development Centre and The Rockefeller Foundation, under the guidance of Bathylle Missika, Acting Head of Policy Dialogue Division, OECD Development Centre. Project co-ordination and additional inputs were provided by Vanessa Fines, Martha Baxter and Federico Recalde-Ovelar. Vararat Atisophon provided statistical assistance and Myriam Andrieux provided administrative support. Fiona Hinchcliffe and Clare Rogers edited the report and the OECD Development Centre's publications team turned the draft into a publication. The cover was designed by Aida Buendia.

The development of the livelihood scenarios featured in the book was led by Angela Wilkinson, Strategic Foresight Counsellor to the OECD Secretary-General, and Betty-Sue Flowers, Professor Emeritus, University of Texas at Austin, who also provided substantial contributions to the report. Jean-Francois Rischard provided text on the financial risks and the agricultural revolution.

This study is an outcome of The Rockefeller Foundation's "Visionaries Unbound" event series and has benefited from funding from The Rockefeller Foundation and the commitment of its team, in particular Claudia Juech, Associate Vice-President and Managing Director for Strategic Research, Kevin O'Neil, Associate Director of Strategic Research, and Robert Garris, former Managing Director.

The work draws on the creative new concepts for securing livelihoods developed by participants at a four-day workshop held at The Rockefeller Foundation's Bellagio Center in August 2014, co-organised by The Rockefeller Foundation, the OECD Development Centre, and the Economist Intelligence Unit. Thanks go to the participants: Janki Andharia, Professor, Tata Institute of Social Sciences, Jean Eric Aubert, Senior Consultant, OECD Development Centre, Sara Bernstein, Executive Director, Centre for Development and Enterprise, Mamadou Biteye, Managing Director, The Rockefeller Foundation, Carl Dahlman, Head of Global Research, OECD Development Centre, Yang Du, Professor, Institute of Population and Labour Economics, Chinese Academy of Sciences, Aidan Eyakuze, Associate Regional Director, Society for International Development, Betty Sue Flowers, Professor Emeritus, University of Texas at Austin, Robert Garris, Managing Director, The Rockefeller Foundation, Ashar Hasan, Founder and Chief Executive Officer, Naya Jeevan, John Irons, Managing Director, The Rockefeller Foundation, Benyamin Lakitan, Senior Advisor, Ministry of Research and Technology, Indonesia, Ahmadou Mbaye, Professor, University Cheikh Anta Diop

Economics, Busisiwe Ntuli, Director, Technology for Sustainable Livelihoods, Department of Science and Technology, South Africa, Kevin O'Neil, Associate Director, The Rockefeller Foundation, Jean-François Rischard, Former Vice President, World Bank, Luis Fernando Sanabria, General Manager, Fundación Paraguaya, Mauricio Santa Maria, former Minister of Health and Social Protection, Colombia, Rachel Slater, Head of Programme, Social Protection, Overseas Development Institute, Conal Smith, Section Head, Well-being/Household Conditions, OECD Statistics Directorate, Eriko Suzuta, Consultant, OECD Development Centre, Imraan Valodia, Dean, Faculty of Commerce, Law and Management, University of Witwatersrand, Johannesburg, Vijay Vaitheeswaran, China Business and Finance Editor, The Economist, Vivek Wadhwa, Fellow, Stanford University Law School, Angela Wilkinson, Strategic Foresight Counsellor, OECD, Adrian Woolridge, Management Editor, The Economist, Tae Yoo, Senior Vice President, Cisco Systems.

The authors are grateful to many OECD colleagues for their participation in workshops and presentations and comments on drafts: Federico Bonaglia, Counsellor, Development Centre, Tracey Burns, Analyst, Directorate for Education and Skills, Anthony Cox, Deputy Director, Environment Directorate, Deirdre Culley, Junior Policy Analyst, Development Centre, Ebba Dohlman, Senior Advisor to the Secretary-General, Nicola Harrington, Deputy Director, Development Centre, Hildegard Lingnau, Senior Counsellor, Development Co-operation Directorate, William Hynes, Senior Economist in the New Approaches to Economic Challenges Unit in the Secretary General's Office, Robin Ogilvy, Advisor to the Secretary-General, Mauro Pisu, Senior Economist, Economics Directorate, Monika Queisser, Head of Social Policy Division, Directorate for Employment, Labour and Social Affairs, Jan Rielaender, Head of Multi-dimensional Country Reviews, Development Centre, Vicente Ruiz, Policy Analyst, Development Centre, Conal Smith, Head of Section, Statistics Directorate, Henri-Bernard Solignac-Lecomte, Head of Europe, Middle East and Africa, Development Centre and Martin von Lampe, Senior Agricultural Policy Analyst, Trade and Agriculture Directorate.

Special thanks also to Kevin O'Neil from The Rockefeller Foundation who provided comments to various drafts of the book.

# *Table of contents*

### Tables



### Figures

### Boxes

# Executive summary

The world has made good progress in improving global livelihoods. More than two billion people emerged from extreme poverty over the last four decades, unskilled workers have seen real increases in their wages, life expectancy has improved, and literacy is more widespread than ever.

Despite these significant improvements, many people remain vulnerable. Furthermore, without action to secure livelihoods, a number of emerging trends threaten to undo much of the improvement made in recent decades. The recent economic and financial crisis already destabilised many people's livelihoods.

This study outlines the status of livelihoods today, and explores emerging trends in the economy, technology, demography, environment, security and governance which could impact livelihoods in the future. It asks how we can build secure livelihoods; how societies will adapt to the coming challenges; and whether there are any innovation opportunities – whether technological or social – that can be exploited?

The considerable livelihood challenges which lie ahead are opportunities for innovation, for seeing the future differently and for bold experiments to move beyond surviving to thriving. It is up to all relevant players – international, national, local and individual – to seize these opportunities.

## Key findings

- Overall economic growth is accompanied by two worrying global trends: a considerable increase in disparity both among and within most countries, and a slowdown in job creation.
- Job creation drives livelihood improvements. The reduction of global extreme poverty over the last decades was made possible by the creation of millions of new productive jobs, particularly in the developing world.
- Yet growth in GDP is not being matched by a rise in employment, leading to the phenomenon of "jobless growth" in almost all countries. This trend has been especially pronounced since the 2000s, reflecting the unemployment problems experienced by a number of countries, as well as significant productivity and technology innovations that release people from repetitive tasks.
- Global growth remains slow and financial fragilities continue. The next major economic shocks may well come from the emerging countries, whose growing corporate sector has benefited from massive lending by the global financial system and whose growth is likely to slow in the coming decades.
- The world is seeing some massive demographic transitions. Ageing populations in most high and middle-income countries are incurring serious pension and health

care costs, while the explosion in young people in most low-income countries will become a source of major stresses if they cannot be provided with enough jobs.

- Environmental degradation will affect us all. The number of natural disasters and extreme weather events has considerably increased over the last three decades and is expected to increase further. Human-induced climate change and related effects are going to significantly disturb living conditions in most parts of the planet.
- Technology appears potentially as the main game changer. With the right policies in place, it can be a source of new activities, improvements in living conditions, and solutions to environment issues. However, it can also be a cause of rising unemployment through the automation and computerisation of labour-intensive jobs.
- Security and peace are essential for livelihoods, yet, 1.5 billion people across the world (about one-fifth of the world's population) live in countries affected by conflict.
- In face of these challenges, governments are unevenly equipped. In a number of high and middle-income countries, trust in governments has fallen, policies are affected by "short-term" views and vested interests, while many states are heavily in debt. In many low-income countries, persistent governance issues limit capacity for action.

## Key recommendations

Addressing these challenges and opportunities requires bold ideas and policy experimentation. There are a number of actions at the global, national and local levels which could help secure livelihoods.

At the **global or multi-national level**, action will be needed on many fronts:

- Act urgently to reach a global agreement for tackling climate change.
- Stabilise the global financial system by strengthening framework conditions; avoiding unhealthy financial activities; and increasing co-ordination and mobility of financial resources among the central banks and international financial institutions.
- Use tax reforms to achieve shared prosperity.
- Develop an inclusive approach to international trade that allows developing countries time for new industries and services to develop and help sustain livelihoods.
- Manage migration better to harness its powerful force for better livelihoods.
- Strengthen responses to disasters and pandemics through more funding and capacity building and greater use of global public partnerships to tackle issues.
- Strengthen water sharing agreements to avert conflict in the developing world in a context of increasing drought.
- Tackle increasing cyber insecurity through an international cyber police force.

- Set up an international research and development agency to promote innovation focused on global "public goods" such as climate, health and the needs of the extremely poor.

At the **national level**, governments can act as a back-stop and enabler of creative and regenerative societies:

- Make education inclusive and livelihood-focused, with a myriad of pathways for skill acquisition and the opportunity for lifelong learning.
- Promote livelihood portfolios made up of part-time work, paid training, and unemployment benefits to help individuals cope with fluid job situations.
- Step up social protection through cost-sharing with the private sector and individuals to share some of the burden.
- Establish a guaranteed minimum income for all in developed countries.
- Use cash transfer programmes in developing countries linked to conditions such as school attendance or immunisation.
- Invest in children and young people, for example by introducing a universal self-investment grant for young people.
- Put green growth at the heart of economies to enhance resilience, reduce emissions, and boost jobs and growth at the same time.

A number of **local initiatives** could also support livelihoods:

- Support a vibrant shared local economy in which individuals can survive through a patchwork of entrepreneurial and social initiatives involving exchanges, barters and virtual service marketplaces.
- Enable initiatives for micro-finance, peer-to-peer lending, and social impact investments which can combat unemployment, and introduce local currencies to cushion people from the turbulences and crises inherent to the globalised financial system.
- Build green and resilient cities to address the issue of economic activity and environmental sustainability at the same time.

# Chapter 1
# Why we need bold action to secure livelihoods

*The world has made good progress in improving global livelihoods; witnessing more than two billion people emerge from extreme poverty over the last four decades, real increases in wages for unskilled workers, better life expectancy, greater gender equality and more widespread literacy. However, a number of daunting challenges threaten to undo this progress, particularly on the demographic and environmental fronts. This chapter provides an overview to the entire book. It outlines the status of livelihoods today and enumerates the main emerging trends which will affect livelihoods in the near future. It envisages a range of possible future scenarios for livelihoods, whose positive or negative outcomes depend on how several emerging challenges are dealt with. It concludes with a wealth of ideas for global, national and local action that hold significant promise for securing resilient and inclusive livelihoods for all.*

## Progress on livelihoods: the end of an era?

Mankind has experienced more than two centuries of almost continuous progress since the Industrial Revolution. The world average life expectancy at birth has increased from below 30 years in the 1880s to almost 70 years in the 2000s (Figure 1.1).[1] In recent decades billions of people have been lifted out of poverty. However, a serious slowdown has occurred with the recent global financial and economic crisis. Other daunting challenges also threaten the future of livelihoods, particularly on the demographic and environmental fronts. How will societies adapt to such challenges? Are there any innovation opportunities – whether technological or social – that can be exploited? More generally, how can we build secure livelihoods? These are the types of questions explored in this book, which builds on discussions during a recent workshop in Bellagio, Italy (Box 1.1). This overview chapter summarises the book's main findings and key messages.

**Box 1.1. Secure Livelihoods: Visions of a Better Future**

To address the looming crisis in livelihoods, and at a time when the international community is taking stock of progress to achieve the Millennium Development Goals (MDGs) and discussing the contours of the post-2015 development framework, The Rockefeller Foundation,[1] the OECD Development Centre[2] and the Economist Intelligence Unit (EIU), supported by The Rockefeller Foundation, organised a conference on "Securing Livelihoods" in August 2014 at the foundation's Bellagio Centre (Italy). Thought leaders from various sectors, disciplines and types of organisations confronted, discussed and generated scenarios on the future means people will dispose of to secure their life's necessities or "livelihoods".

The discussions at Bellagio were wide-ranging and generated many innovative ideas. The EIU moderated the conference and produced a summary of the discussions: *Secure Livelihoods, Visions of a Better Future* (The Rockefeller Foundation, 2014). The OECD Development Centre went on to provide a baseline of the state of livelihoods in the world, develop trends likely to affect livelihoods in the next 15 to 20 years, explore several possible scenarios for the future, and expand on some of the ideas discussed at Bellagio, as well as to highlight some of the global issues affecting livelihoods.

This publication is the outcome of that work, and draws on inputs from the Bellagio workshop, as well as research from the OECD and other organisations (e.g. the *UNDP Human Development Report 2014: Sustaining Human Progress*).

1. The work of The Rockefeller Foundation is deeply rooted in the idea of improving livelihoods, or bolstering the means by which people support themselves, because it believes good livelihoods underpin human progress.

2. The OECD's Development Centre occupies a unique place within the OECD and in the international community. It is a forum where countries come to share their experience of economic and social development policies. The centre contributes expert analysis to the development policy debate. The objective is to help decision makers find policy solutions to stimulate growth and improve living conditions in developing and emerging economies.

## The outlook for livelihoods is fragile

Despite significant recent improvements in well-being, particularly in the areas of income and basic needs, many people remain vulnerable. Without action to build resilient and inclusive global livelihoods, emerging trends in the economy, technology, demography, environment, security and governance could undo much of the progress made to date.

Looking to the future (five years ahead) and compared to their past (five years before) and present situation, people around the world provide interesting insights (Figure 1.2). In all middle and low-income countries, people generally think that the future will be better than the past or the present. The greatest optimism is in the East Asia-Pacific region. People in high-income countries (apart from the Gulf states and the Russian Federation) see their future prospects of life in general only marginally better than the past or present.

**Figure 1.1. Life expectancy has increased sharply around the world during the last 200 years**

Life expectancy at birth (years, decadal averages): 1820s-2000s

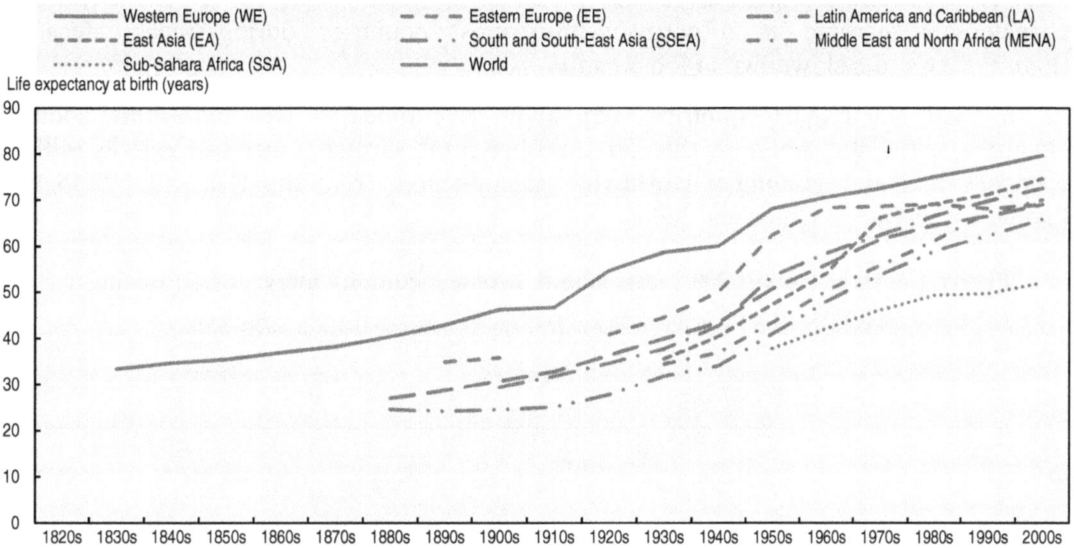


*Source*: van Zanden, J.L. et al. (eds.) (2014), *How Was Life? Global Well-being since 1820*, OECD Publishing, Paris, http://dx.doi.org/10.1787/9789264214262-en.

**Figure 1.2. Thriving, struggling or suffering? Regional perceptions of life**

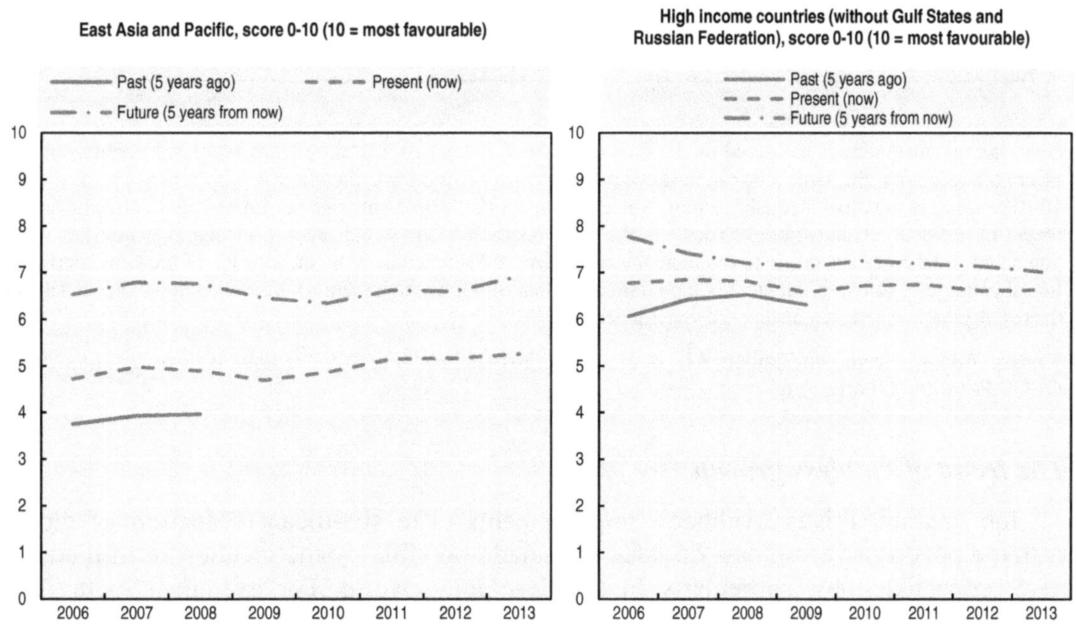


*Notes:* The regions correspond to the 6 developing regions as defined by the World Bank. The category of high income countries does not include the Russian Federation or the Gulf states (Bahrain, Kuwait, Oman, Qatar, Saudi Arabia, and UAE). The index is weighted using the Gallup country weights for each observation and countries' population to calculate regional averages. For more, see Chapter 2, Box 2.2 and Annex 2.A1.

*Source*: Adapted from Gallup (n.d.), Gallup World Poll, Gallup Analytics, Gallup Inc., Washington DC, www.gallup.com/services/170945/world-poll.aspx (accessed 19 January 2015).

### *Economic growth is not benefitting everyone*

Overall economic growth is accompanied by two worrying global trends: a considerable increase in disparity within most countries during recent decades (Figure 1.3), and a slowdown in job creation.

In 1820, the richest countries were about five times as wealthy as the poorest countries; today, they are more than 50 times better off. Growing income disparity within countries is also becoming a worldwide phenomenon, from the UK and US to the People's Republic of China and India.

**Figure 1.3. Over the last 200 years, global income inequality increased significantly**

World income inequality (Gini index, values between 0-100): 1820-2000

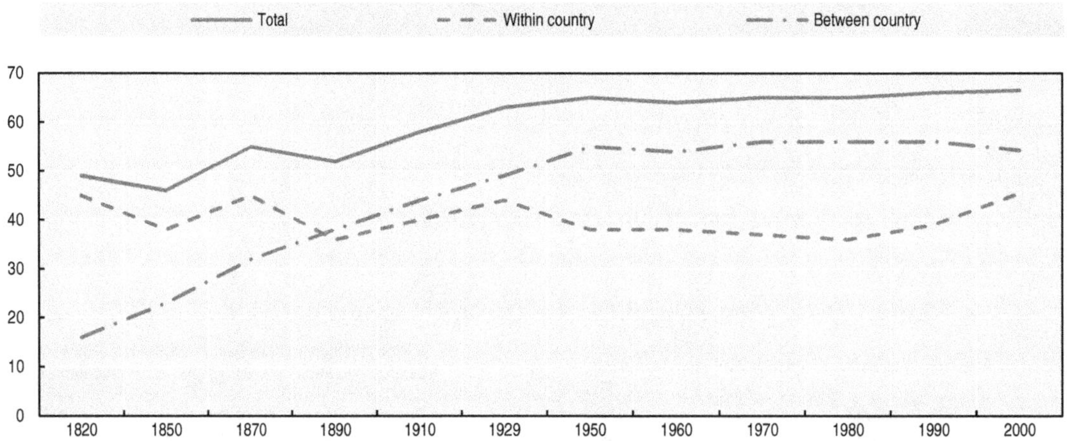


*Note:* Income inequality is measured by the Gini coefficient. A Gini coefficient of zero expresses perfect equality, where all values are the same (for example, where everyone has the same income). A Gini coefficient of one (or 100%) expresses maximal inequality among values (for example, where only one person has all the income and all others have none). In the figure, "Total" is the Gini coefficient for world income inequality when the world population is taken as one group to calculate the coefficient. "Within country" is the average of the Gini coefficient for all countries. "Between country" is the Gini coefficient of the average incomes in each country. For details on the country sample and data quality see van Zanden (2014).

*Source:* Adapted from van Zanden, J.L. et al. (eds.) (2014), *How Was Life? Global Well-being since 1820,* OECD Publishing, Paris, http://dx.doi.org/10.1787/9789264214262-en.

### *The trend of "jobless growth"*

Job creation drives livelihood improvements. The significant reduction of global extreme poverty over the last decades was made possible by the creation of millions of new productive jobs, particularly in the developing world. For example, South Asia created on average 8.5 million new jobs every year between 2009 and 2014. Yet growth in GDP is not being matched by a rise in employment, leading to the phenomenon of "jobless growth" in almost all countries, including the major OECD economies, the BRIICS (Brazil, Russia, India, Indonesia, China and South Africa) and certain low-income countries, such as Bangladesh and Ghana (Figure 1.4). This trend has been especially pronounced since the 2000s, reflecting the unemployment problems experienced by a number of countries, as well as significant productivity and technology innovations that release people from repetitive tasks. In addition, working conditions and job security remain precarious for many, especially women.

**Figure 1.4. Jobless growth: A new normal around the world?**

Indexed GDP (constant 2005 USD), total employment and total labour force, 1991=100 (LHS); labour force participation rate, in % of total population ages 15-64 (RHS)

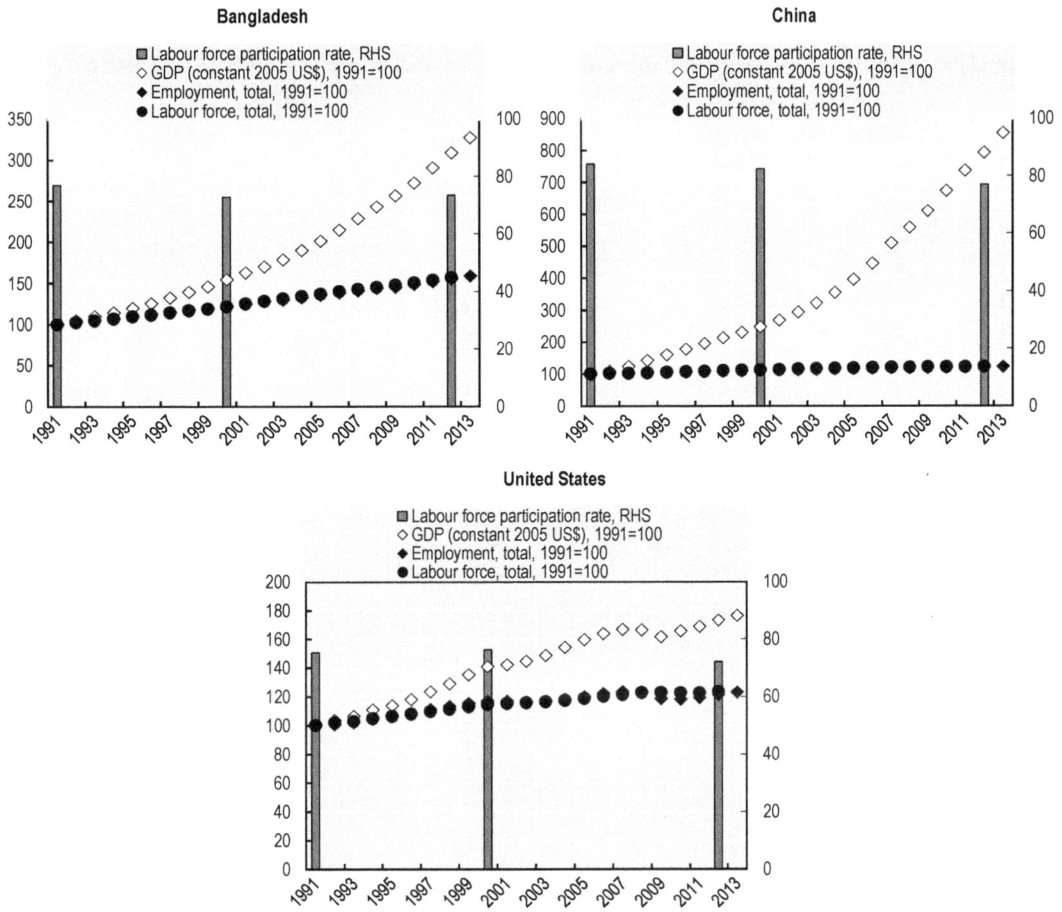


*Notes:* The labour force is the actual number of people available for work. The labour force of a country includes both the employed and the unemployed (that is those looking for a job). RHS means right-hand side axis. LHS means left-hand side axis.

*Source:* World Bank (2014), *World Development Indicators* (database), http://data.worldbank.org/data-catalog/world-development-indicators and ILO (2014), *Global Employment Trends 2014* (data sets), www.ilo.org/global/research/global-reports/global-employment-trends/2014/WCMS_234879/lang--en/index.htm.

## *The global economy remains vulnerable*

Global growth remains slow and financial fragilities continue. The next major economic shocks may well come from the emerging countries, whose growing corporate sector has benefitted from massive lending by the global financial system and whose growth is likely to slow in the coming decades. For example, the bursting of a financial bubble in China could trigger a global crisis.

## *Population dynamics are shifting*

The world is seeing some massive demographic transitions. Ageing populations in most high and middle-income countries are incurring serious pension and health care costs, while the explosion in young people in most low-income countries will become a source of major stresses if they cannot be provided with enough jobs (Figure 1.5). Sub-Saharan Africa's labour force is growing by about 8 million people a year; South Asia's by 12 million a year. How will these enormous contingents of young people be absorbed into the economy? What will be the consequences if they are not? Chronic poverty and unemployment among young people tend to lead to social revolts, as the Arab revolutions of 2011 demonstrated.

**Figure 1.5. The gap is growing between the number of jobs and the working-age population, 1991-2030**

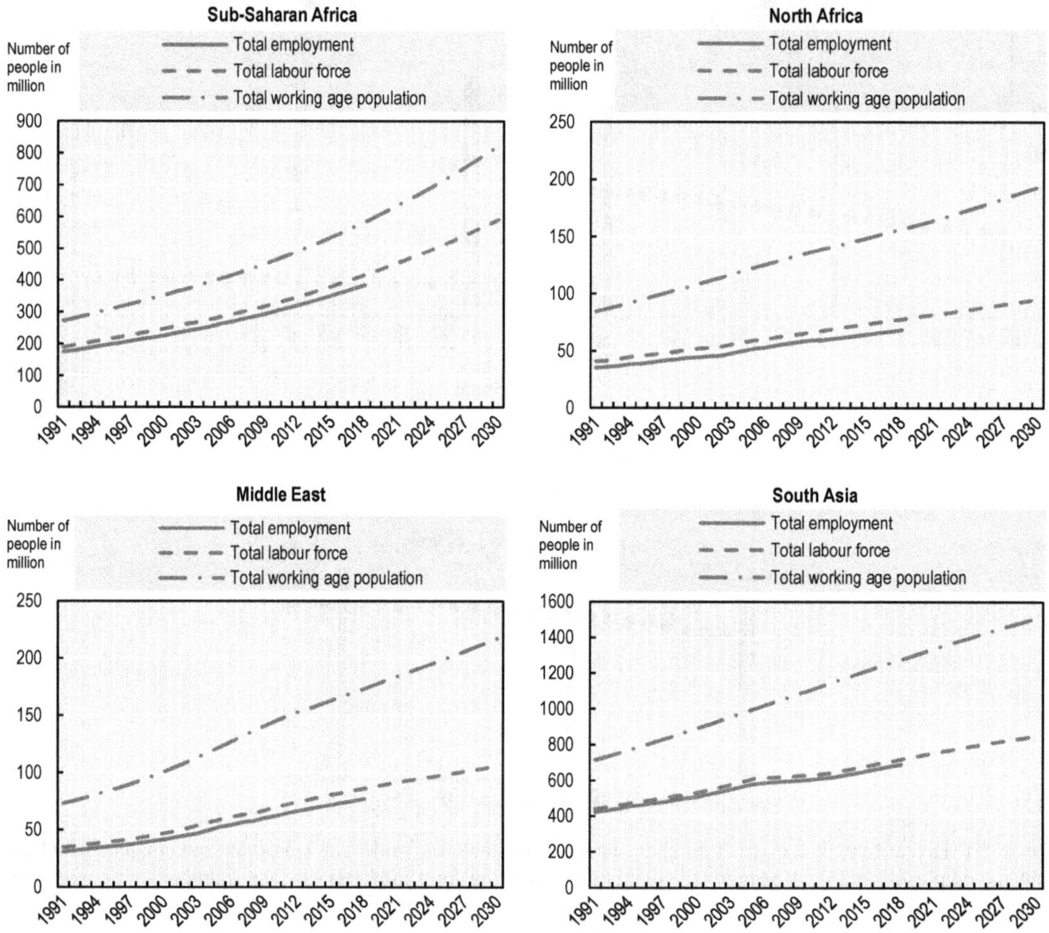


*Note:* Projections start in 2014. The labour force is the actual number of people available for work. The labour force of a country includes both the employed and the unemployed (that is those looking for a job).

*Source:* Adapted from ILO (2014), *Global Employment Trends 2014* (data sets), www.ilo.org/global/research/global-reports/global-employment-trends/2014/WCMS_234879/lang--en/index.htm.

## *Environmental degradation will affect us all*

There is a clear negative correlation between growth in GDP per capita and the quality of the environment. We are living in a world of environmental co-dependencies in which energy, water, food, climate, and other trends are closely linked (Oxford Martin School, 2013). When we consider these trends combined, the future prospects are alarming. The number of natural disasters and extreme weather events has considerably increased over the last three decades (Figure 1.6) and is expected to increase further. Human-induced climate change and related effects are going to significantly disturb living conditions in most parts of the planet, with an increase in the frequency and severity of droughts, floods and extreme weather events. Left unchecked, the impact on economic growth is predicted to be severe.

**Figure 1.6. The increasing incidence of droughts, 1975-2039**

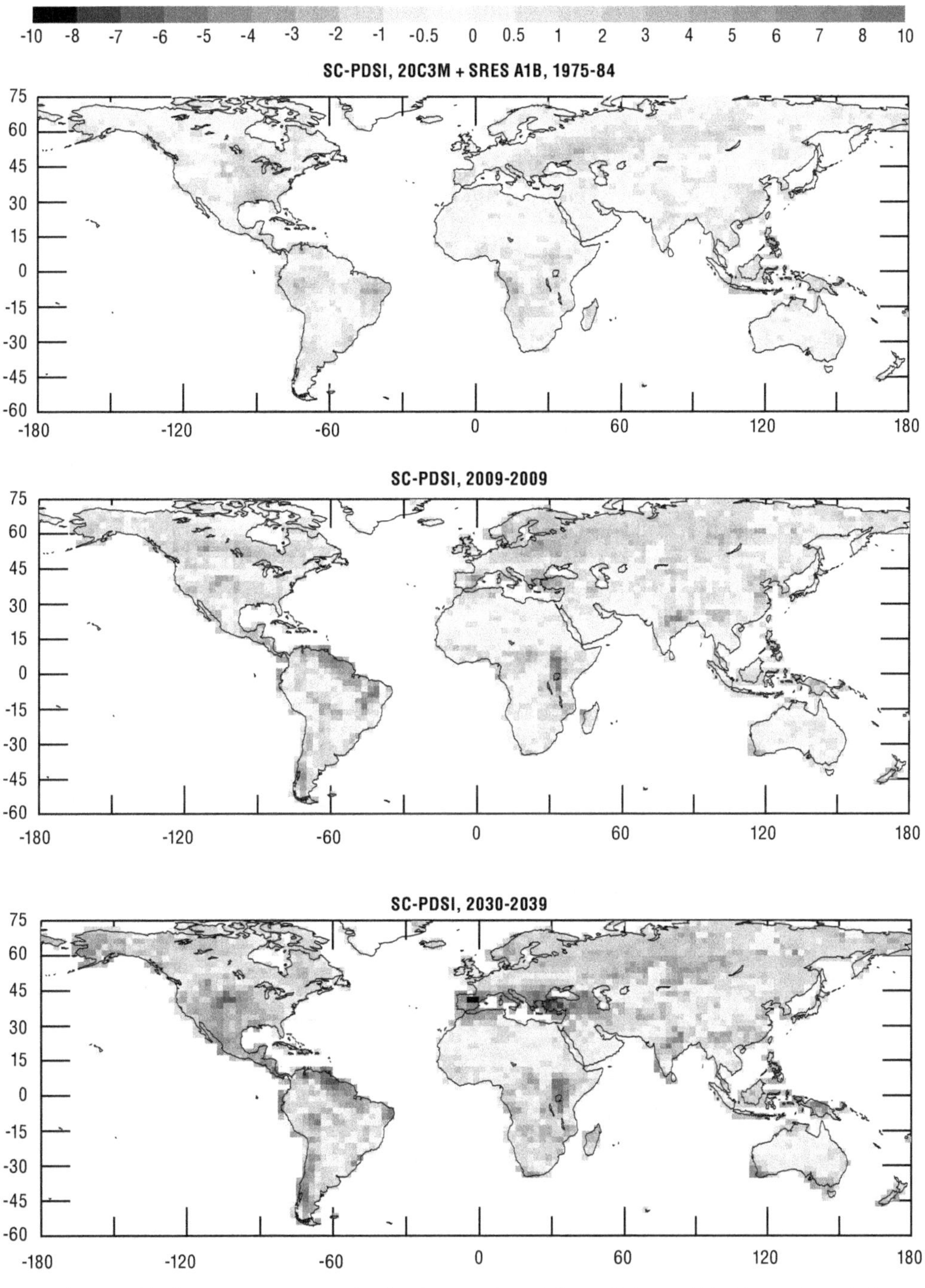


*Notes*: Grey to black areas are extremely dry (severe drought) conditions while blue colours indicate wet areas relative to the 1950–1979 mean. Figures are based on Palmer Drought Severity Index. For technical details on the calculations see Dai (2011). More recent (forthcoming) calculations using a revised method yielded similar drought change patterns but with substantially reduced magnitude.

*Source*: Dai, A. (2011), "Drought under global warming: A review", *WIREs Climate Change*, John Wiley & Sons, New Jersey, Vol 2, pp. 45-65, www.cgd.ucar.edu/cas/adai/papers/Dai-drought_WIRES2010.pdf.

One of the most problematic climate change impacts in the coming decades will probably be the multiplication of droughts. Droughts contribute to higher food prices, famine and social unrest, with strong destabilising effects for the countries involved. To feed the world in 2050, food production may need to rise by some 70%. This may require 50% more water – which will be a challenge, given the changes to precipitation incurred through climate change. Furthermore, 40% of arable land is already degraded to some degree, a problem that will be exacerbated by global warming (Oxford Martin School, 2013). Other emerging environmental challenges include air and water pollution and loss of biodiversity.

### *Technology is both threat and opportunity*

Technology appears potentially as the main game changer. The IT revolution in its most recent developments, notably social media and the "Internet of things", provides opportunities for new production and consumption patterns, and collaborative forms of economy that are more socially and environmentally oriented. With the right policies in place, it can be a source of new activities, improvements in living conditions, and solutions to environment issues. However, it can also be a cause of rising unemployment through the automation and computerisation of labour-intensive jobs. It increases the risk of major man-made accidents; the development and use of weapons of massive destruction; and contributes to cybercrime, the possibility of cyber-attacks or even cyber war.

### *Insecurity and conflict have far-reaching consequences*

Poor livelihood conditions threaten insecurity and insecurity undermines livelihoods. Security and peace are essential for livelihoods. Yet, 1.5 billion people across the world (about one-fifth of the world's population) live in countries affected by conflict. Persistent conflicts in some low-income countries have considerable negative impacts on development, as shown by the strong rise of poverty in such countries (Figure 1.7).

**Figure 1.7. The poverty gap is widening between peaceful and conflict-ridden countries**

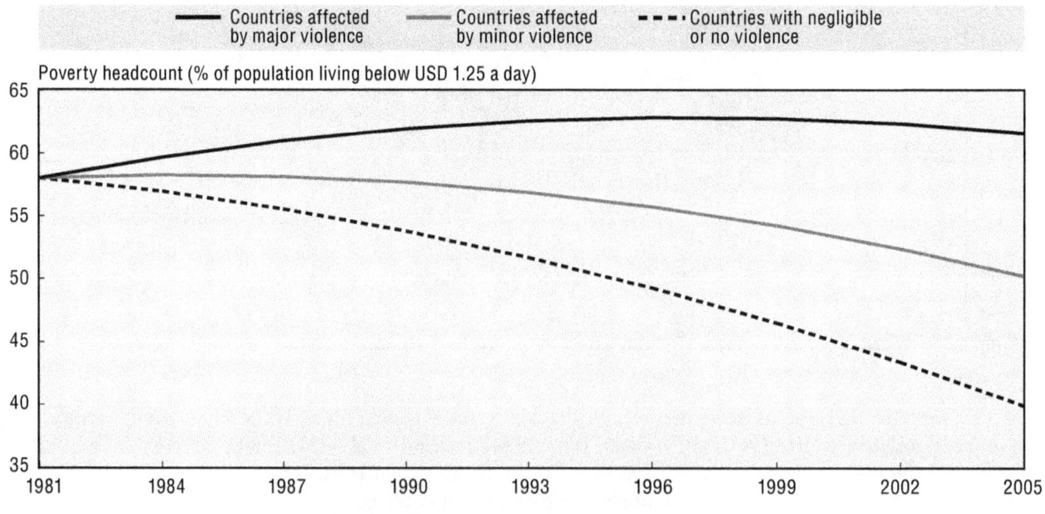


*Note:* Poverty is defined by people living at less than USD 1.25 per day.

*Source:* World Bank (2011), *World Development Report 2011: Conflict, Security and Development*, The World Bank Group, Washington DC, http://siteresources.worldbank.org/INTWDRS/Resources/WDR2011_Full_Text.pdf.

### *Governments are ill-equipped to meet the livelihood challenge*

In the face of these challenges and opportunities, governments are unevenly equipped. In a number of high and middle-income countries, trust in governments has fallen to a low level, policies are affected by "short-term" views and vested interests, while many states are heavily in debt. In many low-income countries, persistent governance issues limit capacity for action and change.

## Five possible livelihood futures

There are many uncertainties as to how these emerging trends may play out and how they will affect livelihoods. Exploring the possibilities – both good and bad – helps us understand what policies may be needed to protect livelihoods against the worst possible scenarios. Chapter 4 of the book presents five future livelihood scenario landscapes in the horizon 2030 (three crisis and two transformational scenarios) and their implications for policy:

### *Scenario 1: "Automated North"*

*Automation proceeds faster than expected and affects ageing societies in particular*

Rapid automation in advanced and some emerging economies means that jobs in most sectors are increasingly taken over by robots and artificial intelligence systems. The process is so fast that most people whose jobs are replaced by technology cannot adapt and find it difficult to secure their livelihoods. Automation is fastest in ageing societies. Inequality increases faster than expected. With fewer jobs available to nationals, pressure is growing to increase barriers to immigration in developed countries. Social tensions and disruptions increase. Lower fiscal revenue combined with more people in need of social security support means that government debt becomes unmanageable. In many developing countries, the automation process is much slower, meaning that these countries are no longer competitive, even in low-cost, low-value added sectors.

### *Scenario 2: "Droughts and joblessness in the South"*

*Droughts become widespread in large parts of the developing world, challenging livelihoods in regions with large youthful populations*

This scenario is particularly relevant for regions with a preponderance of young people (sub-Saharan Africa, North Africa, Middle East and South Asia). Securing livelihoods in these regions becomes yet more challenging as climate change leads to more frequent and longer droughts. Subsistence farming becomes almost impossible. Larger scale farming is also seriously challenged. Famines become normal, not only for small-scale farmers but also for poor people in urban areas as food prices sky-rocket. Migration will primarily take place within countries as rural populations flood to the cities. But international migration also increases as many cities reach their absorption capacities. Guaranteeing equal opportunities for all becomes more challenging. The pace of change – in the youth population explosion as well as in the severity of droughts – is very fast. Countries, communities and individuals are unlikely to be able to adapt livelihoods or support mechanisms fast enough. The result is hunger, increasing inequality and social disruption.

### *Scenario 3: "Global financial crash"*

#### *A new, major financial crisis triggers a collapse of the global trading system and a shift to protectionism*

A housing bubble bursts in China and some other emerging countries. High levels of corporate debt in the developing world become unsustainable and lead to a large financial crisis and capital outflows. A financial crisis results from the unravelling of the European Union. Commodity prices continue to fall rapidly, creating significant challenges for currency stability in countries relying on commodity exports, such as the Russian Federation, Brazil, many African countries, Australia and Canada. These financial disruptions trigger a major global economic crisis, affecting trade, investment and consumption. Protectionist pressure re-emerges but does not help to avoid social disruptions and governments fail to address problems of increasing inequality. In developed and developing countries alike, many people's livelihoods come under pressure. Riots are widespread. Poverty rates increase and at least one billion people fall back into extreme poverty.

### *Scenario 4 "Regenerative economies"*

#### *Technological innovations create enough new jobs for most people and economic activity becomes more sustainable*

Fast technological advances create many new jobs, new products and services, and allow for the greening of economic activity. Many new fields flourish, including cybersecurity, environmentally resilient engineering, robot-enhanced service jobs, and jobs requiring high skills in nanotechnology and biotechnology. Productivity in the world's knowledge economies continues to increase at a fast pace. As the real economy becomes a virtual economy, many sectors undergo a transformation. Country borders and distance become less relevant. Markets become more international than ever before. Countries reshape their education systems so that people can perform in the knowledge economy. Technological innovation in agriculture results in migration from rural to urban areas in many developing countries, but planned, medium-sized cities with energy-efficient infrastructure contribute to sustainable urbanisation. While impacts on livelihoods are positive overall, certain people will still need social security but such systems will be more affordable for nation states under this scenario. This scenario could touch all regions of the world, but would come about faster in advanced and emerging countries (and indeed is already occurring in some).

### *Scenario 5 "Creative societies"*

#### *Diverse experiments and initiatives at the local level focus on individual resilience and social well-being.*

Technology-induced joblessness increases in developed and developing economies alike. Societies evolve towards new ways of living and working, in which individuals and communities are the key actors of change. State income supplements in rich countries assure a basic minimum income. Developed countries learn from experiments in social inclusiveness and adaptive, frugal innovation in developing and emerging economies. In the absence of secure full-time employment, an individual must put together a portfolio of work – part-time jobs, shared work with colleagues, trading skills and services. This portfolio lifestyle is made possible by three important factors: (1) technology, which allows people to work anywhere at any time; (2) the adoption of guaranteed minimum incomes in most developed countries, paid for by higher taxes on capital, rather than labour; and (3) new social attitudes in which young people are not so much interested in the consumer culture, but contribute to what might be called "the experience economy." Cities attempt circular economies and many other green initiatives, especially retrofitting of buildings and water conservation. A robust urban food movement develops, involving many urban community gardens. Public-private livelihood incubators flourish in most cities, providing job counselling, the matching of skills and opportunities, start-up financing, and individually tailored aid packages for young and old. At the national level, much more attention is paid to inclusive growth – growth plus well-being – rather than mere economic growth.

## Bold actions for a brighter future

Why are these scenario landscapes useful? Pushing some hypotheses or fictions to extreme, even dramatic, limits helps open up the policy space to new ideas, and more and different possibilities. They serve to illustrate that a range of forward-looking policies are available to policy makers and stakeholders.

The scenarios serve different purposes and suggest different policy responses. All three of the crisis scenarios raise the spectre of greater inequality – in income, education and other public services – and social disruption in both developed and developing countries. The two transformational scenarios, on the other hand, give hope that many economic, social, environmental or technologically driven crises can be avoided through innovative actions which build more resilient and inclusive livelihoods. The book's final chapter gives a taste of some actions that can help prevent some of the downside scenarios or create more favourable conditions for upside scenarios, drawing on insights from the scenario exercise and from ideas that emerged during the meeting in Bellagio. These actions apply at global, national and local levels:

### *Global preventive and adaptive action*

Global or multi-national action will be needed for many of the preventive policies required to avert crises linked to the financial system, to climate change, to pandemics and many other challenges, and to help ensure inclusiveness and resilience in livelihoods. For example:

- **Act urgently to reach a global agreement for tackling climate change:** The Conference of the Parties to the United Nations Framework Convention on Climate Change, to be held in Paris in November 2015, could cement the recent US-China deal to reduce carbon dioxide emissions.
- **Stabilise the global financial system:** by strengthening global and regional framework conditions; avoiding unhealthy financial activities; and increasing co-ordination and mobility of financial resources among the central banks, the International Monetary Fund, the World Bank and regional development banks.
- **Use tax reforms to achieve shared prosperity:** Possible actions include entering into appropriate multilateral agreements to prevent tax evasion by multinational enterprises and improving the progressiveness of tax systems.

- **Develop an inclusive approach to international trade:** Free global trade could initially have negative consequences for a number of industries and activities. Implementing new trade regimes and agreements in developing countries gradually could allow time for new industries and services to develop and help sustain livelihoods.
- **Manage migration better:** International migration can be a powerful force for better livelihoods as long as it is well co-ordinated. To prepare policies which respond to international migration, an informed discussion of possible trends and their impacts in the future is essential.
- **Strengthen responses to disasters and pandemics:** More funding and capacity building at both international and local levels are needed, and greater use of global public partnerships to tackle issues like immunisation.
- **Strengthen water sharing agreements:** to avert conflict in the developing world in a context of increasing drought.

---

What if…?
…there was a globally funded research organisation for innovation in technologies for resilient livelihoods: renewable energy, low-input farming, health etc.? See Box 5.3 in Chapter 5

---

- **Tackle increasing cyber insecurity:** through an international cyber police force.
- **Set up an international research and development agency:** to promote innovation in livelihood-focused technology. Technology is a potential game changer for global livelihoods, especially if focused on global "public goods" such as climate, clean energy, environment, health and the needs of the extremely poor.

### *Sustaining livelihoods calls for innovative national policies*

Control and responsibility for livelihoods are increasingly shifting from governments to communities and individuals themselves, suggesting a new role for government as back-stop and enabler of creative and regenerative societies.

---

What if…?
…there was a Global Open University for Livelihoods available to everyone? See Box 5.5 in Chapter 5

---

- **Make education inclusive and livelihood focused:** Secure livelihoods require a myriad of pathways for skill acquisition, and the opportunity for lifelong learning in open-access virtual classrooms. Education should also build basic livelihood skills – to help people meet their basic needs and cope with diverse financial, social or environmental challenges.
- **Promote livelihood portfolios:** As full employment becomes an illusion for an increasing number of people, "livelihood portfolios" made up of part-time work, paid training, and unemployment benefits can help individuals cope with fluid job situations.

- **Establish a guaranteed minimum income for all in developed countries:** by building on and rationalising existing welfare programmes and expenditures and a general reorganisation of tax systems, including the introduction of a negative income tax.
- **Use cash transfer programmes in developing countries:** Cash payments linked to conditions such as school attendance or immunisation can be a powerful force for well-being improvements.
- **Invest in children and young people:** The "youth bulge" in developing countries offers an unprecedented opportunity to enhance human capital to create a large, well-educated and potentially productive labour force. Investments in education and skills at this critical age bring high returns. Bold ideas include a universal self-investment grant for young people.

---

What if…?
…a new Green Revolution focused on livelihoods to stimulate a more localised, self-sufficient and resilient agriculture? See Box 5.8 in Chapter 5

---

- **Put green growth at the heart of economies:** Green growth can enhance resilience, reduce emissions, and boost jobs and growth at the same time. This will require policies for greener cities, sustainable farming, renewable energy, the removal of fossil fuel subsidies and funding for low-carbon infrastructure (such as "green bonds").

### *Local initiatives are central to resilient societies*

While prevention of global shocks is best carried out at the global level, and adaption at the national level, the local level should aim for autonomy from those shocks. Having autonomy (such as a local currency, which can act as a cushion during a global financial crisis) is a central element of resilience. Societies need to evolve towards new ways of living and working in which individuals and communities are the key actors of change. The economy could be driven by local experiments in well-being, supported at the national level, where much more attention is paid to inclusive growth – growth plus well-being – rather than merely economic growth. Initiatives to support greater resilience and more positive outcomes include the following:

- **Support a vibrant shared local economy:** In a world of technology-induced joblessness, individuals can survive through a patchwork of entrepreneurial and social initiatives involving exchanges, barters and virtual service marketplaces. Governments can do much to encourage and scale up such activities through fiscal arrangements, regulation, quality control and assurance.
- **Enable initiatives for micro-finance and local currencies:** Micro-finance, peer-to-peer lending, and social impact investments etc. can combat unemployment and be more efficient and livelihood-enhancing than state unemployment benefits. Local currencies cushion people from the turbulences and crises inherent to the globalised financial system and are particularly adapted to local exchanges between individuals and providers of local products and services.
- **Build green and resilient cities:** Cities are critical drivers of economic growth, being where most jobs are created. With 60% of the world's population likely to

be living in urban areas by 2030, cities need to become part of the solution, not part of the problem for livelihoods. Green and resilient cities address the issue of economic activity and environmental systems at the same time.

## A call for action

This book sees the considerable livelihood challenges which lie ahead as opportunities for innovation, for seeing the future differently and for bold experiments to move beyond surviving to thriving. These innovations or experiments might be technological or social, implying new modes of consumption and production, and new forms of organisations or institutions.

It is up to all relevant players – international, national, local and individual – to seize these opportunities. There is plenty to be done and many places to start. Coalitions of interested stakeholders should come together to start the process. Others will catch up and the momentum will grow.

## Note

1. Although there are still significant gaps between regions, and the difference in life expectancy between sub-Saharan Africa and Western Europe has actually increased.

# *References*

Dai, A. (2011), "Drought under global warming: A review", *WIREs Climate Change*, John Wiley & Sons, New Jersey, Vol 2, pp. 45-65, www.cgd.ucar.edu/cas/ adai/papers/Dai-drought_WIRES2010.pdf.

Gallup (n.d.), *Gallup World Poll*, Gallup Analytics, Gallup Inc., Washington DC, www.gallup.com/services/170945/world-poll.aspx (accessed 19 January 2015).

ILO (2014), *Global Employment Trends 2014* (data sets), www.ilo.org/global/research/global-reports/global-employment-trends/2014/WCMS_234879/lang--en/index.htm.

Oxford Martin School (2013), *Now for the Long Term: The Report of the Oxford Martin Commission for Future Generations*, Oxford University Press, Oxford, www.oxfordmartin.ox.ac.uk/downloads/commission/Oxford_Martin_Now_for_the_Long_Term.pdf.

The Rockefeller Foundation (2014), *Securing Livelihoods: Visions of a Better Future,* The Rockefeller Foundation, www.visionariesunbound.com/static/pdf/EIU-Rockefeller_Livelihoods%20report_Dec%202014.pdf

UNDP (2014), *UNDP Human Development Report 2014: Sustaining Human Progress,* United Nations Development Programme, New York, http://hdr.undp.org/sites/default/files/hdr14-report-en-1.pdf.

van Zanden, J.L., et al. (eds.) (2014), *How Was Life? Global Well-being since 1820*, OECD Publishing, Paris, http://dx.doi.org/10.1787/9789264214262-en.

World Bank (2014), *World Development Indicators* (database), http://data.worldbank.org/data-catalog/world-development-indicators

World Bank (2011), *World Development Report 2011: Conflict, Security and Development*, The World Bank Group, Washington DC, https://openknowledge.worldbank.org/handle/10986/4389.

# Chapter 2
# The state of the world's livelihoods

*Global progress in improving people's livelihoods has been remarkable over the past two centuries, especially in reducing extreme poverty, improving health, increasing literacy and moving towards gender equality. This chapter outlines progress in the core dimensions of livelihoods – income, work and basic needs – and shows that although living conditions have improved on many fronts, progress is slowing down. It also asks how people feel about their own livelihoods – are they thriving, surviving or suffering, and how does this vary across regions? Thus, the chapter looks at livelihoods beyond simple monetary measures and includes the many other factors which influence people's lives, from education, living conditions and health to people's own sense of well-being. This approach reflects the need to seek resilient and inclusive livelihoods.*

**Highlights**

- Livelihoods are defined as the ability to support oneself now and in the future. Livelihoods go beyond sheer survival to include people's potential to thrive.
- The world has made significant progress in improving livelihoods, especially living standards and health. Yet inequality is once again on the rise.
- Job creation has been the main driver of livelihood improvements in emerging and developing countries. However, work conditions remain mediocre in most low-income and some middle-income countries.
- Following the global economic crisis of 2008/9, unemployment has risen around the world, with the poor and young people particularly hard-hit. The progress made on securing basic needs in health, nutrition, access to basic services and education has slowed down.
- Many people feel dissatisfied with life, particularly the poor, and satisfaction has deteriorated in several regions following the economic crisis. People are nevertheless optimistic about the future, although less so in high-income countries.
- To sum up, though progress towards better livelihoods has been remarkable, the gains made are fragile and many people risk falling back into extreme poverty.

## Livelihoods are not just about surviving but also thriving

In this book we define livelihoods as the ability to support oneself now and in the future. People's livelihoods are founded on the underlying condition that their basic needs are met. Basic needs include adequate nutrition, healthcare, shelter, water, sanitation, education, etc. Income, work and basic needs together form the core elements of livelihoods. Jobs are central as they are the main source of income for most people.

Livelihoods go beyond sheer survival, however, to include people's potential to thrive. Thriving can increase life satisfaction. People who are thriving are likely to have more sustainable livelihoods and greater resilience to upsets and challenges. They are more likely to have more accumulated wealth, more work opportunities and greater choice over their own lives. On the other hand, someone who subsists under poor living conditions over which he or she has no influence or choice is vulnerable to even small shocks such as sickness, job loss, failed harvests, etc. Such livelihoods may not be sustainable. Building people's ability to thrive depends not only on income and available resources, but also on the competences and capacities people need to create the life of their choosing.

### *Promoting resilience and inclusiveness requires a more rounded understanding of livelihoods*

The most basic indicators for evaluating livelihoods tend to be gross domestic product (GDP) per capita and the World Bank's USD 1.25 a day extreme poverty threshold. But these statistics do not provide policy makers with a sufficiently detailed picture of people's living conditions. Income or consumption alone may not capture the multiple ways in which people can be poor. For example, economic growth has been strong in India in recent years and poverty in monetary terms has fallen. However, the prevalence of child malnutrition, for example, has remained at nearly 50%, which is among the highest rates worldwide. Moreover, poor people themselves describe their experience of poverty as multidimensional. Participatory exercises reveal that poor people describe a lack of well-being to include poor health and nutrition, lack of adequate sanitation and clean water, social exclusion, low education, bad housing conditions, violence, shame, and disempowerment, among others (Oxford Poverty and Human Development Initiative).

The quest for secure livelihoods and inclusiveness calls for a better way of measuring the contributing factors. The way that livelihoods are assessed is therefore evolving rapidly. For example, the United Nations Human Development Index complements the GDP per capita indicator with some indicators of basic needs (life expectancy and education level).[1]

The Multidimensional Poverty Index (MPI),[2] developed by the United Nations Development Programme (UNDP) with the University of Oxford, complements a purely monetary measure of poverty by considering other deprivations. The index identifies deprivations across the same three dimensions as the Human Development Index – namely education, health and standard of living (Kovacevic and Calderon, 2014). A person is considered as "multidimensionally poor" if they are deprived in 33% or more of the weighted indicators. Another advantage of a multidimensional perspective on poverty is that it allows policy makers to make better-informed policy decisions. For example, if many people are deprived of education, a different poverty reduction strategy will be required to a situation where people lack adequate housing.

But these objective measures need to be complemented by more subjective measures to get a fuller understanding of people's well-being. People's subjective evaluations of their own life (life satisfaction) help to see beyond survival and take into account their potential to thrive.

Richer countries, whose citizens' basic needs have been met, are now starting to look at happiness or life satisfaction as indicators of well-being; basic economic needs are no longer the main drivers of social change. However, greater wealth does not necessarily result in greater life satisfaction. This has been confirmed by the "Easterlin paradox": although people in wealthier countries are on average happier or more satisfied with life than people in poor countries, happiness seems only to rise with income up to a point, but not beyond it (Graham, 2009; Senik, 2014).

The Gallup World Poll measures life satisfaction based on extensive surveys of people's own perceptions of their livelihoods around the world (see Box 2.2 later in this chapter).[3] Their indicators give a view of overall life satisfaction as well as more specific aspects of individuals' subjective well-being, such as their evaluations of social capital, food and shelter security, health status, job climate, income/wealth status and environmental conditions.

The OECD Better Life initiative, launched in 2011, captures both objective and subjective aspects of people's individual well-being along 11 dimensions. This includes material conditions – namely income and wealth, jobs and housing – as well as quality of life dimensions: health, work-life balance, education and skills, social connections, civic engagement and governance, environmental quality, security, and subjective well-being (OECD, 2013a). A set of indicators is used to construct the score for each of the 11 dimensions. An interactive online tool allows users to set their own weights for each dimension.[4] So far, the Better Life Index has only been developed for the 34 OECD countries. The OECD is currently developing an adjusted framework for developing countries (Boarini et al., 2014).

The OECD Better Life Index also acknowledges that the sustainability and resilience of livelihoods over time is built on different types of capital, although indicators for these are not part of the index. These types of capital include:

- Human capital: the stock of populations' competencies, knowledge and skills which constitute a potential workforce to meet employment or production needs.
- Social capital: the networks and social behaviours that contribute to civic and community life. It can also include institutional capital, such as trust in government action, transparency, corruption-clean policies, etc.
- Natural capital: the overall environment, including all its environmental and geological resources, as well as broader ecosystems, biodiversity, etc.
- Economic capital: the material aspect of livelihoods. It can be "produced physical capital" (such as infrastructure and buildings), knowledge assets (such as intellectual property), or financial assets (such as financial wealth).

This chapter uses both objective and subjective measures of livelihoods (including the types of capital contributing to them) to assess evolutions in the three core dimensions of livelihoods – income, work and basic needs – across all regions of the world. The assessment of income gives special emphasis to the analysis of poverty, while the focus on basic needs is mainly on health, education and basic infrastructure.

The chapter also looks at people's perspectives of their own lives – as a whole, and of specific aspects ranging from jobs to health and the environment – as subjective measures of the various types of capital mentioned above. Different aspects of livelihoods are compared with each other across regions and countries to identify possible correlations.

## Progress in global well-being since 1820 has been remarkable

A recent OECD study of livelihoods (van Zanden, 2014) shows that the last two centuries have seen significant improvement in global well-being, particularly in the areas of income and basic needs. GDP per capita in purchasing power parity has increased by a factor of 10 between 1820 and 2010. Real wages of unskilled workers are about eight times the level attained at the start of the 19th century. Health status, measured as life expectancy, has also improved. Overall progress has been accompanied by greater gender equality. At lower levels of per capita GDP (below USD 5000, in 1990 purchasing power party; see Box 2.2 for a discussion of PPP-based poverty measures), an improvement in per capita income has been associated with bigger gains in overall well-being compared to income improvements at higher income levels (Figure 2.1).

Yet this growth has been accompanied by a considerable increase in disparity among countries, and a serious deterioration in the quality of the environment. In 1820, the richest countries were about five times as wealthy as the poorest countries; in 1950, they were more than 30 times as well off, thanks to rapid industrialisation. Today, they are more than 50 times better off (World Bank, 2014). Inequality within countries, measured by the Gini coefficient, has increased (Figure 2.2, Panel A). In Western countries, after a decline from the end of the 19th century, inequality started to rise again in the 1970s, following a U-shaped curve (Figure 2.2, Panel B). This rise is sharp in Anglo-Saxon countries and relatively modest in continental Western Europe. The disintegration of communism in the 1980s was also followed by a sharp increase in inequality in Eastern Europe. In other parts of the world, China in particular, recent trends have also led to greater income inequality.

**Figure 2.1. Improvements in well-being slowed down when the world became richer**

Relation between a composite well-being indicator and GDP per capita

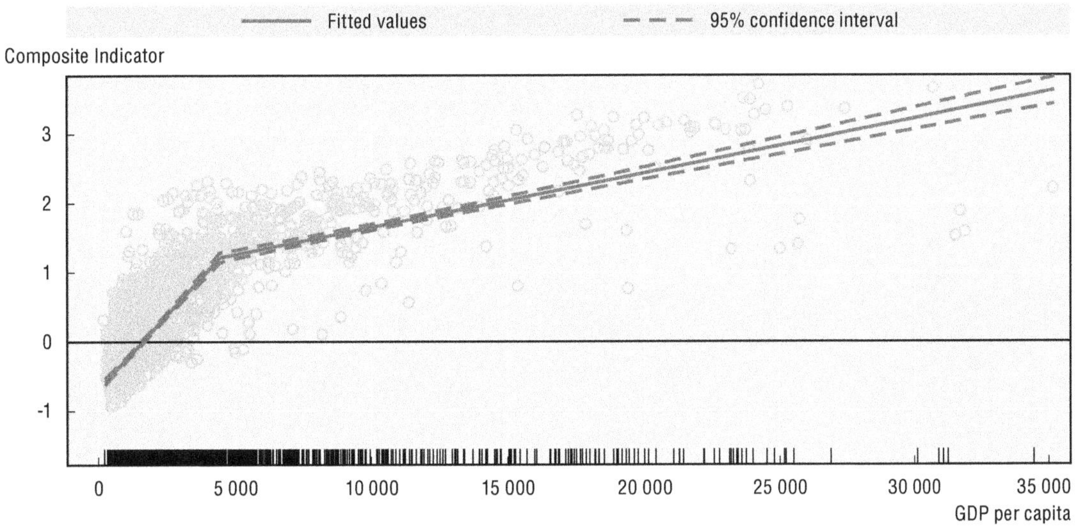


*Notes:* Higher values of the composite indicator correspond to higher average well-being. Grey circles represent one country for a given year (between 1820 and 2000). GDP per capita is based on USDs at 1990 PPP, decadal averages. For more details on the calculations see van Zanden (2014). The composite indicator of well-being includes the following measures: GDP per capita, real wages, physical height, life expectancy, average years of education, income inequality, polity, mean species abundance, homicide rate.

*Source*: van Zanden, J.L., et al. (eds.) (2014), *How Was Life? Global Well-being since 1820*, OECD Publishing, Paris, http://dx.doi.org/10.1787/9789264214262-en.

Progress in basic needs such as health and education has been significant, often linked with the growth in GDP. This is particularly the case for health. Since industrialisation began, average life expectancy at birth has almost doubled in wealthier countries, from 40 years to almost 80 years, and from around 30 years to 65 years in other parts of the world. Universal access to education has become a global phenomenon, leading to literacy rates rising from less than 20% in 1820 to around 80% in the 2000s. The only exception to this widespread livelihood progress is sub-Saharan Africa, which is lagging behind in life expectancy (around 52 in the 2000s) and literacy rates (65% in 2010) (van Zanden, 2014).

This general progress has been accompanied by greater gender equality – although much still remains to be done as highlighted by OECD Development Centre's Social Institutions & Gender Index (SIGI) (see Box 2.1). Women's life expectancy has increased from a world average of 36 years in 1900 to 71 in 2000. Since 1960, countries such as Afghanistan and India, which were characterised by large gender differences in life expectancy, have almost closed the gap. There are also regional differences: in Asia, women's life expectancy grew faster than men's. In education, the last five decades have seen a significant closing of the gap. In South and Southeast Asia, average years of schooling of females have more than doubled since the 1980s. Overall, however, the relationship between per capita GDP and gender equality is not very clear-cut.

**Figure 2.2. Inequality is on the rise**

World income inequality (Gini coefficient, values between 0-100%): 1820-2000

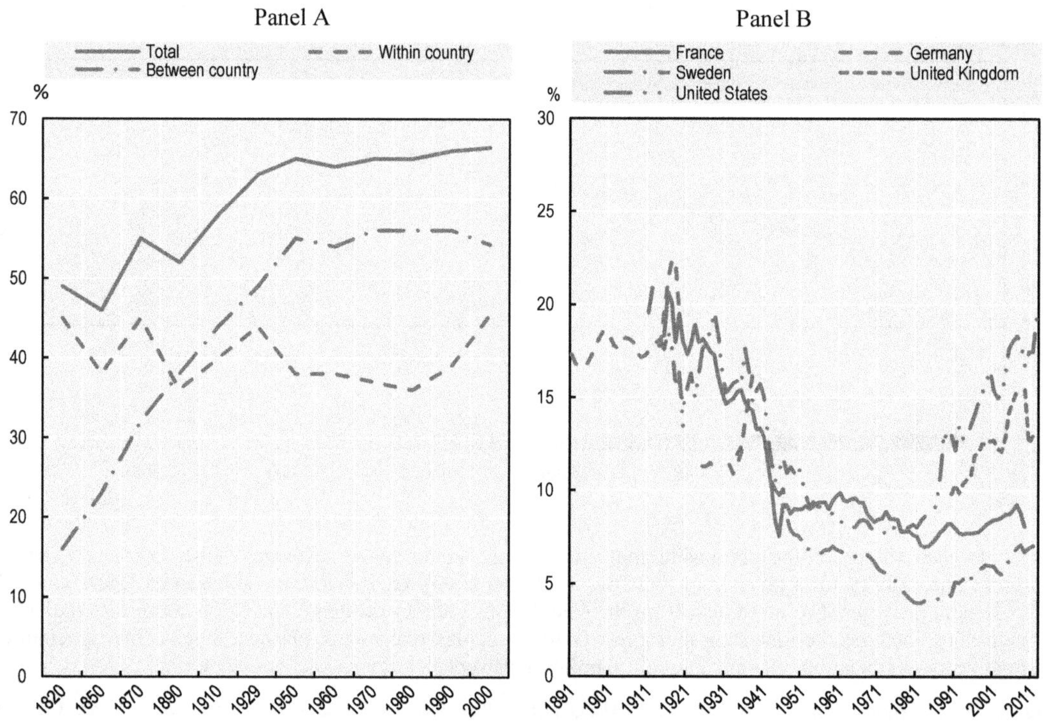


*Notes:* Panel A: Income inequality is measured by the Gini coefficient. A Gini coefficient of zero expresses perfect equality, where all values are the same (for example, where everyone has the same income). A Gini coefficient of one (or 100%) expresses maximal inequality among values (for example, where only one person has all the income and all others have none). In the figure, "Total" is the Gini coefficient for world income inequality when the world population is taken as one group to calculate the coefficient. "Within country" is the average of the Gini coefficient for all countries. "Between country" is the Gini coefficient of the average incomes in each country. For details on the country sample and data quality see van Zanden, J.L., et al. (eds.) (2014). Panel B: For details on data, see Alvaredo et al. (2015).

*Source*: Panel A: Adapted from van Zanden, J.L., et al. (eds.) (2014), *How Was Life?: Global Well-being since 1820*, OECD Publishing, http://dx.doi.org/10.1787/9789264214262-en. Panel B: Alvaredo F., A. B. Atkinson, T. Piketty and E. Saez (2015), *The World Top Incomes Database*, Paris School of Economics, Paris, http://topincomes.parisschoolofeconomics.eu/#Database.

### Box 2.1. Key results of the 2014 Social Institutions & Gender Index (SIGI)

The OECD Development Centre's Social Institutions and Gender Index (SIGI) is a cross-country measure of discrimination against women in social institutions (formal and informal laws, social norms, and practices) across 160 countries. Discriminatory social institutions intersect across all stages of girls' and women's life, restricting their access to justice, rights and empowerment opportunities and undermining their agency and decision-making authority over their life choices. As underlying drivers of gender inequalities, discriminatory social institutions perpetuate gender gaps in development areas, such as education, employment and health, and hinder progress towards rights-based social transformation that benefits both women and men.

The 2014 edition of the SIGI shows that countries have made great strides in reducing discrimination through ambitious target setting and promising initiatives. However, gaps and challenges remain across some key areas affecting women's socio-economic and political rights and freedom from violence. Below are some global, regional and national trends which highlight the universal challenge of discriminatory social institutions and norms:

- **Early marriage**: The number of early marriages is decreasing in developing countries (from 36% in 2004 to 26% in 2010 in Malawi, for example), but the practice remains pervasive: on average in non- OECD countries 16% of girls 15-19 years old are married, ranging from less than 1% in Lithuania to 60% in Niger.
- **Unpaid care work**: Caring responsibilities are mainly performed by women, who typically spend three times more of their time on unpaid care work than men, ranging from 1.3 times in Denmark (where women spend on average four hours and men three hours on unpaid care activities) to 10 times in Pakistan (where women spend on average five hours and men less than 30 minutes on unpaid care activities).
- **Inheritance**: Only 55 countries in the SIGI's 160 accord women the same inheritance rights as men, both in law and in practice.
- **Domestic violence**: 35% of women believe that domestic violence is justified under certain conditions, ranging from 3% in Jamaica to 92% in Guinea, and 30% of women have been victims of gender-based violence in their lifetime, ranging from 7% in Canada to almost 80% in Angola.
- **Female genital mutilation**: In the 28 countries where female genital mutilation is a widespread practice (Egypt, Yemen and some Sub-Saharan African countries), 47% of women and girls have been victims.
- **Missing women**: Over 90 million women are missing around the world, 80% of these missing women are from India and the People's Republic of China.
- **Secure access to land**: The laws or customary practices of 102 countries still deny women the same rights to access land as men.
- **Political participation**: Only one member of parliament in five is a woman (no woman in Qatar and Yemen versus 63% in Rwanda). Even with legislative quotas, women occupy less than 10% of parliamentary seats in Brazil, the Democratic Republic of the Congo, Egypt and the Republic of the Congo.

*Source*: OECD (2014c), *Social Institutions & Gender Index, 2014 Synthesis report*, www.genderindex.org/sites/default/files/docs/BrochureSIGI2015.pdf.

## The poverty picture is complex

More than two billion people have moved out of extreme poverty over the last four decades, largely thanks to the growth of the emerging economies, especially China. Extreme poverty is measured as people living on less than USD 1.25 a day (in 2005 purchasing power parity; see Box 2.2 for a discussion of PPP-based poverty measures). At the beginning of the 1980s, more than 50% of the developing world's population was below the USD 1.25 a day poverty threshold. This headcount ratio was reduced to 17% by 2010. China alone has reduced the number of extreme poor by 700 million since 1981.

### *Poverty is concentrated in a few regions*

The world's poor are mainly concentrated in South Asia, sub-Saharan Africa, East Asia and the Pacific (Figure 2.3, Panel A), although poverty reduction in East Asia and the Pacific is proceeding at a fast pace. South Asia and sub-Saharan Africa still have rapidly growing populations, making it challenging to reduce the absolute poverty headcount. Although South Asia reduced the number of extreme poor from around 600 million in 1990 to around 500 million in 2010, this still makes up more than 40% of the world's poor. In sub-Saharan Africa, the number of extremely poor people increased over the same period by more than 100 million, coming close to the absolute number of poor in South Asia. The growth spurt in some emerging economies of East Asia and the Pacific, particularly in China, but also for example in Indonesia, Thailand and Malaysia, resulted in an impressive reduction of absolute poverty from more than 800 million to just above 200 million between 1990 and 2010. This reduction accounts for around 20% of the world's poor people.

A closer look at individual countries reveals that poverty today is largely concentrated in just five countries: Bangladesh, China, Democratic Republic of Congo, India and Nigeria (Figure 2.3, Panel B). In each of these five countries, the extreme poverty headcount was above 50 million in 2010. The headcount is highest in India, with more than 400 million poor, or 35% of the world's poor population.

### *Poverty relative to total population is decreasing in all regions*

Poverty headcount ratios – the share of the population living below USD 1.25 a day – decreased in all developing regions between 1990 and 2010 (Figure 2.4, Panel A). In 1990 in developing sub-Saharan Africa, South Asia and East Asia and the Pacific, where the world's poverty is concentrated, the ratios were above 50%. By 2010 they had fallen to below 50% in sub-Saharan Africa, to approximately 30% in South Asia and to 10% in East Asia and the Pacific. In the other three developing regions (Latin America and the Caribbean, the Middle East and North Africa, and Europe and Central Asia), poverty headcount ratios also decreased during the same period and were below 10% in 2010.

Mapping the poverty headcount ratios by country reveals that in most countries on the African continent, poverty remains a concern (Figure 2.4, Panel B). Extreme poverty is most widespread in the Democratic Republic of Congo (85%), Liberia (83%), Madagascar (81%), Burundi (80%) and Zambia (75%). It appears to be less prevalent in northern and southern Africa. In Asia, poverty headcounts remain above 20% in Bangladesh, India, the Philippines and Lao PDR. In Central and South America, only Haiti is left with a high poverty headcount ratio of 65%. All other countries in that region have figures below 20%.

**Figure 2.3. Poverty is concentrated in a few regions and countries**

A. Poor people by region according to poverty thresholds, in millions

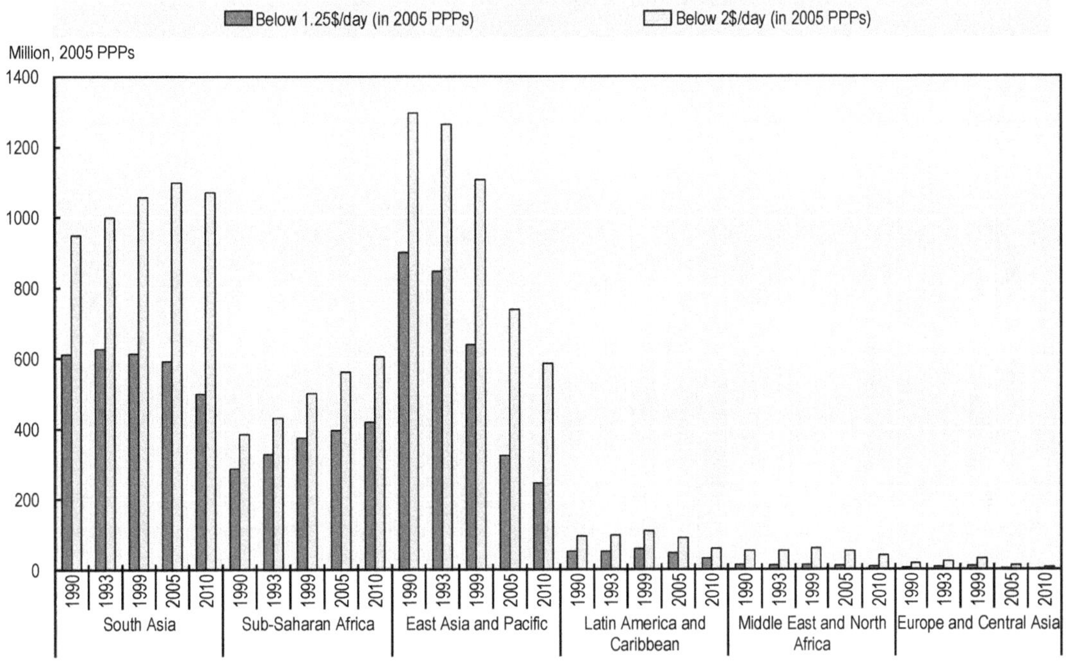


B. Numbers of poor people by country, 2010

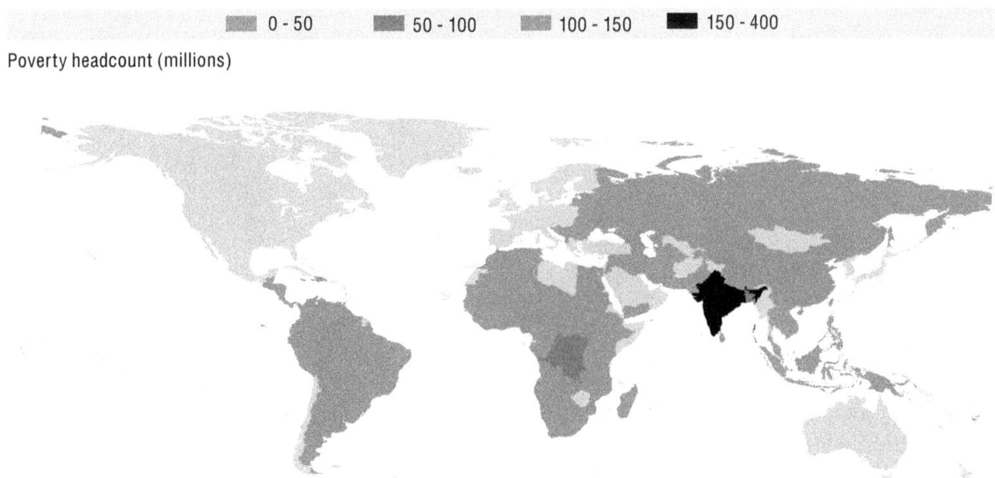


*Notes:* Panel B: PPP: purchasing power parity. Poverty figures for countries in light grey are not available. This is usually the case for developed countries where extreme poverty is low or inexistent. Reference year 2010.

*Source:* World Bank (2014), 2014 World Development Indicators, The World Bank Group, Washington DC, http://data.worldbank.org/indicator.

**Figure 2.4. All developing regions have reduced the share of their populations living in extreme poverty, 1990-2010**

**A. Poverty headcount ratio by region according to poverty thresholds, in %**

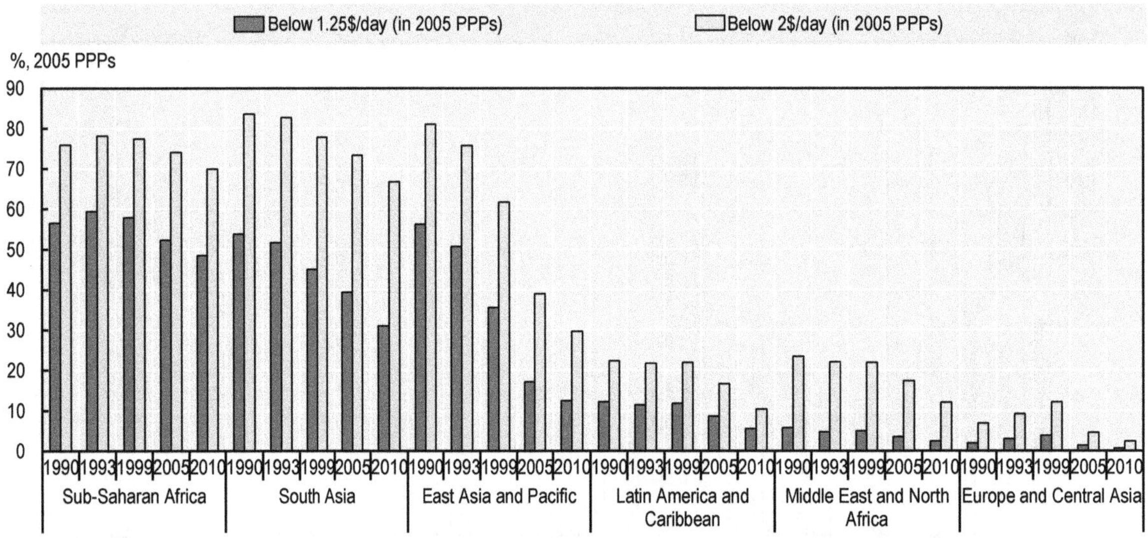


B. Poverty headcount ratio by country, in %, 2005 PPPs, 2010

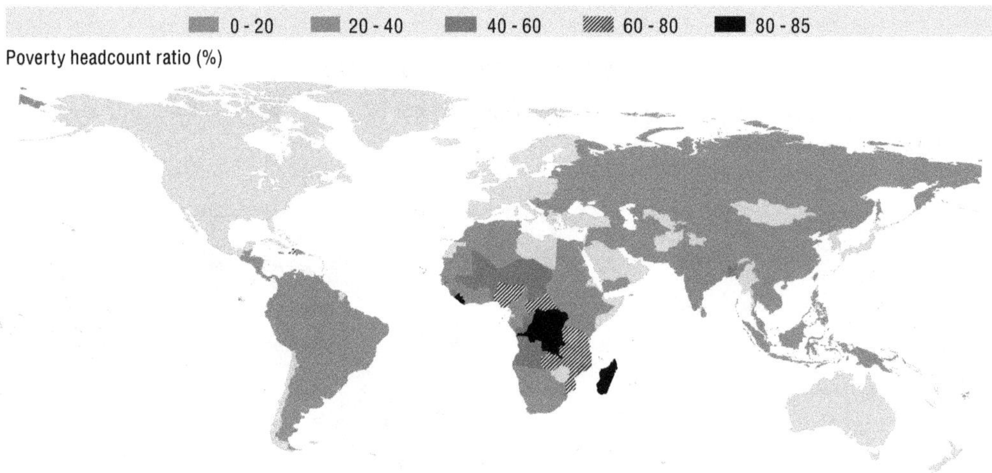


*Notes:* Panel B: PPP: purchasing power parity. Poverty figures for countries in light grey are not available. This is usually the case for developed countries where extreme poverty is low or inexistent. Reference year 2010.

*Source:* World Bank (2014), 2014 World Development Indicators, The World Bank Group, Washington DC, http://data.worldbank.org/indicator.

## *A large share of the world's population is at risk of falling back into extreme poverty*

Many people who have managed to move out of extreme poverty remain at risk of falling back into it. When looking at the higher poverty line of USD 2 a day, the regional trends in poverty again reveal a strong concentration of poverty and higher poverty headcount ratios in South Asia, sub-Saharan Africa and East Asia and the Pacific (Figures 2.3 and 2.4). It is significant that the number of poor people in all regions increases considerably for each year when using the USD 2 a day line compared to the USD 1.25 a day line. This illustrates that even if many people have moved out of extreme poverty in South Asia or East Asia and the Pacific, they are still at risk of falling back into it. Also, while many emerging economies do have rising middle classes (sometimes defined by people living on USD 10 or more a day; see Annex 3.A1 in Chapter 3), it is clear that sub-Saharan Africa and South Asia are far from that situation, with more than 65% of their populations still living on less than USD 2 a day (Figure 2.4, Panel A).

### *Alternative poverty measures provide additional insights*

Dollarised poverty measures have an important limitation: poverty counts change in every round of purchasing power parity (PPP) benchmarks. For example, the latest PPP benchmark figures published in the first of half of 2014 dramatically change the poverty landscape (Box 2.2). According to calculations by Brookings researchers, the poverty headcount in South Asia is cut in half from around 500 million in 2010 to 250 million when using the new PPP benchmark, while poverty in East Asia and Pacific as well as in sub-Saharan Africa would be reduced much less (Chandy and Kharas, 2014). For example, for India, the new PPP benchmark reduces the poverty headcount from around 400 million to just 180 million in 2010. Overall, this large discrepancy between poverty figures calculated using different PPP benchmarks illustrates that poverty is indeed very difficult to quantify; figures should therefore be taken with a pinch of salt.

**Box 2.2. The limitations of PPP-based poverty measures**

Standard exchange rates measure the relative values of different currencies for goods, services and financial assets traded internationally. In contrast, PPP exchange rates measure the relative values (purchasing power) of currencies in domestic markets, including the cost of services – haircuts, housing, local transportation, etc. – that are not traded across international borders. Consumption PPPs – which are used to convert the international poverty line into local currencies – measure the relative cost of a representative bundle of goods and services in each country, weighted by the share of each item in overall consumer spending. Using PPP exchange rates to convert the international poverty line into local currencies helps ensure that the calculated values correspond to a similar standard of living in each country. The key word here is "helps," because there is much room for error in this calculation. In addition, a particular problem with PPP exchange rates is that they are only valid for the year in which the price comparisons were made. For this reason, they must be treated with caution when looking at changes over time (OECD, 2013d).

The International Comparison Program (ICP) updated purchasing power parities around the world in 2014 based on detailed price data for the benchmark year 2011. The previous benchmark was 2005. The ICP 2011 estimates benefited from a number of methodological improvements over past efforts to calculate PPPs. More details on this update can be found online: www.worldbank.org/en/news/press-release/2014/04/29/2011-international-comparison-program-results-compare-real-size-world-economies.

How does the poverty picture change when using the multidimensional poverty index (MPI)? Although multidimensional poverty headcounts across countries are often closely tied to counts using the standard USD 1.25 a day poverty line, some significant deviations can be observed (Figure 2.5). For example, none of the five poorest countries identified using the standard poverty line (Burundi, Democratic Republic of Congo, Liberia, Madagascar and Zambia) is among the poorest when using the MPI. Instead these are Burkina Faso, Ethiopia, Guinea, Mali and Niger. Around 1.5 billion people in the 91 countries covered by the MPI live in multidimensional poverty. This exceeds the estimated 1.2 billion people in those countries who live on USD 1.25 a day or less (UNDP, 2014a), and accounts for more than one-third of their population.

The alternative measures of poverty discussed above provide valuable insights into the situation of people who may not immediately appear to be poor according to the USD 1.25 extreme poverty line. It is also important to consider the vulnerability of such people, revealed by their deprivations in basic services or risk of falling back into extreme poverty.

**Figure 2.5. A mismatch in poverty measures: Multidimensional and the "USD 1.25-a-day" poverty measures compared**

In % of total population

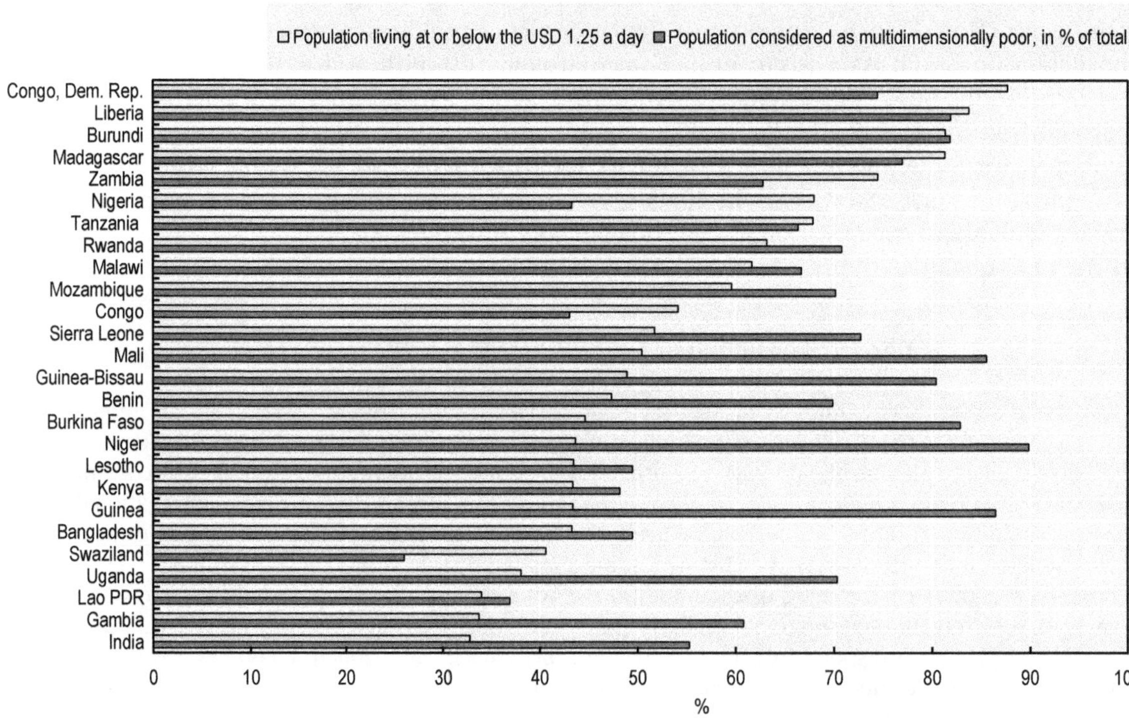


*Notes:* The Multidimensional Poverty Index complements a purely monetary measure of poverty by considering overlapping deprivations suffered by people at the same time. The index identifies deprivations across education, health and standard of living. A person is considered as multi-dimensionally poor if they are deprived in 33% or more of the weighted indicators (see Endnote 2 of this chapter for more details). The most recent year is used (from 2000-12) for which the MPI is available.

*Source*: UNDP (2014a), *The 2014 Human Development Report – Sustaining Human Progress: Reducing Vulnerabilities and Building Resilience*, United Nations Development Programme, New York, http://hdr.undp.org/sites/default/files/hdr14-report-en-1.pdf.

## Global unemployment is on the rise

Increased employment is the largest contributor to poverty reduction (Figures 2.6 and 2.7). The significant reduction of poverty around the globe was made possible by the creation of millions of new productive jobs, particularly in the developing world. Indeed, South Asia created on average 8.5 million new jobs every year between 2009 and 2014 (ILO, 2014a). Africa has created over 37 million wage-paying jobs within the past 10 years (UNECA, 2013).

Today there are about three billion people who have jobs around the world, of which around half are working for a wage or salary and the other half are working in farming or are self-employed (World Bank, 2012a). But there are almost two billion working-age adults who are not participating in the labour force; that is, neither working nor looking for work.

In 2013, 202 million people were unemployed worldwide, up five million from the year before. Forty-five percent of these jobseekers are from East Asia and South Asia, followed by sub-Saharan Africa and Europe (ILO, 2014a). Since the economic crisis, the global unemployment rate has stabilised at around 6% – a level expected to remain constant until 2017 (ILO, 2014a). Almost 30 million net jobs were lost during the financial crisis and have not been recovered (Oxford Martin School, 2013).

**Figure 2.6. Jobs are the most important source of household income**

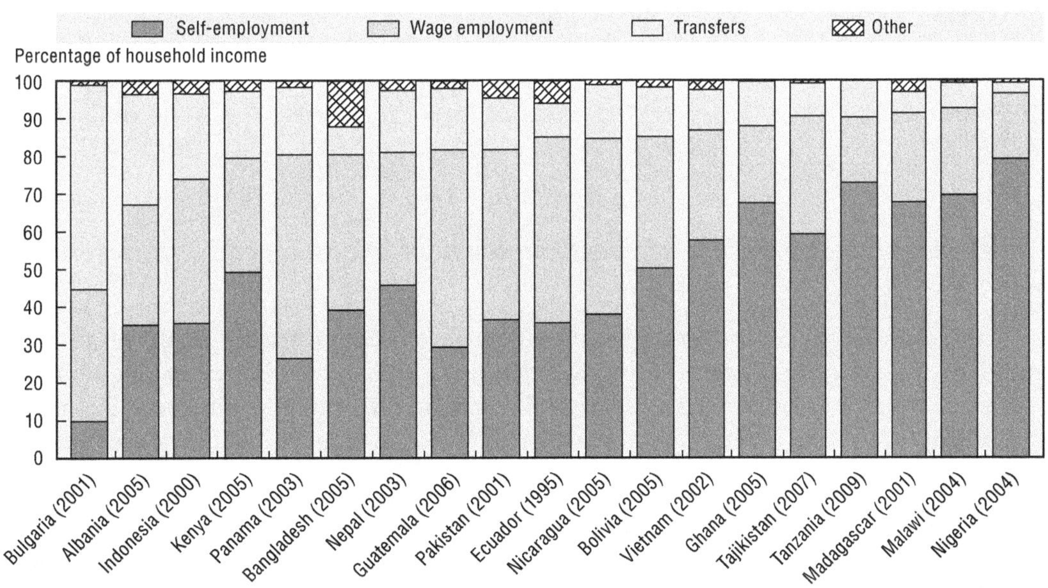


*Source:* World Bank (2012a), *World Development Report 2013: Jobs*, The World Bank Group, Washington DC, http://siteresources.worldbank.org/EXTNWDR2013/Resources/8258024-1320950747192/8260293-1322665883147/WDR_2013_Report.pdf.

**Figure 2.7. Jobs account for much of the decline in extreme poverty**

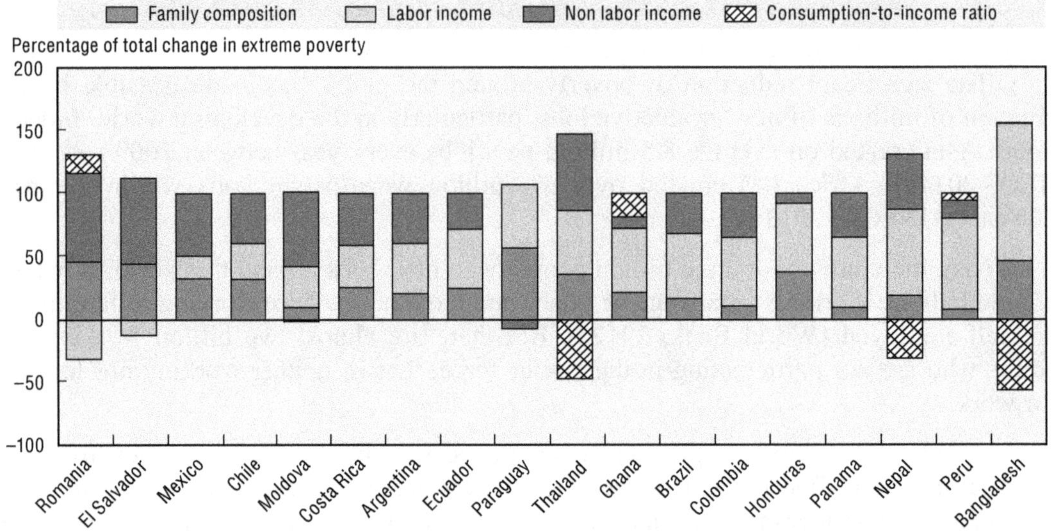


*Notes:* Extreme poverty is defined as people living at or below USD 1.25 a day. Family composition indicates the change in the share of adults (ages 18 and older) within the household. Labour income refers to the change in employment and earnings for the each adult. Non-labour income refers to changes in other sources of income such as transfers, pensions, and imputed housing rents. If a bar is located below the horizontal axis, it means that the source would have increased, instead of decreased, poverty. The changes are computed for Argentina (2000-10); Bangladesh (2000-10); Brazil (2001-09); Chile (2000-09); Colombia (2002-10); Costa Rica (2000-08); Ecuador (2003-10); El Salvador (2000-09); Ghana (1998-2005); Honduras (1999-2009); Mexico (2000-10); Moldova (2001-10); Panama (2001-09); Paraguay (1999-2010); Peru (2002-10); Nepal (1996-2003); Romania (2001-09); and Thailand (2000-09). The changes for Bangladesh, Ghana, Moldova, Nepal, Peru, Romania, and Thailand are computed using consumption-based measures of poverty, while the changes for the other countries are based on income measures.

*Source:* World Bank (2012a), *World Development Report 2013: Jobs*, The World Bank Group, Washington DC, http://siteresources.worldbank.org/EXTNWDR2013/Resources/8258024-1320950747192/8260293-1322665883147/WDR_2013_Report.pdf.

## *The economic recession has affected employment in developed countries more severely*

The economic crisis and low growth have affected countries differently in terms of employment. After an increase during the crisis, unemployment in developing countries has decreased to around pre-crisis levels of 5.5% today. Meanwhile, advanced economies are still suffering from unemployment rates of 8.5% on average, higher than the pre-crisis 5.8% rate.

A number of high-income countries are facing serious unemployment problems. They vary in their capacity to adapt to such problems. On the one hand, countries that have traditionally flexible labour markets, such as the US and UK, are better able to adapt to business cycles, albeit with potentially significant losses of income for laid-off workers. On the other hand, countries with rigid labour markets and significant compensation for jobless people, such as France, are experiencing persistently high levels of unemployment.

People living in advanced economies also struggle with precarious employment. The financial crisis has led to a significant increase in temporary employment as employers have become cautious about hiring permanent workers. Employees under temporary contracts tend to be the first to be laid off. Moreover, employment protection legislation is weakening (OECD, 2013b).

### *Unemployment affects the poorest most*

In developing and emerging countries, trends since 2008 reveal that it is the poor who have been the most affected by job losses (Figure 2.8). The middle classes have fared much better, benefitting the most from job creation. Job creation in Latin America and Africa has been particularly remarkable, benefitting all income groups except the extreme poor. The situation is not as positive in East Asia and South Asia. Projections for 2013-2018 suggest a continuation of past trends, with employment growth mainly benefiting the middle classes (ILO, 2014b).

**Figure 2.8. The changing face of employment in the developing world, 2008-18**

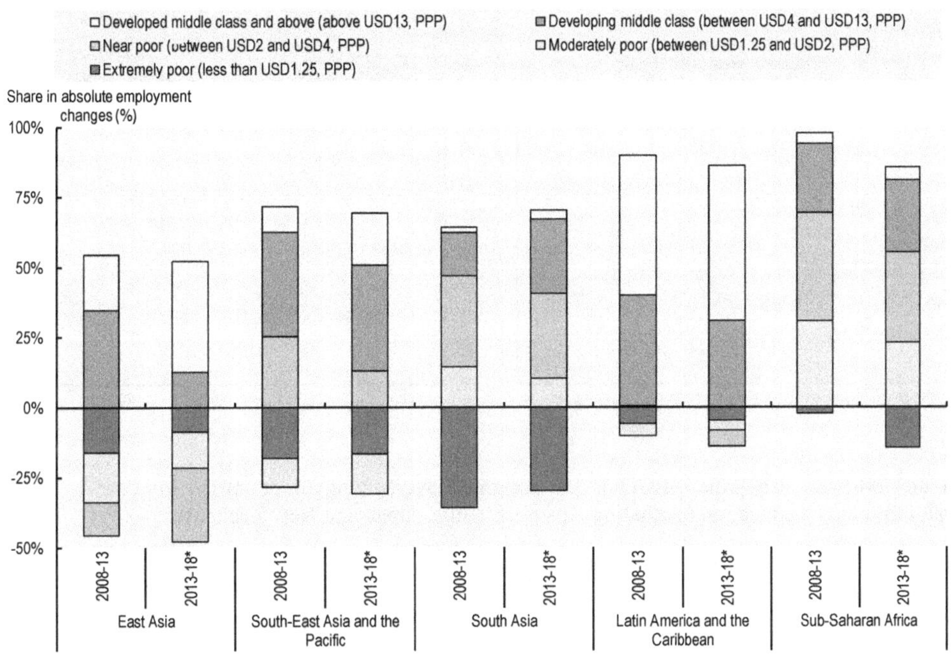


*Note:* * 2013 to 2018 are projections. The absolute changes in employment add up to 100%.

*Source:* ILO (2014b), *Global Employment Trends 2014: Risk of a Jobless Recovery?* International Labour Organization, Geneva, http://ilo.org/global/research/global-reports/global-employment-trends/2014/lang--en/index.htm.

### *Unemployment is particularly high among the young*

Worldwide, unemployment is particularly high among the young (aged 15-24), with the youth unemployment rate reaching 13.1% – three times as high as the adult unemployment rate in 2013 (ILO, 2014a). The number of young people who are not in employment, education or training (described as "idle") has also increased since the start of the crisis, to 621 million. In certain countries, almost a quarter of young people aged 15 to 24 are not in employment, education or training (Figure 2.9 for the situation in OECD countries).

In OECD countries, low-skilled young men have been the most affected by declining employment and labour force participation, while low-skilled men are seeing the greatest increase in unemployment (OECD, 2013b). Employment rates among low-skilled men were 7 percentage points lower at the end of 2012 than at the start of the crisis. In contrast, the employment rate among older individuals increased, continuing a trend apparent before the crisis. Furthermore, the young (aged 18 to 25) in OECD countries have suffered the most severe income losses, suggesting that their risk of income-poverty is higher than for people over 65. Analysis by household type also shows the most vulnerable to be jobless or single-worker households, and single parent households (OECD, 2014a).

**Figure 2.9. The young and low-skilled are worst affected by unemployment in OECD countries**

A. Employment rate of different groups relative to that of the overall population, Q1 2008=100

B. Percentage of youth population not in education and not employed (NEETs), 2006=100

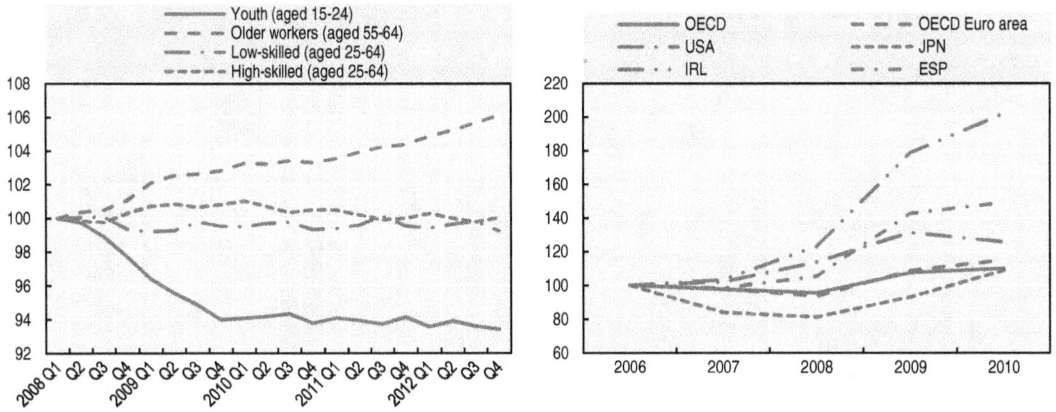


*Note*: In the left-hand panel the OECD is the weighted average of 34 countries for data by age, and 30 countries for data by education (excluding Australia, Chile, Japan and New Zealand).

*Source*: OECD (2012a), *Employment Outlook 2012*, OECD Publishing, Paris, http://dx.doi.org/10.1787/empl_outlook-2013-en (Panel A); OECD (2012b), *Education at a Glance 2012: OECD Indicators*, OECD Publishing, Paris, http://dx.doi.org/10.1787/eag-2012-en (Panel B).

### *Conditions are precarious for the working poor in developing countries*

In developing countries, labour markets have three main characteristics. First, there is the prevalence of self-employment, which often makes measures of unemployment inadequate. Second, the coexistence of traditional and modern modes of production leads to large variations in the nature of work, from subsistence agriculture and menial work to technology-driven manufacturing and services. Finally, the majority of workers in the poorest countries are engaged in informal working relationships (World Bank, 2012a).

In many developing countries, most poor people can barely earn a living despite long working hours. Around 400 million people aged 15 and older were estimated to be employed but still living in households earning less than USD 1.25 per person a day – the so-called working poor. Three-quarters of the world's poor live in rural areas. The regions with the highest rate of the working poor as share of total employment are South Asia (25.7%) and sub-Saharan Africa (41.7%). Their number, according to the International Labour Organization, is estimated to have increased by 50 million with the financial crisis (ILO, 2012).

The economic crisis has had a significant impact on the working poor. There were 50 million more working poor in 2011 than in 2007. Of these, only 24 million climbed above the USD 1.25 a day poverty line between 2007 and 2011, compared with 134 million between 2000 and 2007 (UNDP, 2014a).

People in such precarious forms of employment usually have lower and more volatile earnings, lack social protection, and often work outside the jurisdiction of labour legislation. Worldwide, of the more than 3 billion people who have jobs, only 1.65 billion have regular wages or salaries. Another 1.5 billion work in farming and small household enterprises (World Bank, 2012a). Agricultural workers suffer the highest prevalence of poverty. They are caught in cycles of low productivity, seasonal unemployment and low wages and are particularly vulnerable to changing weather patterns.

People's working conditions therefore deserve special attention. Salaries, and the benefits associated with jobs, tend to increase with economic development (Figure 2.10). Part of the change stems from the greater skills that people gain as their economies become more developed, and part comes from improved wages and benefits for people at any skills level.

Working conditions are particularly important as the share of labour in national GDP is declining in a majority of countries, both developed and developing. This trend, which has been observed since the mid-1980s, has been attributed to various factors, from technological progress biased towards skilled workers to global competition undermining workers' bargaining power. The entrance of China and India into world trade has doubled the size of the globalised labour force, reducing the price of labour relative to other factors of production (see Chapter 3 for more on this).

**Figure 2.10. Jobs provide higher earnings and benefits as countries grow**

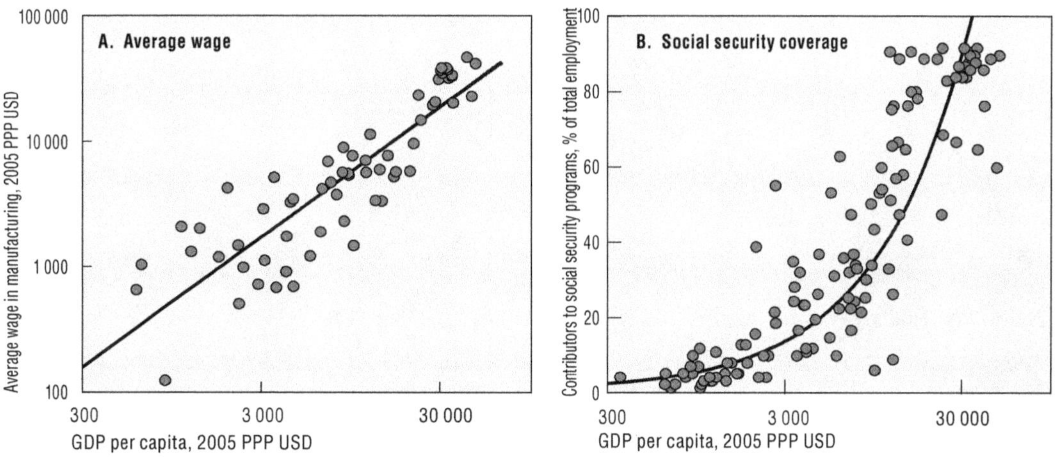


*Notes:* GDP is gross domestic product; PPP is purchasing power parity. Each dot represents a country.

*Source*: World Bank (2012a), *World Development Report 2013: Jobs*, The World Bank Group, Washington DC, http://siteresources.worldbank.org/EXTNWDR2013/Resources/8258024-1320950747192/8260293-1322665883147/WDR_2013_Report.pdf.

## *Wages in developing countries are catching up with developed countries*

Since the mid-1990s, wages in developing countries have begun to grow faster than in developed countries, regardless of skill levels. This trend is more pronounced for tradable products and services, whereas low-skilled workers in non-tradable sectors (e.g traditional service sectors such as housekeeping or hairdressers) remain the most disadvantaged (Figure 2.11). The lower wages for low-skilled workers, particularly in non-tradable sectors in developing countries, underline the importance of better education.

**Figure 2.11. Wages in developing countries are catching up**

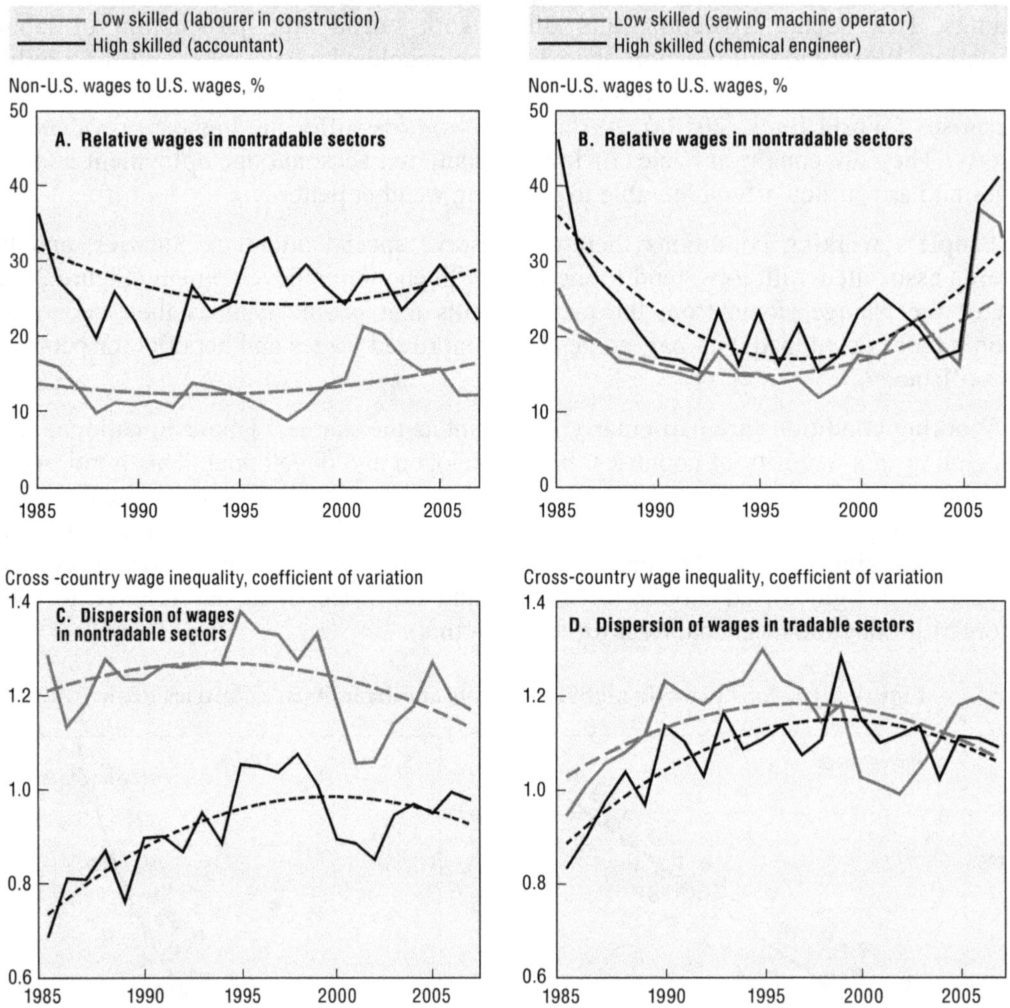


*Notes:* For details on the calculations, see World Bank (2012a), Figure 1.8.

*Source*: World Bank (2012a), *World Development Report 2013: Jobs*, The World Bank Group, Washington DC, http://siteresources.worldbank.org/EXTNWDR2013/Resources/8258024-1320950747192/8260293-1322665883147/WDR_2013_Report.pdf, p.59.

## *Women's access to paid work remains low*

Recent work shows that circumstances of birth and education play important roles in explaining unequal access to jobs. A study of 29 countries in Europe and Central Asia indicates that factors such as gender, ethnicity, parental education attainment and political affiliation contributed substantially to inequality (World Bank, 2012a).

Gender differences in employment are striking. Worldwide, fewer than 50% of women have jobs, compared to about 75% of men. Women are significantly underrepresented in wage employment in low and lower middle-income countries. Non-wage work represents more than 80% of women's employment in sub-Saharan Africa, whereas it is less than 20% in Eastern European and Central Asian countries. Furthermore, women continue to earn significantly less than men – even when they are equals in terms of education, experience or work sector (World Bank, 2012a).

Unpaid employment and self-employment account on average for more than half of total women's employment; the shares are particularly high in Southeast Asia (61%), South Asia (77%), and sub-Saharan Africa (77%). Non-income generating activities are shown to be a high proportion of women's total activities in countries as diverse as India, Guatemala, Spain and the US (Figure 2.12). According to the UNDP, women perform 66% of the world's work, but earn just 10% of the income and own only 1% of the property (UNDP, 2011, cited in Oxford Martin School, 2013).

**Figure 2.12. Women spend more time in activities that do not directly generate income**

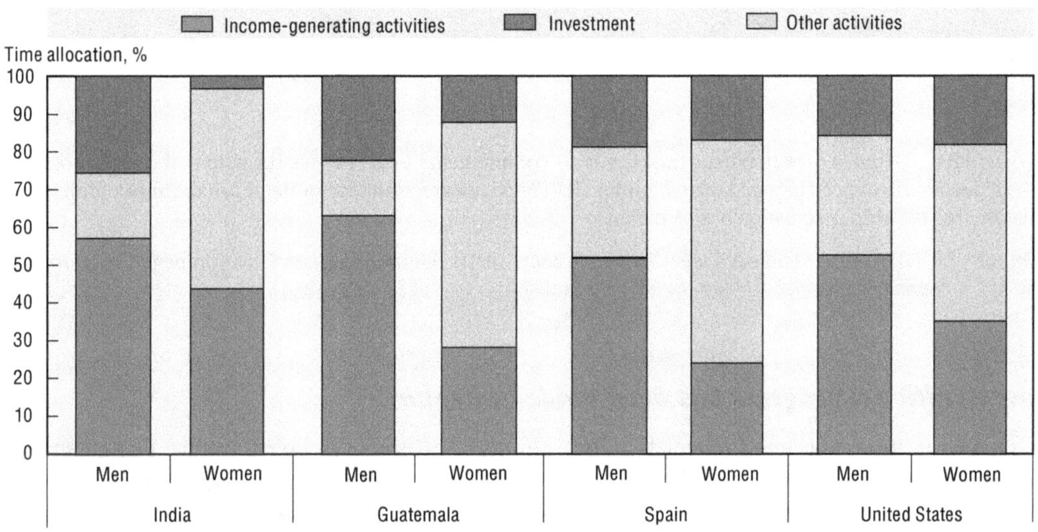


*Notes:* The figure refers to people aged 15 years and more. *Income-generating activities* is the time devoted to wage or salaried employment; farming, own-account work, self-employment with hired labour, and unpaid family labour in household enterprises; *investment* refers to time allocated to education, health care, and job search; *other activities* included work outside the system of national accounts, for example child care, housework. Leisure and other activities associated with consumption (for example, shopping and social interactions), as well as sleep, are not includes.

*Source*: World Bank (2012a), *World Development Report 2013: Jobs*, The World Bank Group, Washington DC, http://siteresources.worldbank.org/EXTNWDR2013/Resources/8258024-1320950747192/8260293-1322665883147/WDR_2013_Report.pdf.

## Progress towards basic needs is variable

Certain basic needs are essential for people to survive. These include education, health (including good nutrition) and infrastructure (water and sanitation, shelter, electricity, and information and communication technologies). However, basic needs provision does not automatically increase with economic growth (Figure 2.13). To secure basic needs, additional specific policies are required, as proposed in Chapters 4 and 5.

**Figure 2.13. The relationship between economic growth and changes in health and education is weak**

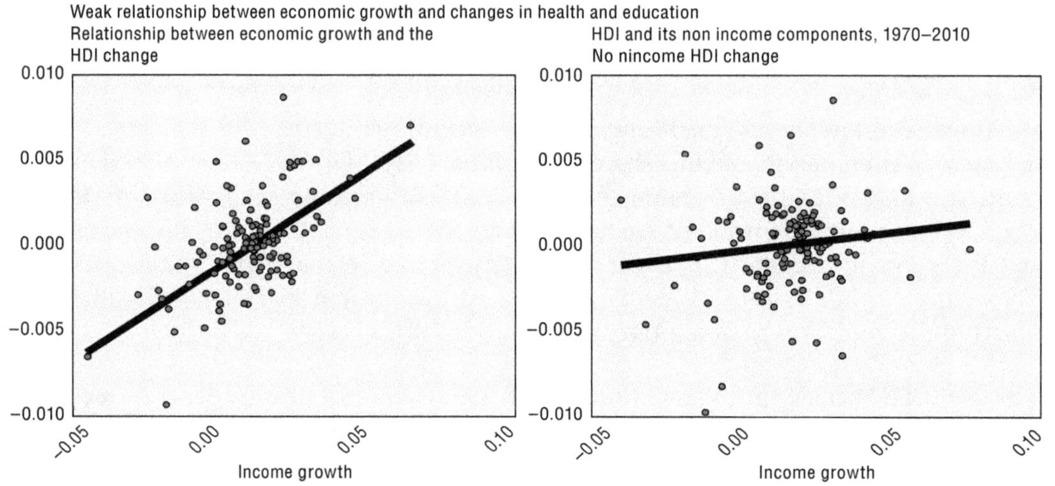


*Notes*: HDI – Human Development Index, which complements GDP per capita with some indicators of basic needs (life expectancy and education level). Thicker regression line in the left-hand figure indicates that the relationship is statistically significant.

*Source:* UNDP (2010), Human Development Report 2010, United Nations Development Programme, New York, http://hdr.undp.org/sites/default/files/reports/270/hdr_2010_en_complete_reprint.pdf, Figure 3.1.

## *Most significant progress has been made in health*

Health is the basic need towards which greatest progress is being made. For example, maternal mortality fell by 45% between 1990 and 2013 worldwide, from 380 to 210 deaths for every 100 000 live births. An estimated 3.3 million deaths from malaria were averted worldwide between 2000 and 2012 thanks to the substantial expansion of malaria interventions. About 90% of those averted deaths (3 million) were children under five living in sub-Saharan Africa (UNDP, 2014b). The global under-five mortality rate has declined by nearly half (49%) since 1990, dropping from 90 to 46 deaths for every 1 000 live births in 2013. In 1990, 12.7 million children under five died. In 2013 that number fell to 6.3 million (UNICEF, 2014a). Progress is accelerating in some regions of the world, particularly in East Asia and the Pacific, Latin America and the Caribbean, and sub-Saharan Africa (Figure 2.14).

There are still important discrepancies among countries, however. While the under-five mortality rate in sub-Saharan Africa has improved, it is nearly 15 times the average rate of high-income countries. Half of all under-five deaths in 2013 occurred in just five countries: India (21%), Nigeria (13%), Pakistan (6%), Democratic Republic of the Congo (5%) and China (4%) (UNICEF, 2014b).

**Figure 2.14. Good global progress in reducing under-five mortality rates, 1990-2013**

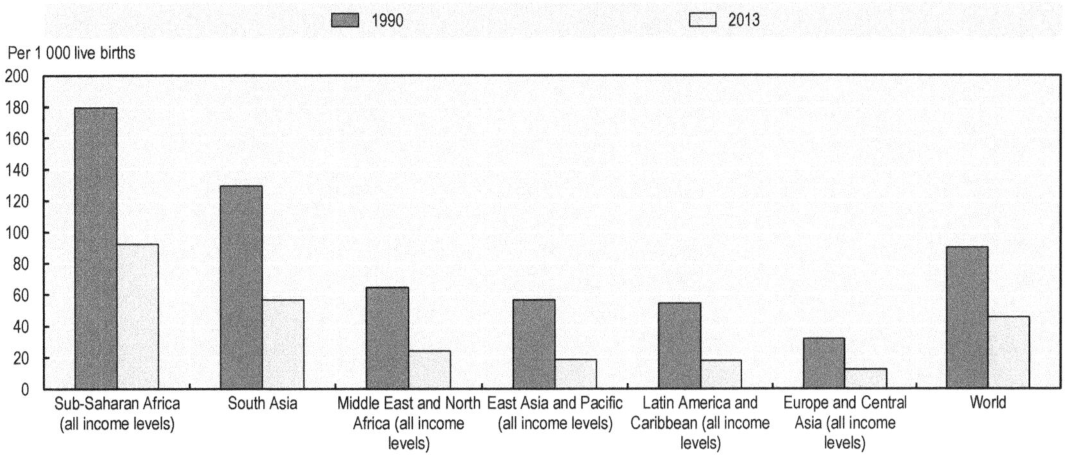


*Source:* World Bank (2014), *2014 World Development Indicators*, The World Bank Group, Washington DC, http://data.worldbank.org/indicator.

## *Hunger still affects the developing world*

Although the *share* of the population in developing countries that is undernourished, (according to UNICEF) has fallen significantly over the past two decades – from 23% in 1990/92 to 15% in 2010/12 (Figure 2.15) – population growth has meant that the total *number* of undernourished people in developing countries has fallen more slowly. Around 12% of people globally (850 million) have no secure source of food, and one in four children are still affected by chronic malnutrition (162 million children) (UNICEF, 2014a).

Around 70% of the world's undernourished live in middle-income countries. Asian countries accounted for 65% of the world's total in 2010/12, with China and India alone contributing 40%, despite significant progress in China in the last ten years. On the other hand, the prevalence of undernourishment is highest in low-income countries. Countries in Africa are the worst affected, with 34% of people undernourished on average (OECD, 2013c). Developed countries may not be completely spared from undernourishment. In OECD countries, rising numbers of families also say they cannot afford enough food (OECD, 2014b).

In low-income countries, food consumption expenditures typically account for 50% or more of households' budgets. In lower middle-income countries, such as China and India, the figure is about 40% (OECD, 2013c). As countries develop, the challenge of ensuring food security and good nutrition becomes progressively less a question of income, and more one of modifying behaviour: unhealthy eating is a significant issue in both developed and developing countries.

**Figure 2.15. The number of undernourished people is unacceptably high**

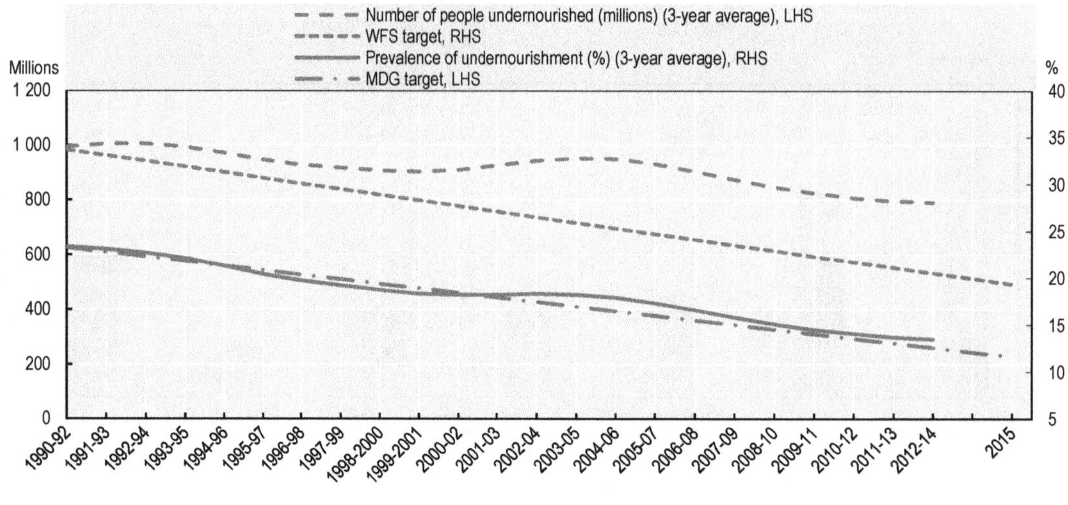


*Note:* WFS: World Food Summit; MDG: Millennium Development Goals.

*Source:* OECD (2013c), *Global Food Security: Challenges for the Food and Agricultural System*, OECD Publishing, Paris, http://dx.doi.org/10.1787/9789264195363-en using FAO data.

## Access to basic infrastructure remains very uneven in the developing world

The Millennium Development Goal (MDG) target of halving the proportion of people without access to an improved drinking water source was achieved in 2010, five years ahead of schedule. In 2012, 89% of the world's population had access to an improved source, up from 76% in 1990. This means that worldwide, over 2.3 billion more people have access to an improved source of drinking water. However, in Africa, fewer than 60% of people have access to a clean water source (WHO/UNICEF, 2000). Between 1990 and 2012, almost 2 billion people gained access to an improved sanitation facility. But 2.5 billion still do not have access to an improved sanitation facility (UNDP, 2014b).

Infrastructure that is essential for people's basic needs includes shelter, electricity, transport, telecommunications and the technology that can enable people to access vital services such as education and health. Infrastructure is often transversal and affects many areas. For example, electricity not only enables us to heat our houses, but it also allows people to make better use of time at night (including working, reading, and education) and can also power hospitals and refrigerators for vaccines. Roads in rural areas can boost movement of goods, school attendance, and access to health services. Information and communication technology (ICT) can provide education and training opportunities, and transmit a wealth of information and knowledge to people. Water systems, electricity, roads, and ICTs all have implications for the environment.

Low and middle-income countries have the greatest gap in infrastructure provision (Table 2.1). In Africa, only 30% of the population has access to electricity. Of the estimated 7 000 megawatts (MW) of new power generation capacity required, only 1 000 MW has been achieved in recent years.[5] While only 10% of the continent's population uses the Internet, 56% of people are already covered by a mobile cellular network (World Bank, 2012b).

**Table 2.1. Global variations in access to infrastructure**

Access to utilities services and communication technologies

| | % of population with access to | | | |
|---|---|---|---|---|
| | Electricity | Improved water sources | Improved sanitation facilities | Mobile phone subscribers (%) |
| Low-income countries | 32.9 | 69 | 37 | 53 |
| Lower middle-income countries | 72.9 | 88 | 48 | 85 |
| Upper middle-income countries | 98.2 | 93 | 74 | 100 |

*Source*: World Bank (2014), *2014 World Development Indicators*, The World Bank Group, Washington DC, http://data.worldbank.org/indicator.

## *Education attainment improved but quality concerns remain significant*

Enrolment in primary education across the developing world increased from 83% to 90% between 2000 and 2012. By 2012, all developing regions had almost achieved gender parity in primary education. The number of out-of-school children has fallen from 108 million to 60 million in the past 20 years, largely thanks to a 66% reduction in South and West Asia (Oxford Martin School, 2013).

However, high inequalities persist, particularly in South Asia, the Arab states, and sub-Saharan Africa. In 2012, of the around 60 million out-of-school children, more than 50% were in sub-Saharan Africa or in conflict-affected areas (Oxford Martin School, 2013). Three-quarters of illiterate adults lived in just 10 countries; 37% of all illiterate adults lived in India (Oxford Martin, 2013). Of the 781 million adults and 126 million youth worldwide lacking basic literacy skills, more than 60% are women (UNDP, 2014a).

**Figure 2.16. In 29 countries there is a big gap between the number of pupils per teacher and per trained teacher**

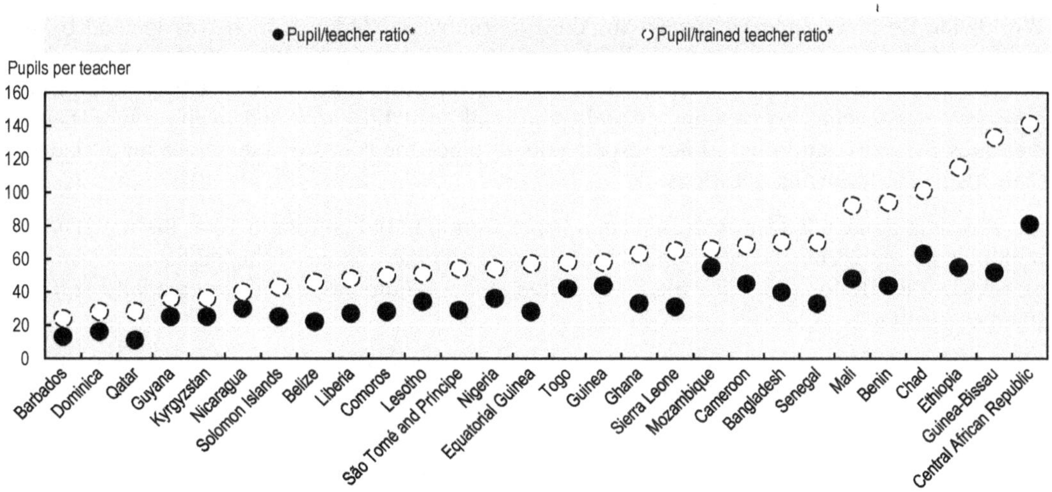


*Note:* * Based on headcounts of pupils and teachers.

*Source:* UNESCO (2014), *EFA Global Monitoring Report 2013/4 – Teaching and Learning: Achieving Quality for All*, United Nations Educational, Scientific and Cultural Organization, UNESCO publishing, Paris, http://unesdoc.unesco.org/images/0022/002256/225660e.pdf.

Even in countries that have reached a fair level of educational attainment, quality can still be a problem. Out of 250 million children globally who are unable to read, 130 million are in school (UNESCO, 2014). In low and lower-middle income countries, one in three children is still not able to read despite five or six years of schooling. Teacher recruitment lags behind growth in pupil enrolment: in 2011, 16% of all countries in the world had a pupil/teacher ratio exceeding 40:1 in primary education. Twenty-three of these countries were in sub-Saharan Africa (Figure 2.16).

In secondary schools, in half of the countries for which data is available, at least 25% of all teachers lack appropriate training. In one fifth of the countries, more than 50% of all teachers lacked appropriate training (UNESCO, 2014); similar trends can be seen in primary schools (Figure 2.16). Good quality material is also scarce in developing countries. In Tanzania, only 3.5% of all grade 6 pupils had sole use of a reading textbook. Poor physical infrastructure is another problem, with young children squeezed into overcrowded classrooms. In Malawi, there are on average 130 children per class in grade 1. In Chad, only one in four schools has a toilet.

## Progress in life satisfaction stagnates, but optimism remains

The previous sections have outlined the status of more objective measures of livelihoods (income, employment, access to basic needs). But as we have seen, people's subjective evaluations of their own livelihoods can complement these measures. This section analyses how people's own perceptions of and satisfaction with their lives vary according to region and over time, and how they correlate with more objective livelihood conditions (such as income and inequality). The data are mainly derived from the Gallup Worldwide Research Indexes (Box 2.3 and Annex 2.A1).

### Box 2.3. The Gallup Worldwide Research Indexes: Measuring people's perceptions around the world

All the indexes used for the analysis in this chapter were directly derived from the Gallup Worldwide Research Indexes; except for the Environmental Index, which was created by the authors of this publication using individual Gallup questions (Gallup, 2014). Most of the analysis presented here draws on data from the Life Evaluation Index. The Life Evaluation Index measures respondents' perceptions of their own quality of life, now and in the future. Gallup measures life satisfaction by asking respondents to place the status of their lives on a "ladder" scale, using the following questions:

Please imagine a ladder, with steps numbered from 0 at the bottom to 10 at the top. The top of the ladder represents the best possible life for you and the bottom of the ladder represents the worst possible life for you. On which step of the ladder would you say you personally feel you stand at this time?

Just your best guess – on which step of the same ladder do you think you will stand in the future, say about five years from now?

Individuals who rate their current lives a "7" or higher AND their future an "8" or higher are "thriving". Individuals are "suffering" if they report their current AND future lives as "4" and lower. All other individuals are "struggling". A respondent must have answered both questions to have indexes calculated. The final country-level index is a variable that codes respondents into one of these three categories of well-being and represents the percentage of respondents in each category. Country-level weights are applied to this calculation.

For more detail on the Gallup research methodology, see Annex 2.A1 and Gallup (2013), *Worldwide Research Methodology and Codebook*, Gallup Inc., Washington DC.

## *Most people in the developing world are struggling or even suffering*

In most developing regions, 80% of people – in some regions even more – feel they are struggling or even suffering in their daily lives (Figure 2.17, Panel A). In developing South Asia, Middle East and North Africa, and Europe and Central Asia, around 20% of people feel they are suffering. In all other regions (including the high-income group of countries), this share is around 10%.

**Figure 2.17. Thriving, struggling or suffering? Regional perceptions**

A. Life evaluation index, 2012

B. Changes in life satisfaction, 2006-13, people thriving as % of total, by region

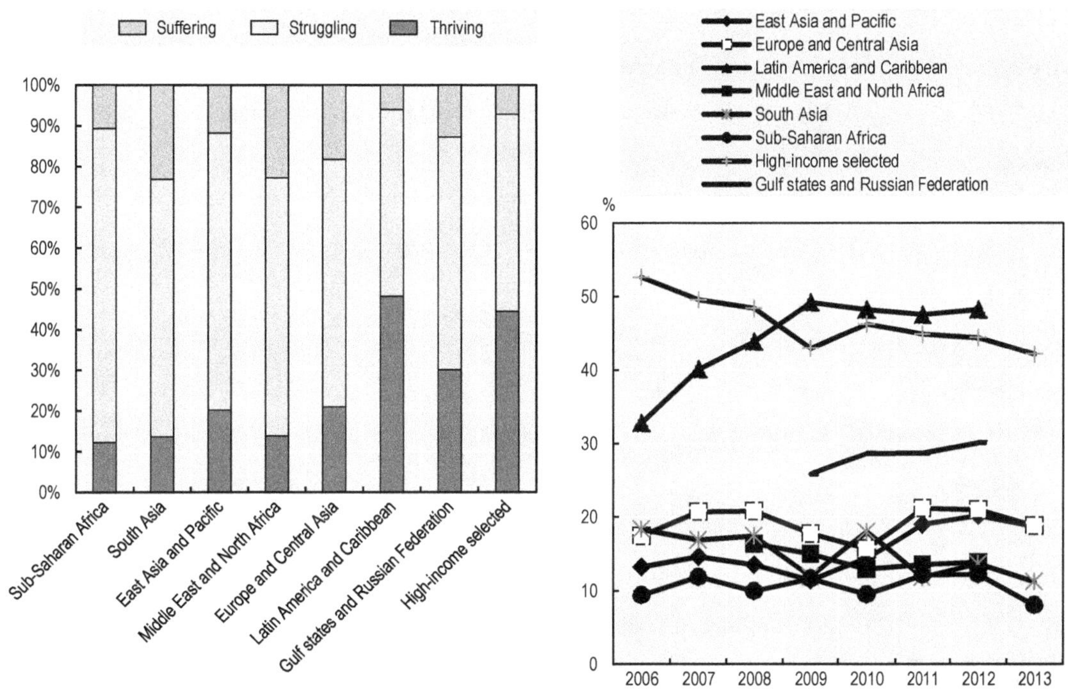


*Notes*: The regions correspond to the 6 developing regions as defined by the World Bank, plus the Gulf states (Bahrain, Kuwait, Oman, Qatar, Saudi Arabia, and UAE) and the Russian Federation, and other high-income countries. Sub-Saharan Africa includes data for 28 countries, Middle East and North Africa for 11, Europe and Central Asia for 21, Latin America and Caribbean for 18, South Asia for 6, East Asia and Pacific for 10, high-income countries for 38 and the Gulf states and the Russian Federation for 6. The regions are ordered by their average GDP per capita in purchasing power parity (PPP). The index is weighted using the Gallup country weights for each observation and countries' population to calculate regional averages. For more, see Box 2.2 and Annex 2.A1.

*Source:* Adapted from Gallup (n.d.), Gallup World Poll, Gallup Analytics, Gallup Inc., Washington DC, www.gallup.com/services/170945/world-poll.aspx (accessed 19 January 2015).

In Latin America and the Caribbean, people appear to be more satisfied than in all other regions of the world. Here, 50% of people consider themselves to be thriving – a higher share than in high-income countries. In the high-income group (excluding the Gulf states and the Russian Federation) around 45% feel they are thriving, while in the Gulf states and the Russian Federation, the share is 30%. Between 2006 and 2009 the share of people increased in Latin America and the Caribbean who feel they are thriving (Figure 2.17, Panel B).

Since 2009, life seems to have become harder for most people. More and more people in the developed world feel they are either struggling or suffering. While more than half of all people in the developed world felt they were thriving in 2006, the share had fallen to just over 40% in 2013. It is only in the Gulf states and the Russian Federation that more people have become satisfied with their life in recent years.

### *Wealth is not enough to achieve life satisfaction*

Generally, the richer a country, the more people are satisfied with their life. But additional income in poorer countries plays a more important role than additional income in richer countries (see Figure 2.18's concave trend line in Panel A, and convex trend lines in Panels B and C).

**Figure 2.18. Additional income plays a greater role in life satisfaction for people in poorer countries**

A. Share of people that are thriving compared with GDP per capita

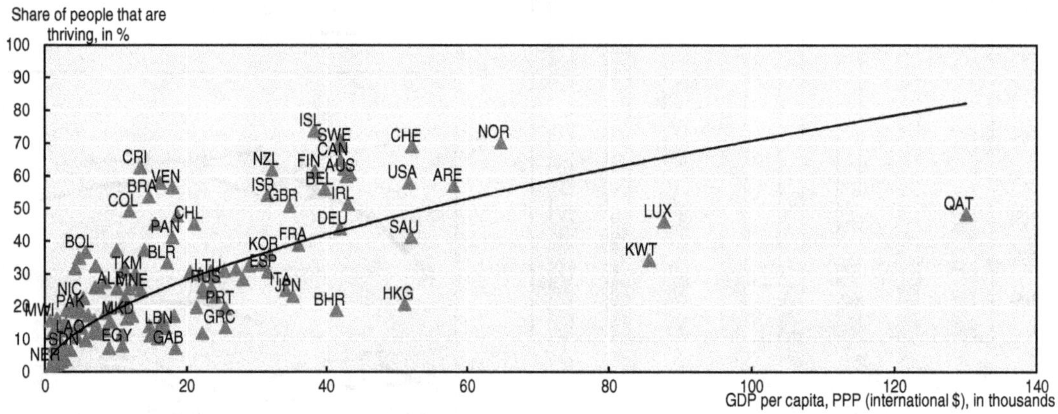


B. Share of people that are struggling compared with GDP per capita

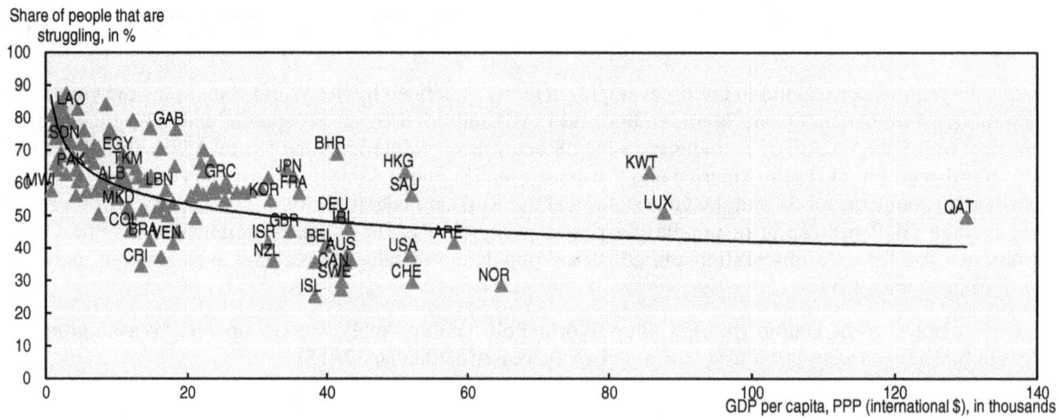

**Figure 2.18. Additional income plays a greater role in life satisfaction for people in poorer countries** *(cont.)*

C. Share of people that are suffering compared with GDP per capita

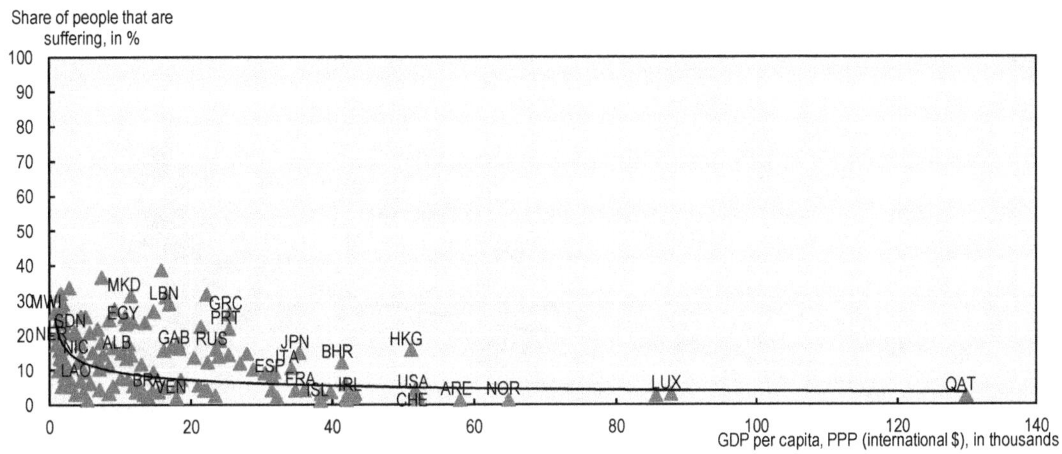


*Notes:* The reference year is 2012. For more information on the life satisfaction index, see Box 2.2 and Annex 2.A1. For a key to the 3-letter ISO country codes see http://unstats.un.org/unsd/ methods/m49/m49alpha.htm.

*Source:* Adapted from Gallup (n.d.), Gallup World Poll, Gallup Analytics, Gallup Inc., Washington DC, www.gallup.com/services/170945/world-poll.aspx (accessed 19 January 2015) and World Bank (2014), *2014 World Development Indicators*, The World Bank Group, Washington DC, http://data.worldbank.org/sites/default/files/wdi-2014-book.pdf.

Factors other than income also matter for people's well-being. For example, people in many Latin American countries – such as Brazil, Chile, Colombia and Panama – seem to be clearly more satisfied with their lives than people in other countries at similar per capita income levels; the same holds true for people in European countries such as Iceland, Norway, Sweden and Switzerland. People in high-income countries like Kuwait, Luxembourg and Qatar, on the other hand, seem to have more difficult lives than would be expected given their high per capita incomes.

Comparing people's life satisfaction with the more multidimensional Human Development Index (HDI) also shows a clear positive relationship (Figure 2.19, Panel A). However, there are still significant deviations from this overall trend, calling for an even deeper exploration of the other factors that affect people's life satisfaction. The *World Happiness Report 2013* shows that community trust, mental and physical health as well as the quality of governance and rule of law also matter for life satisfaction and potentially offset the benefits felt from higher income (Helliwell, Layard and Sachs, 2013). Inequality, measured by the Gini index, is – surprisingly – a very bad predictor of a country's average life satisfaction (Figure 2.19, Panel B).

**Figure 2.19. The links between life satisfaction, human development and income inequality**

A. People's life satisfaction tends to be higher in countries that score well on the Human Development Index

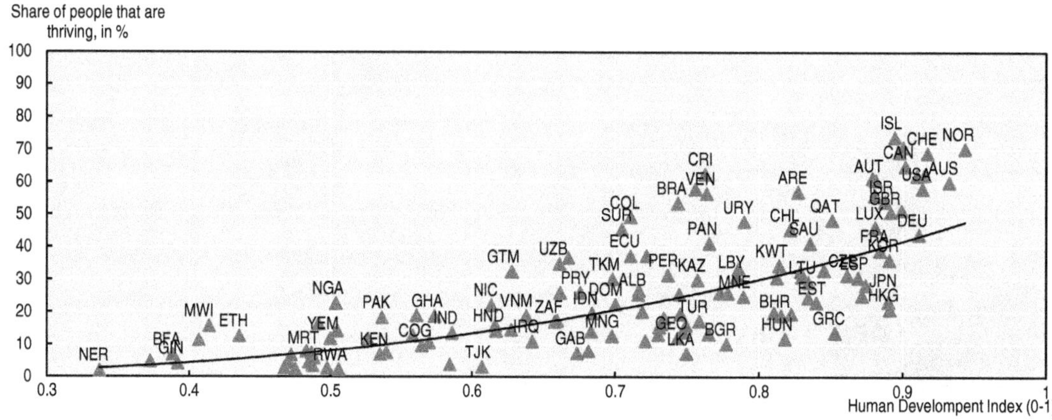


B. There is no clear link between life satisfaction and a country' level of income inequality

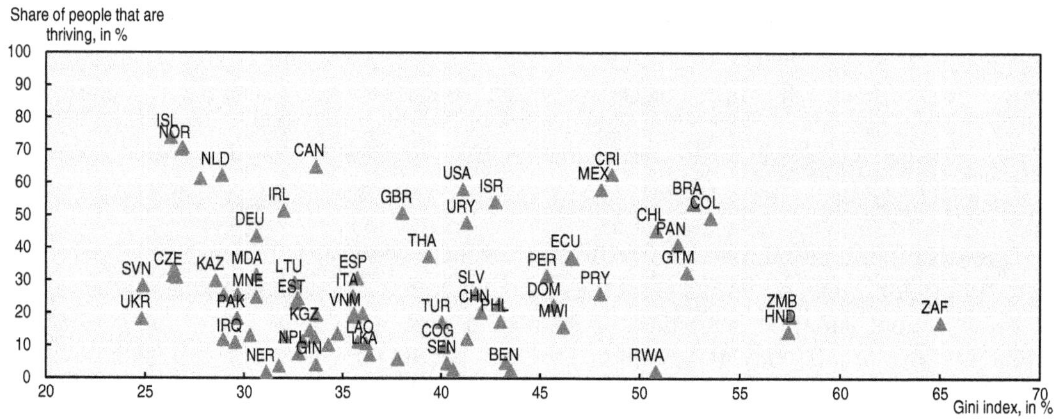


*Notes:* The reference year is 2012. For more information on the life satisfaction index, see Box 2.2 and Annex 2.A1. Income inequality is measured by the Gini coefficient. A Gini coefficient of zero expresses perfect equality, where all values are the same (for example, where everyone has the same income). A Gini coefficient of one (or 100%) expresses maximal inequality among values (for example, where only one person has all the income and all others have none). Link for 3-digit ISO country codes: http://unstats.un.org/unsd/methods/m49/m49alpha.htm.

*Sources:* Adapted from Gallup (n.d.), Gallup World Poll, Gallup Analytics, Gallup Inc., Washington DC, www.gallup.com/services/170945/world-poll.aspx (accessed 19 January 2015); World Bank (2014), *2014 World Development Indicators*, The World Bank Group, Washington DC, http://data.worldbank.org/sites/default/files/wdi-2014-book.pdf and UNDP (2014a), *The 2014 Human Development Report – Sustaining Human Progress: Reducing Vulnerabilities and Building Resilience*, United Nations Development Program, New York, http://hdr.undp.org/sites/default/files/hdr14-report-en-1.pdf.

## *Lack of jobs and money are people's greatest concerns worldwide*

In addition to the life evaluation index, this analysis has drawn on seven sub-indexes which explore individuals' perceptions of their livelihoods across a range of issues. Individuals' evaluations of these more specific aspects of their livelihoods provide subjective proxies for the value of the various types of capital (social, human, economic and natural capital). The sub-indexes include the following (see Annex 2.A1 for details):

1. The Environmental Index indicates whether current and future local environmental issues (such as pollution, floods, droughts, heat or cold) are perceived as a problem.
2. The Social Well-Being Index shows whether individuals can count on relatives or friends to support them, if needed.
3. The Food and Shelter Index indicates whether people have enough money to buy food and provide adequate shelter or housing.
4. The Physical Well-Being Index gives an indication of people's physical and mental health.
5. The Youth Development Index represents people's evaluation of opportunities for younger generations in their home city or town.
6. The Job Climate Index gives an indication of people's perspectives of job prospects in their area.
7. The Financial Well-Being Index is an indicator of people's living conditions in terms of income or other financial means.

**Figure 2.20. Jobs and money are people's greatest concerns**

Subjective livelihood indexes 2012, 0-100

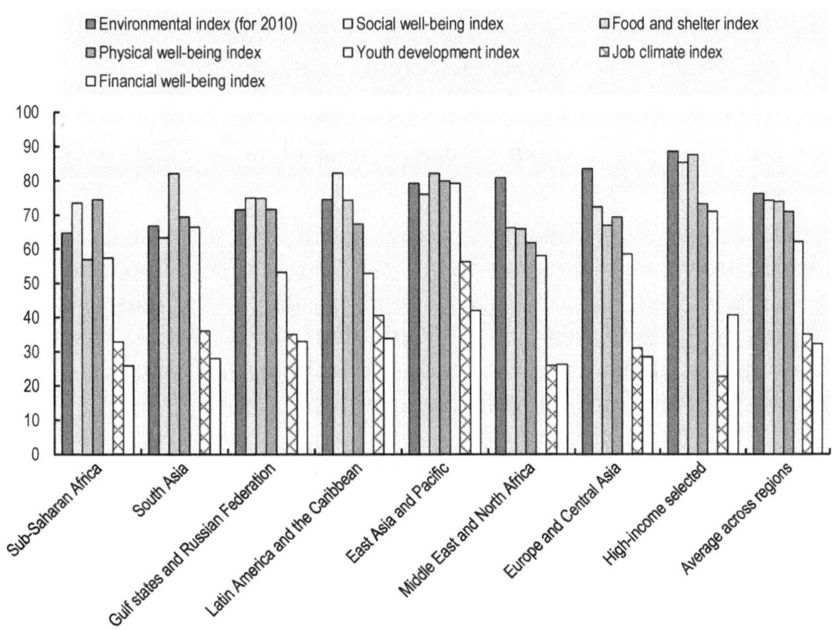


*Notes:* The higher the index score the more positive people feel.

*Source*: Adapted from Gallup (n.d.), Gallup World Poll, Gallup Analytics, Gallup Inc., Washington DC, www.gallup.com/services/170945/world-poll.aspx (accessed 19 January 2015).

For each country, the indexes can have values between 0 and 100, representing the percentage of people with favourable evaluations of a given aspect. The higher the score, the more positive the perception (see Annex 2.A1). Worldwide, the scores are most favourable for the Environmental Index, the Social Well-Being Index, the Food and Shelter

Index and the Physical Well-Being Index (all either at or above 70%), followed by the Youth Development Index, which scores around 60% (Figure 2.20). Jobs and income seem to be the biggest concerns for people around the globe, averaging less than 40%.

Looking more closely, however, concerns vary by country grouping. Individuals in high-income countries (except the Gulf states and the Russian Federation) feel most secure about the local environment, social well-being and food and shelter, yet they worry most about the job climate. The East Asia and Pacific region has the highest percentage of people who feel positive about several aspects of life, including physical and financial well-being, youth development and the job climate. While people in sub-Saharan Africa worry most about almost all seven aspects, they seem to be less worried about their physical and mental health than almost any other region.

### *Most people are optimistic about the future, except in high-income countries*

Looking to the future (five years ahead) and compared to their past (five years before) and present situation, people around the world provide interesting insights (Figure 2.21). In all middle and low-income countries, people generally think that the future will be better than the past or the present, except in Central Asia, where the past is now perceived as better than the present. The greatest optimism is in the East Asia-Pacific region. In Latin America, optimism about the future has been increasing. This positive perception, confirmed by other evaluations, can be explained by the good economic and job performance experienced by most economies on the continent. There is also a positive trend in the Gulf States, which enjoy wealth generated by their oil and gas reserves; and to a lesser extent in the Russian Federation (although its economy changed significantly in 2014).

However, in those high-income countries that have been affected by the economic crisis or in regions with other problems (such as the Middle East and North Africa), there is little optimism about the future.

To conclude, despite significant progress to improve people's livelihoods around the world and particularly in low-income countries, there are still important efforts to be made. Moreover, with slow economic growth continuing to affect most parts of the world and shocks potentially increasing, it is likely that much of this progress could be threatened by some of the emerging trends described in the next chapter. This underlines the need to build more resilient and inclusive societies.

**Figure 2.21. Life perceptions – past, present and future**

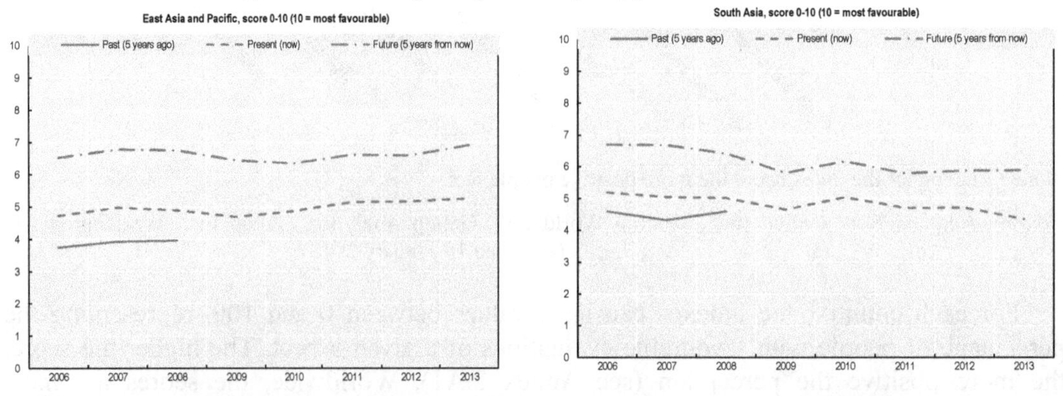

**Figure 2.21. Life perceptions – past, present and future** *(cont.)*

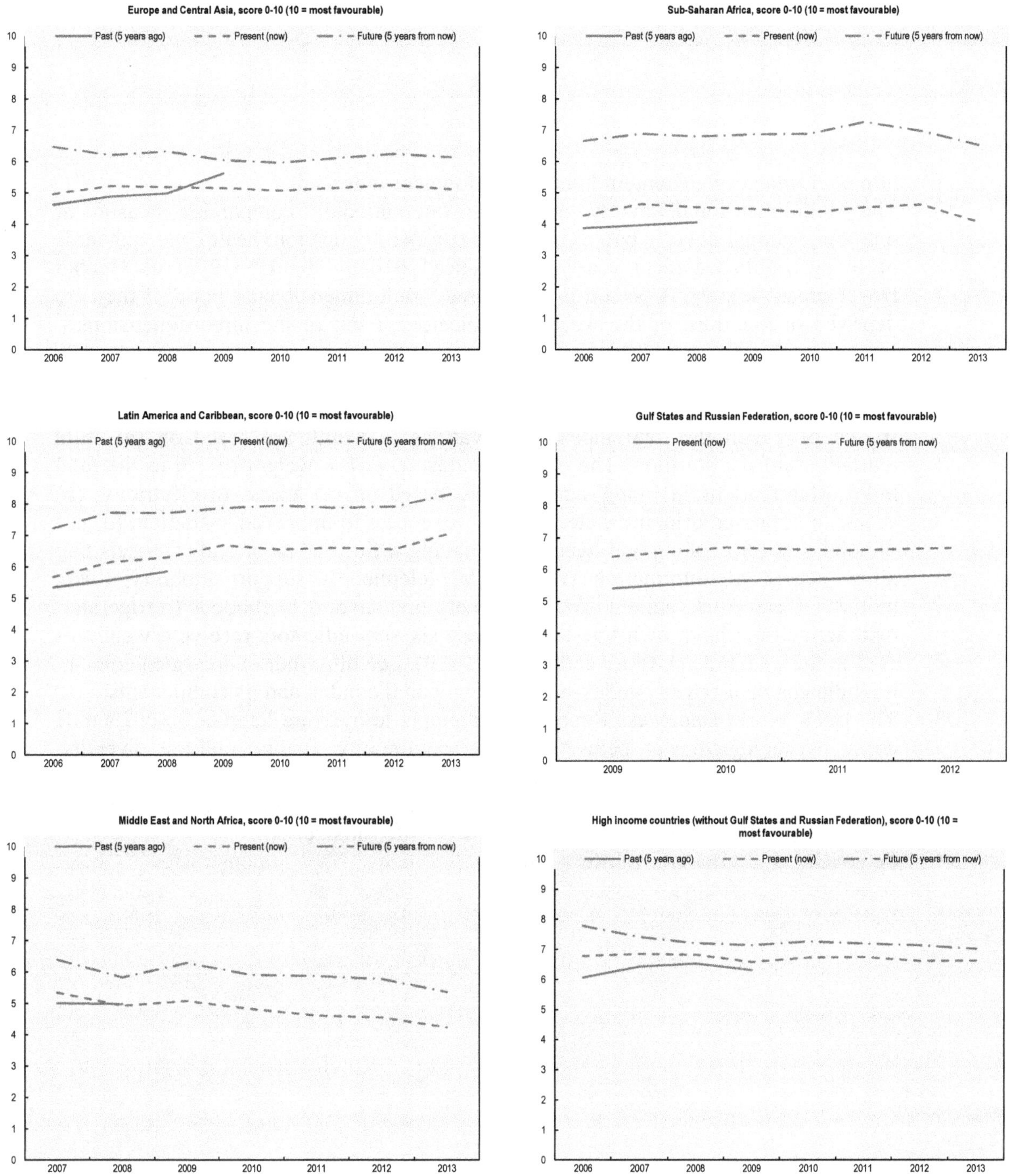


*Source*: Adapted from Gallup (n.d.), Gallup World Poll, Gallup Analytics, Gallup Inc., Washington DC, www.gallup.com/services/170945/world-poll.aspx (accessed 19 January 2015).

## Notes

1. http://hdr.undp.org/en/content/human-development-index-hdi
2. The Multidimensional Poverty Index is an internationally comparable measure of multidimensional poverty based on ten indicators of education, health and standards of living, published on a yearly basis since 2010 by the UNDP in its Human Development Report. A person is considered "multidimensionally poor" if they are deprived in one-third of the weighted indicators. Each of the three dimensions – education, health and living standards – receives an equal weight of 1/3. Deprivations in education are based on (a) school attendance for school-age children and (b) school attainment for household members. The two indicators receive a weight of 1/6 in the total index. Deprivations in health are based on (a) child mortality and (b) nutrition. The two indicators receive a weight of 1/6 in the total index. Deprivations in living standards are based on (a) access to electricity, (b) access to improved drinking water sources, (c) access to improved sanitation, (d) use of solid fuel for cooking and heating, (e) having a finished floor and (f) assets that allow access to information (radio, TV, telephone), support mobility (bike, motorbike, car, truck, animal cart, motorboat), and support livelihoods (refrigerator, own agricultural land, own livestock). These six sub-indicators receive a weight of 1/18 in the total index (Alkire and Santos, 2010). See http://hdr.undp.org/en/content/multidimensional-poverty-index-mpi to download the index and its components.
3. The UN's World Happiness Report also attempts to measure happiness across nine areas: psychological well-being, time use, community vitality, cultural diversity, ecological resilience, living standards, health, education and good governance (for example, see Helliwell et al., 2013). This Happiness Report makes extensive use of Gallup World Poll data to measure "happiness"/ life satisfaction.
4. Personalized Better Life Indexes can be constructed here: www.oecdbetterlifeindex.org.
5. See http://siteresources.worldbank.org/INTAFRICA/Resources/aicd_factsheet_energy.pdf

# *References*


Alvaredo F., A. B. Atkinson, T. Piketty and E. Saez (2015), The World Top Incomes Database, Paris School of Economics, Paris, http://topincomes.parisschoolofeconomics.eu/

Alkire, S. and M.E. Santos (2010), "Acute Multidimensional Poverty: A New Index for Developing Countries", *OPHI Working Paper*, No. 38, Oxford Poverty and Human Development Initiative, University of Oxford, Oxford, www.ophi.org.uk/wp-content/uploads/ophi-wp38.pdf.

Boarini, R., A. Kolev and A. McGregor (2014), "Measuring Well-being and Progress in Countries at Different Stages of Development: Towards a More Universal Conceptual Framework", *OECD Development Centre Working Papers*, No. 325, OECD Publishing, Paris, http://dx.doi.org/10.1787/5jxss4hv2d8n-en

Chandy L. and H. Kharas (5 May 2014), "What Do New Price Data Mean for the Goal of Ending Extreme Poverty?" Up Front blog, The Brookings Institution, www.brookings.edu/blogs/up-front/posts/2014/05/05-data-extreme-poverty-chandy-kharas.

The Economist (2012), "For richer, for poorer", Special Report: The World Economy, *The Economist*, 13 October 2012, www.economist.com/node/21564414.

Gallup (2014), *State of Global Well-Being,* Gallup-Healthways Well-Being Index, Gallup Inc., Washington DC, http://info.healthways.com/wellbeingindex.

Gallup (2013), *Worldwide Research Methodology and Codebook*, Gallup Inc., Washington DC.

Gallup (n.d.), *Gallup World Poll*, Gallup Analytics, Gallup Inc., Washington DC, www.gallup.com/services/170945/world-poll.aspx (accessed 19 January 2015).

Graham, C. (2009), *Happiness Around the World: The Paradox of Happy Peasants and Miserable Millionaires*, Oxford University Press, Oxford, https://global.oup.com/academic/product/happiness-around-the-world-9780199549054?cc=fr&lang=en&.

Helliwell, John F., Richard Layard, and Jeffrey Sachs (2013), *World Happiness Report 2013*, United Nations Sustainable Development Solutions Network, New York, http://unsdsn.org/wp-content/uploads/2014/02/WorldHappinessReport2013_online.pdf.

ILO (2014a), *World of Work Report 2014: Developing with Jobs*, revised edition, International Labour Organization, Geneva, www.ilo.org/wcmsp5/groups/public/---dgreports/---dcomm/documents/publication/wcms_243961.pdf.

ILO (2014b), *Global Employment Trends 2014: Risk of a Jobless Recovery?* International Labour Organization, Geneva, http://ilo.org/global/research/global-reports/global-employment-trends/2014/lang--en/index.htm.

ILO (2012), *Global Employment Trends 2012: Preventing a Deeper Jobs Crisis*, International Labour Organization, Geneva, www.ilo.org/global/research/global-reports/global-employment-trends/2012/lang--en/index.htm.

Kovacevic, M. and C. Calderon (2014), *UNDP's Multidimensional Poverty Index: 2014*, Human Development Report Office Occasional Paper, United Nations, New York, http://hdr.undp.org/sites/default/files/specifications_for_computation_of_the_mpi.pdf

OECD (2014a), *Income Inequality Update, June 2014,* Insights from the OECD Income Distribution Database, OECD Publishing, Paris, www.oecd.org/els/soc/OECD2014-Income-Inequality-Update.pdf.

OECD (2014b), *Society at a Glance 2014: OECD Social Indicators*, OECD Publishing, Paris, http://dx.doi.org/10.1787/soc_glance-2014-en.

OECD (2014c), *Social Institutions & Gender Index, 2014 Synthesis report*, OECD Publishing, www.genderindex.org/sites/default/files/docs/BrochureSIGI2015.pdf.

OECD (2013a), *How's Life? 2013: Measuring Well-being*, OECD Publishing, Paris, http://dx.doi.org/10.1787/9789264201392-en.

OECD (2013b), *OECD Employment Outlook 2013*, OECD Publishing, Paris, http://dx.doi.org/10.1787/empl_outlook-2013-en.

OECD (2013c), *Global Food Security: Challenges for the Food and Agricultural System*, OECD Publishing, Paris, http://dx.doi.org/10.1787/9789264195363-en.

OECD (2013d), Development Co-operation Report 2013: Ending *p*overty, OECD Publishing, Paris, http://dx.doi.org/10.1787/dcr-2013-en.

OECD (2012a), *OECD Employment Outlook 2012*, OECD Publishing, Paris, http://dx.doi.org/10.1787/empl_outlook-2013-en.

OECD (2012b), *Education at a Glance 2012: OECD Indicators*, OECD Publishing, Paris, http://dx.doi.org/10.1787/eag-2012-en.

Oxford Martin School (2013), *Now for the Long Term: The Report of the Oxford Martin Commission for Future Generations*, Oxford University Press, Oxford, www.oxfordmartin.ox.ac.uk/downloads/commission/Oxford_Martin_Now_for_the_Long_Term.pdf.

Oxford Poverty and Human Development Initiative, *Missing Dimensions of Poverty*, Oxford Department of International Development, Queen Elizabeth House, University of Oxford, www.ophi.org.uk/research/missing-dimensions/ (accessed 6 February 2015).

Senik, C. (2014), *L'Économie du Bonheur,* Coédition Seuil-La République des idées, Paris, www.seuil.com/livre-9782021186239.htm.

UNDP (2014a), *The 2014 Human Development Report – Sustaining Human Progress: Reducing Vulnerabilities and Building Resilience*, United Nations Development Programme, New York, http://hdr.undp.org/sites/default/files/hdr14-report-en-1.pdf.

UNDP (2014b), *The Millennium Development Goals Report 2014*, United Nations Development Programme, New York, http://www.un.org/millenniumgoals/2014%20MDG%20report/MDG%202014%20English%20web.pdf.

UNDP (2011), "Gender Equality and UNDP", Fast Facts, July, United Nations Development Programme, New York, www.undp.org/content/dam/undp/library/corporate/fast-facts/english/FFGender-Equality-and-UNDP.pdf.

UNDP (2010), *Human Development Report 2010*, United Nations Development Programme, New York, http://hdr.undp.org/sites/default/files/reports/270/hdr_2010_en_complete_reprint.pdf.

UNECA (2013), *The Millennium Development Goals Report 2013 – Food Security In Africa: Issues, Challenges and Lessons,* United Nations Economic Commission for Africa, Addis Ababa, www.uneca.org/sites/default/files/publications/mdgreport2013_eng.pdf.

UNESCO (2014), *EFA Global Monitoring Report 2013/4 – Teaching and Learning: Achieving Quality for All*, United Nations Educational, Scientific and Cultural Organization, UNESCO publishing, Paris, http://unesdoc.unesco.org/images/0022/002256/225660e.pdf.

UNICEF (2014a), "Under-five and infant mortality rates and number of deaths" (dataset) UNICEF, New York, http://data.unicef.org/child-mortality/under-five#sthash.F62DHfP4.dpuf.

UNICEF (2014b), *Committing to Child Survival: A Promise Renewed - Progress report 2014*, UNICEF, New York, http://files.unicef.org/publications/ files/APR_2014_web_15Sept14.pdf.

van Zanden, J., et al. (eds.) (2014), *How Was Life? Global Well-being since 1820*, OECD Publishing, Paris, http://dx.doi.org/10.1787/9789264214262-en.

WHO and UNICEF (2000), *Global Water Supply and Sanitation Assessment 2000 Report*, WHO/UNICEF, Geneva/New York, www.who.int/water_sanitation_health/monitoring/jmp2000.pdf?ua=1.

World Bank (2014), *2014 World Development Indicators*, The World Bank Group, Washington DC, http://data.worldbank.org/sites/default/files/wdi-2014-book.pdf.

World Bank (2012a), *World Development Report 2013: Jobs*, The World Bank Group, Washington DC, http://siteresources.worldbank.org/EXTNWDR2013/Resources/8258024-1320950747192/8260293-1322665883147/WDR_2013_Report.pdf.

World Bank (2012b), *Transformation Through Infrastructure: Infrastructure Strategy Update, FY 2012-2015*, The World Bank Group, Washington DC, http://siteresources.worldbank.org/INTINFRA/Resources/Transformationthroughinfrastructure.pdf.

# Annex 2.A1. Methodology for the subjective well-being indexes

Gallup Worldwide Research continually surveys residents in more than 150 countries, representing more than 98% of the world's adult population, using randomly selected, nationally representative samples. Gallup typically surveys 1 000 individuals in each country through face-to-face or telephone interviews, using a standard set of core questions that has been translated into the major languages of the respective country.

The Gallup Worldwide Research measures key indicators such as law and order, food and shelter, job creation, migration, financial well-being, personal health, civic engagement, and evaluative well-being and demonstrates their correlations with world development indicators including GDP. These indicators assist leaders in understanding the broad context of national interests and establishing organisation-specific correlations between leading indexes and lagging economic outcomes.

All the indexes used for the analysis in this chapter were derived from the Gallup Worldwide Research Indexes (Gallup, 2014), except for the Environmental Index, which was created by the OECD based on Gallup data. For more detail on the methodology and the Gallup research, see Gallup (2013), *Worldwide Research Methodology and Codebook*, Gallup Inc., Washington DC.

### *Life Evaluation Index*

As explained in Box 2.1, the Life Evaluation Index measures respondents' perceptions of their own quality of life, now and in the future. Gallup measures life satisfaction by asking respondents to place the status of their lives on a "ladder" scale:

- Please imagine a ladder, with steps numbered from 0 at the bottom to 10 at the top. The top of the ladder represents the best possible life for you and the bottom of the ladder represents the worst possible life for you. On which step of the ladder would you say you personally feel you stand at this time?
- Please imagine a ladder, with steps numbered from 0 at the bottom to 10 at the top. The top of the ladder represents the best possible life for you and the bottom of the ladder represents the worst possible life for you. Just your best guess, on which step do you think you will stand in the future, say about five years from now?

Index scores are calculated at the individual record level. For each individual record the following procedure applies. Individuals who rate their current lives a "7" or higher AND their future an "8" or higher are "thriving". Individuals are "suffering" if they report their current AND future lives as a "4" and lower. All other individuals are "struggling". A respondent must have answered both questions to have indexes calculated. The final country-level index is a variable that codes respondents into one of these three categories of well-being and represents the percentage of respondents in each category. Country-level weights are applied to this calculation.

### *Food and Shelter Index*

The Food and Shelter Index measures whether a respondent has experienced deprivation in the areas of food and shelter. It is composed of two questions that ask about respondents' ability to afford food or shelter in the past year:

- Have there been times in the past 12 months when you did not have enough money to buy food that you or your family needed?
- Have there been times in the past 12 months when you did not have enough money to provide adequate shelter or housing for you and your family?

Index scores are calculated at the individual record level. For each individual record the following procedure applies: The two items are recoded so that positive (or favorable) answers are scored a "1" and all other answers (including don't know and refused) are assigned a score of "0." If a record has no answer for an item, then that item is not eligible for inclusion in the calculations. An individual record has an index calculated if it has valid scores for both questions. A record's final index score is the mean of valid items multiplied by 100. The final country-level index score is the mean of all individual records for which an index score was calculated. Country-level weights are applied to this calculation.

Lower scores on this index indicate that more respondents reported struggling to afford food and shelter in the past year, while higher scores indicate fewer respondents reported such struggles.

### *Financial Well-Being Index*

The Financial Well-Being Index measures respondents' personal economic situations and the economics of the community where they live. The subjective measures of financial well-being that make up the index are an important complement to traditional macroeconomic indicators such as GDP and unemployment rates, particularly in cases in which these data are difficult to obtain or the quality is suspect.

- Which one of these phrases comes closest to your own feelings about your household's income these days: living comfortably on present income, getting by on present income, finding it difficult on present income, or finding it very difficult on present income?
- Are you satisfied or dissatisfied with your standard of living, all the things you can buy and do?
- Right now, do you feel your standard of living is getting better or getting worse?
- Right now, do you think that economic conditions in the city or area where you live, as a whole, are getting better or getting worse?

### *Job Climate Index*

The Job Climate Index measures the attitudes about a community's efforts to provide economic opportunities.

- Right now, do you think that economic conditions in the city or area where you live, as a whole, are getting better or getting worse?

- Thinking about the job situation in the city or area where you live today, would you say that it is now a good time or a bad time to find a job?

### *Physical Well-being Index*

The Physical Well-Being Index measures perceptions of one's own health. Attempts to assess the state of a country's overall health usually involve the accumulation of health-related statistics such as life expectancy, infant mortality, and disease infection rates. Additionally, many government studies in individual countries collect health data via surveys from their own residents. Less numerous are survey projects that collect consistent health-related data from respondents across several countries, and in most cases those multinational efforts focus on Western countries. Gallup Worldwide Research has now measured self-reported personal health using the same questions and representative sample frames in more than 150 countries and areas. The object of the Physical Well-Being Index was to produce an overview of respondents' perceptions of their own health status. Individuals with high Physical Well-Being scores also tend to be more optimistic about the future and in terms of well-being are less likely to be "suffering."

- Do you have any health problems that prevent you from doing any of the things people your age normally can do?
- Now, please think about yesterday, from the morning until the end of the day. Think about where you were, what you were doing, who you were with, and how you felt. Did you feel well-rested yesterday?
- Did you experience the following feelings during a lot of the day yesterday? Physical pain? Worry? Sadness?

### *Social Well-being Index*

The Social Well-Being Index assesses a respondent's social support structure and opportunities to make friends in the city or area where he or she lives.

- If you were in trouble, do you have relatives or friends you can count on to help you whenever you need them, or not?
- In the city or area where you live, are you satisfied or dissatisfied with the opportunities to meet people and make friends?

### *Youth Development Index*

The Youth Development Index measures a community's focus on the welfare of its children. This index includes general measures of development of youth and respect for youth, along with satisfaction with the educational system.

- In the city or area where you live, are you satisfied or dissatisfied with the educational system or the schools?
- Do you believe that children in (country) are treated with respect and dignity, or not?
- Do most children in (country) have the opportunity to learn and grow every day, or not?

### *Environmental Index*

This index was constructed by this book's authors, using data from individual Gallup survey questions. It was constructed in exactly the same way as the indexes described above.

- In the past 12 months, have there been any severe environmental problems in your city or area, or not? For example, pollution, floods, droughts, or long periods of extreme heat or cold?
- In the next five years, do you think you will need to move because of severe environmental problems?

# Chapter 3
# Emerging trends and threats to livelihoods

*This chapter surveys emerging global trends in the economy, technology, demography, environment, security and governance that could have a significant impact on future livelihoods. Economic trends include the continuing economic weight of emerging and developing economies; plus the prospects of jobless economic growth, rising inequality, and the climbing costs of social protection. Technology offers both threat and opportunity: increasing automation of jobs could destabilise livelihoods, while innovation could bring greater access to education and global markets, and medical breakthroughs. Demographic shifts – such as too many old people in advanced and emerging economies and too many young people in developing countries – will all influence future livelihoods. Climate change and natural resource degradation are already affecting people, as are conflict, crime, terrorism and cybercrime. The chapter concludes with some of the governance weaknesses – such as resistance to change, lack of trust, and poor global and national co-ordination and delegation – which are hindering an adequate response to these emerging trends.*

The statistical data for Israel are supplied by and under the responsibility of the relevant Israeli authorities. The use of such data by the OECD is without prejudice to the status of the Golan Heights, East Jerusalem and Israeli settlements in the West Bank under the terms of international law.

## Key messages

Major trends in the economy, technology, demography, environment, security and governance will affect the future of livelihoods throughout the world:

- The global economy remains fragile. The next major shocks may well come from the emerging countries, whose growing corporate sector has benefited from massive lending by the global financial system and whose growth is likely to slow in the coming decades.
- Jobless growth is a worrying phenomenon. Statistics clearly demonstrate that job increases – whether in high, middle or low-income countries – are not keeping pace with growth. Over the past three decades, labour's share in output has shrunk globally from 64% to 59%.
- Inequality seems to be on the rise. For example, the wealth generated by the digital revolution has gone overwhelmingly to the owners of capital and the highest-skilled workers.
- Technology is changing the nature of employment. Jobs that are low-skilled, routine and repetitive are at risk from automation, while ICT-intensive occupations now account for more than 20% of all employment in OECD countries.
- Demographic trends are a concern in both developing and developed countries. The large share of young people in many developing countries could be a destabilising influence if they cannot be productively employed. Ageing populations in developed countries lead to high pension and health costs that will weigh heavily on private and public budgets.
- Social protection systems are under stress from budget cuts, ageing populations and increasing unemployment. Only 20% of the world's population has adequate social security coverage, and more than half lack any coverage at all.
- Livelihoods are increasingly threatened by climate change; extreme weather events such as droughts and floods are increasing in many regions of the world.
- Conflicts, which are taking new forms, undermine livelihoods, while poverty drives criminality. More than 1.5 billion people live in countries affected by conflict – about one-fifth of the world's population.
- Policy action by governments to improve livelihoods may be hampered by resistance to change, low levels of trust in government by their citizens, and difficulties in constructing an effective global governance architecture.

The previous chapter has emphasised that despite considerable global progress in improving people's lives around the world, many remain vulnerable. This chapter considers some emerging trends that are likely to affect livelihoods in the different parts of the world in the areas of economy, technology, demography, environment, security and governance. As indirect as they may seem, there is a need to understand such forces as they shape the context of livelihoods. It is essential to have a clearer view of the "big picture" in order to address relevant policy issues for the improvement of livelihoods.

## Global economic trends are of concern

The coming decades will be characterised by a few major economic trends that will have considerable consequences for future livelihoods. The global economic shift towards emerging economies will continue. Jobless growth, experienced in most parts of the world, will persist, with a continuous quest for greater productivity, often supported by automation. Inequalities are likely to continue to rise, as capital tends to be remunerated more than labour, and the trend towards a knowledge economy – a major source of growth – is likely to polarise incomes. Social and welfare expenses will continue to mount with increased demands for social protection, pensions, health, and unemployment benefits. Finally, financial fragilities may not be reduced enough to avoid severe financial crises recurring.

### *The growth of emerging economies will continue, but more slowly*

A major feature of recent decades has been the shift in the economic balance towards emerging countries, especially those in Asia (Figure 3.1). This is forecast to continue: by 2030 China's GDP is likely to represent more than 25% of the world economy, and India's more than 10% (Figure 3.2). The United States' share may fall to 17%, matched by similar decreases in other OECD countries (including all European countries, Japan and Korea).

However, the gap in the economic growth rate between OECD and non-OECD countries has narrowed recently and there has been a significant slowdown in the rate of growth of emerging countries. At current rates (average growth between 2000 and 2012) several lower middle-income countries (e.g. India, Indonesia and Viet Nam) as well as countries in the upper middle-income bracket (such as Brazil, Colombia, Hungary, Mexico and South Africa) will fail to catch up with average OECD income levels by 2050. Their challenge is deepened by the slowdown in China, whose rapid growth has also benefited its neighbours and suppliers, in particular exporters of natural resources (OECD, 2014a).

**Figure 3.1. Non-OECD countries' share in the global economy has been steadily rising**

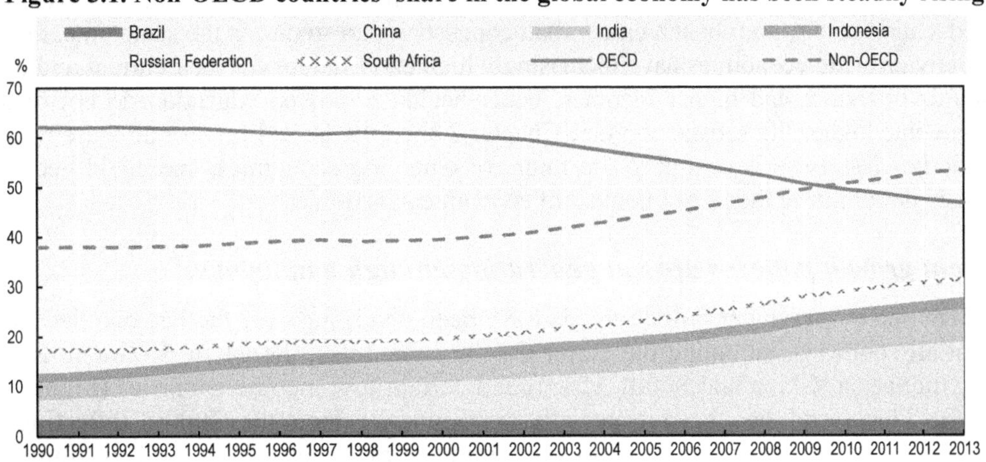


*Sources:* OECD (2014a), *Perspectives on Global Development 2014: Boosting Productivity to Meet the Middle-Income Challenge*, OECD Publishing, Paris, http://dx.doi.org/10.1787/persp_glob_dev-2014-en and World Bank (2014), *World Development Indicators* (database), http://data.worldbank.org/data-catalog/world-development-indicators (accessed on 5 February 2015).

**Figure 3.2. The growing share of the emerging economies in global GDP**

% of global GDP

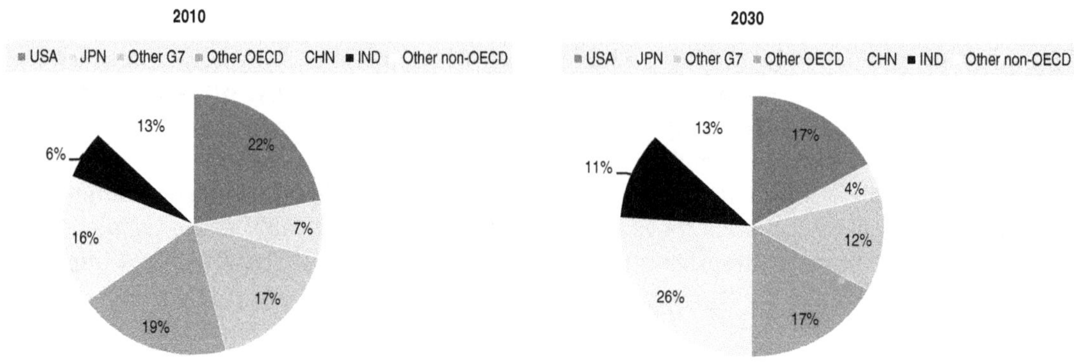


*Note:* Non OECD consists of Argentina, Brazil, China, India, Indonesia, Russian Federation, Saudi Arabia and South Africa.

*Source*: Braconier, H. and G. Nicoletti (2014), "OECD@100: Policies for a Shifting World", Working Party No. 1 on Macroeconomic and Structural Policy Analysis, Economics Department, 69th Meeting of the Economic Policy Committee, Paris, 7 February 2014 ECO/CPE/WP1(2014)2, OECD, Paris.

Such growth slowdowns are often associated with significant slowdowns in growth of total factor productivity. Productivity slowdowns in middle-income countries can be caused by difficulties in moving up the value chain away from a growth path driven by factor accumulation and low labour costs to one driven by innovation (OECD, 2014a). Escaping from this trap requires determined policy action in many fields (education, industry, finance, etc.) to raise the technological level of the economy, while at the same time facilitating restructuring processes and expanding social protection and other measures for the growing middle classes.

The middle classes of emerging countries are fragile in many ways (OECD, 2014a). The lower layers of the middle classes are at risk of economic and social exclusion, experiencing low education levels, poor health care, urban congestion and so on. At the same time, citizens of rapidly growing economies have increasingly high expectations for their current and future standards of living; and higher incomes, better health, improved education do not directly translate into higher life satisfaction (see Chapter 2 and OECD, 2014a). For all these reasons, the middle class issue is central to the future of emerging economies, and could become a seriously destabilising factor in a context of economic slowdown.

## *Current growth patterns are not generating enough employment*

GDP and employment growth trends have been diverging over the last two decades in almost all countries, including the major OECD economies, the BRIICS (Brazil, Russia, India, Indonesia, China and South Africa) and certain low-income countries (Figures 3.3 to 3.6). This trend has been especially pronounced since the 2000s, reflecting the unemployment problems experienced by a number of countries, as well as significant productivity increases that release people from repetitive and boring tasks. Looking forward, unemployment is seen as a major global risk for the next decade, and one which could have a significant impact, especially as it can translate into profound social instability (WEF, 2015).

**Figure 3.3. Growth in GDP is not matched by employment growth across the OECD**

Indexed GDP (constant 2005 USD), total employment and total labour force, 1991=100 (LHS); labour force participation rate, total in % of total population ages 15-64 (RHS)

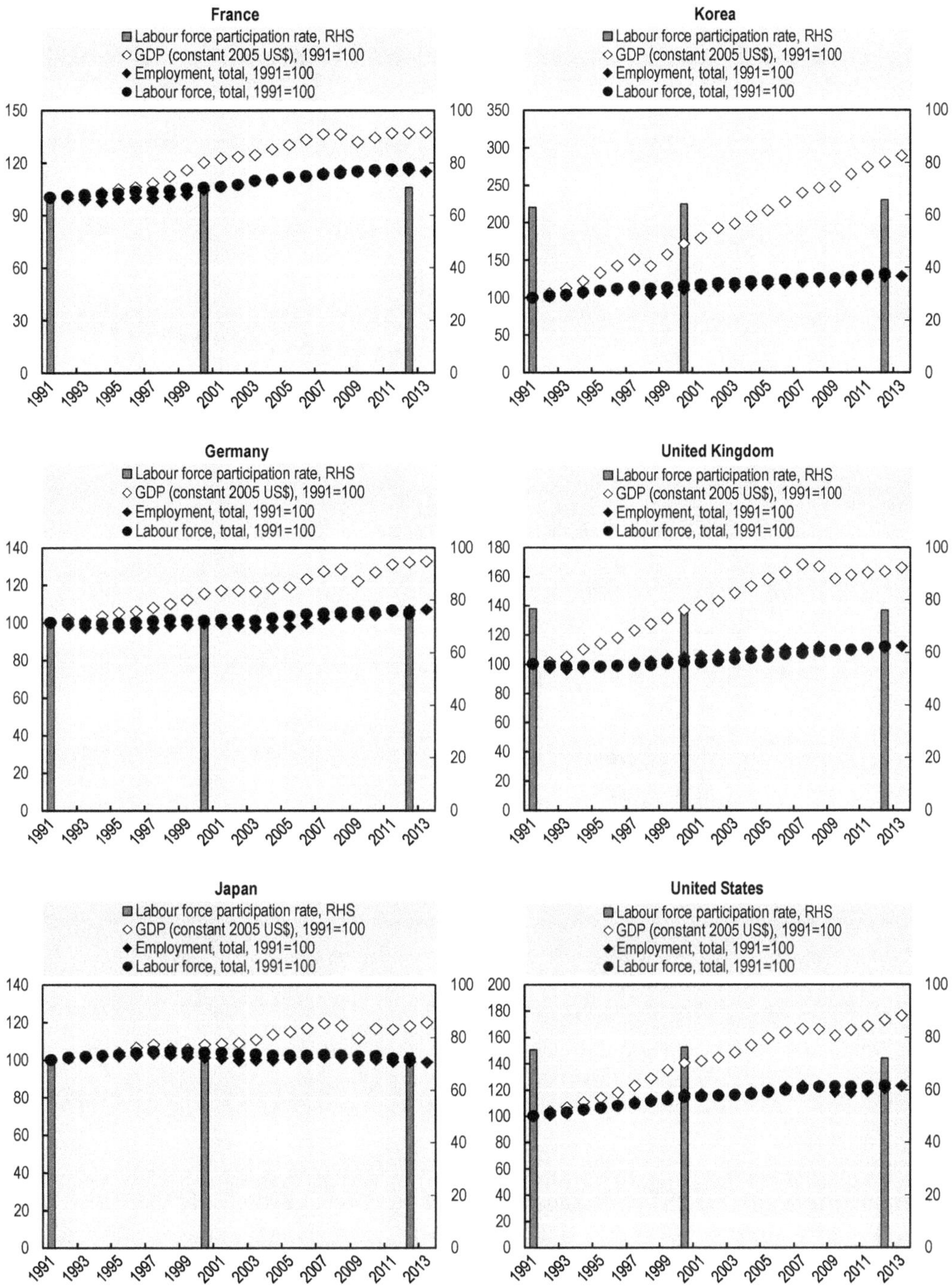


*Notes:* Total employment figures in 2013 are based on preliminary estimates. The labour force is the actual number of people available for work. The labour force of a country includes both the employed and the unemployed (that is those looking for a job).

*Source*: World Bank (2014), *World Development Indicators* (database) http://data.worldbank.org/data-catalog/world-development-indicators (accessed on 3 February 2015) and ILO (2015), *Employment Trends* (database), http://www.ilo.org/empelm/units/employment-trends/lang--en/index.htm (accessed on 6 February 2015).

**Figure 3.4. Employment growth is flat lining in China, India and Indonesia**

Indexed GDP (constant 2005 USD), total employment and total labour force, 1991=100 (LHS); labour force participation rate, total in % of total population ages 15-64 (RHS)

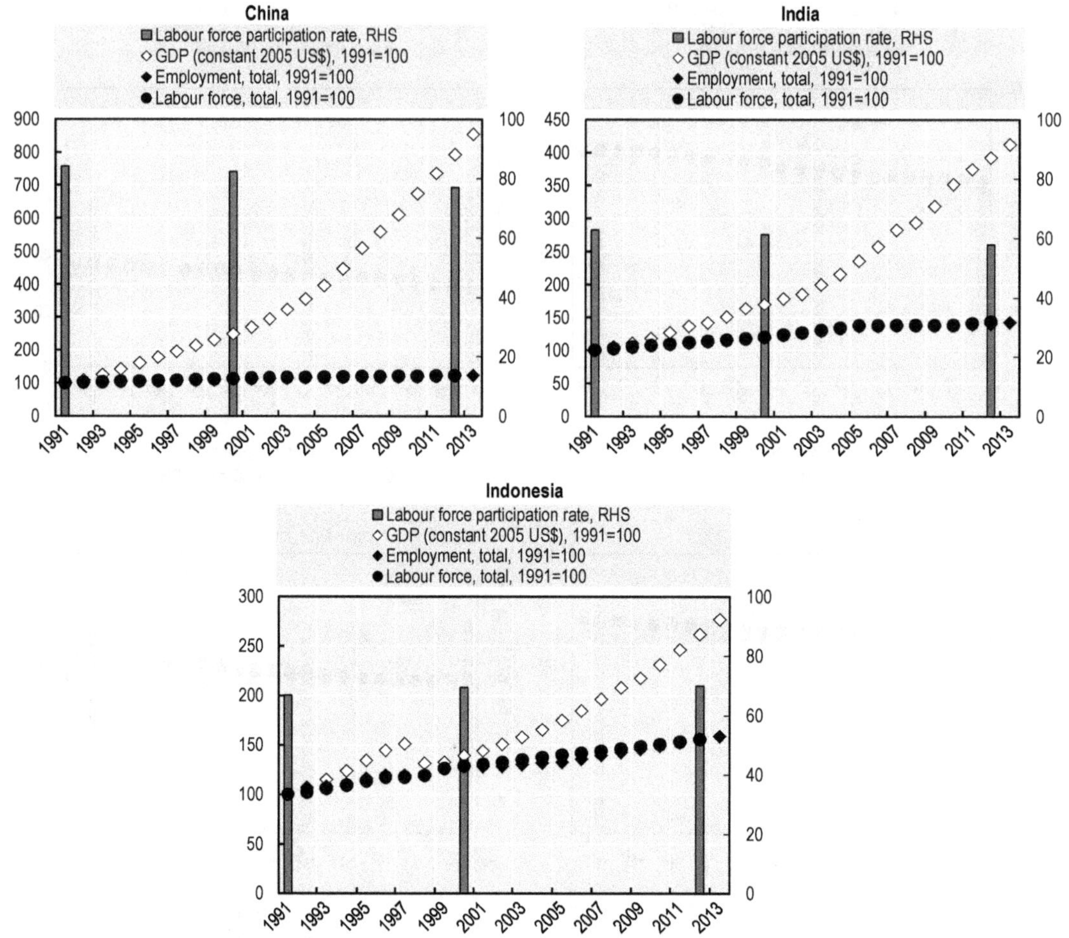


*Notes:* Total employment figures in 2013 are based on preliminary estimates. The labour force is the actual number of people available for work. The labour force of a country includes both the employed and the unemployed (that is those looking for a job).

*Source*: World Bank (2014), *World Development Indicators* (database), http://data.worldbank.org/data-catalog/world-development-indicators (accessed on 3 February 2015) and ILO (2015), *Employment Trends* (database), http://www.ilo.org/empelm/units/employment-trends/lang--en/index.htm (accessed on 6 February 2015).

Among the major OECD countries, the phenomenon is particularly visible in the US, UK, and Korea, and to a lesser – but still significant – extent in Japan, Germany and France. In the US, GDP rose by more than 70% from 1992 to 2012 (adjusted for inflation), while employment grew by just 20%. The UK shows similar trends, with GDP up by more than 60% but employment by only 15%. In the US there has been a significant decline in the workforce participation rate for the 24-65 age group, indicating that the population has adjusted to a decline in job supply by extending studies, retiring earlier, or simply stopping looking for a job.

Among the BRIICS, China's case is particularly striking (Figure 3.4): between 1991 and 2012, GDP multiplied by a factor of almost nine (adjusted for inflation), while total employment remained practically static. Meanwhile, the workforce participation rate diminished by some 10 percentage points (from 85% of the 24-65 age group to 77% in 2012). In India, the phenomenon is similarly impressive, although here the workforce participation rate declined less steeply than in China, reflecting the greater size of the informal economy and lower literacy levels. After a later start caused by the severe impact of the Asian crisis of the late 1990s, Indonesia is now following the same path as China and India. However its workforce participation rate is increasing.

**Figure 3.5. Jobless growth is now emerging in Brazil, Russian Federation and South Africa**

Indexed GDP (constant 2005 USD), total employment and total labour force, 1991=100 (LHS); labour force participation rate, total in % of total population ages 15-64 (RHS)

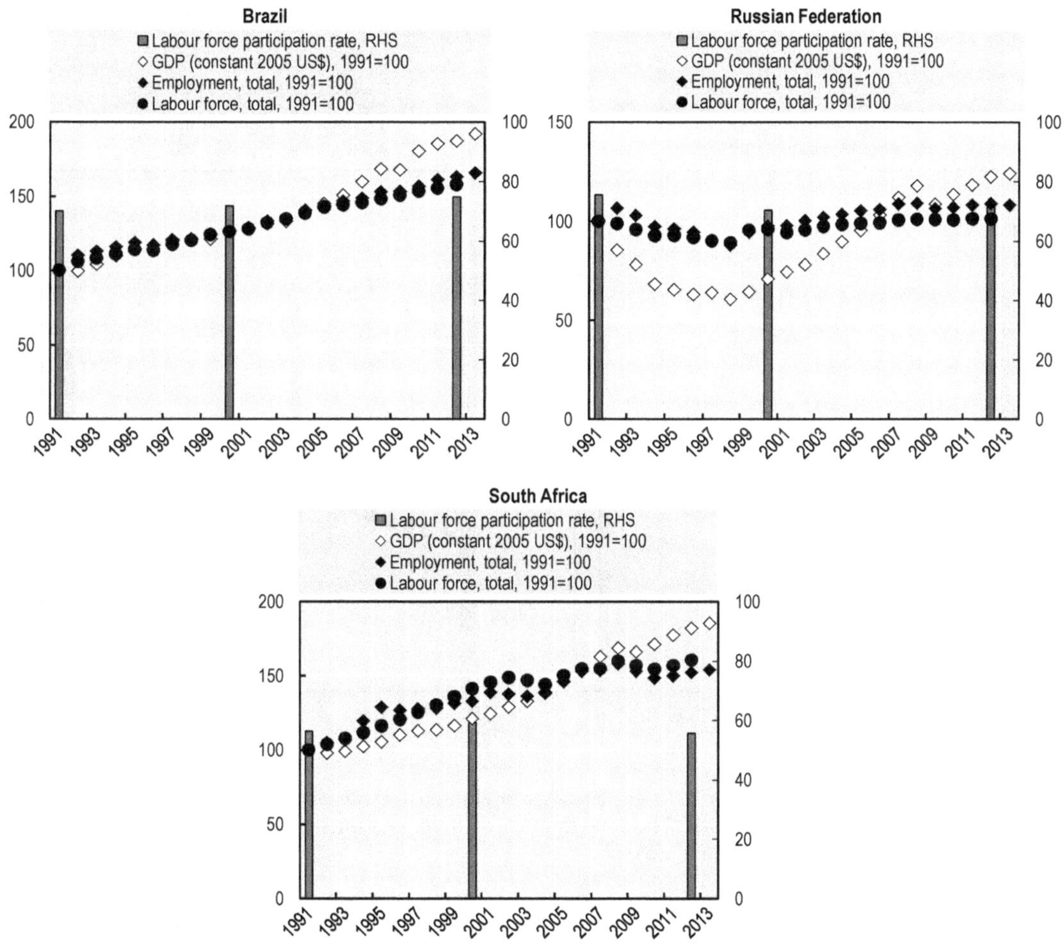


*Notes:* Total employment figures in 2013 are based on preliminary estimates. The labour force is the actual number of people available for work. The labour force of a country includes both the employed and the unemployed (that is those looking for a job).

*Source*: World Bank (2014), *World Development Indicators* (database) http://data.worldbank.org/data-catalog/world-development-indicators (accessed on 3 February 2015) and ILO (2015), *Employment Trends*, www.ilo.org/empelm/units/employment-trends/lang--en/index.htm (accessed 6 February 2015).

In Brazil, the Russian Federation and South Africa, the trend of "jobless growth" has only emerged since around 2007/08, marking the beginning of the global economic crisis (Figure 3.5). In the case of Brazil, GDP and employment have both grown in parallel for many years – as in a number of Latin America countries. In Russia and South Africa, the GDP fall experienced in the difficult transition years of the 1990s was not accompanied by a corresponding reduction in employment, which remained stable overall.

Similar trends can be seen in all other countries – including low-income ones – which have had sustained engagement in productive activities (notably manufacturing) accompanied by relatively stable growth rates (Figure 3.6 shows the examples of Bangladesh and Ghana).

**Figure 3.6. Jobless growth is also occurring in low-income countries: Bangladesh and Ghana**

Indexed GDP (constant 2005 USD), total employment and total labour force, 1991=100 (LHS); labour force participation rate, total in % of total population ages 15-64 (RHS)

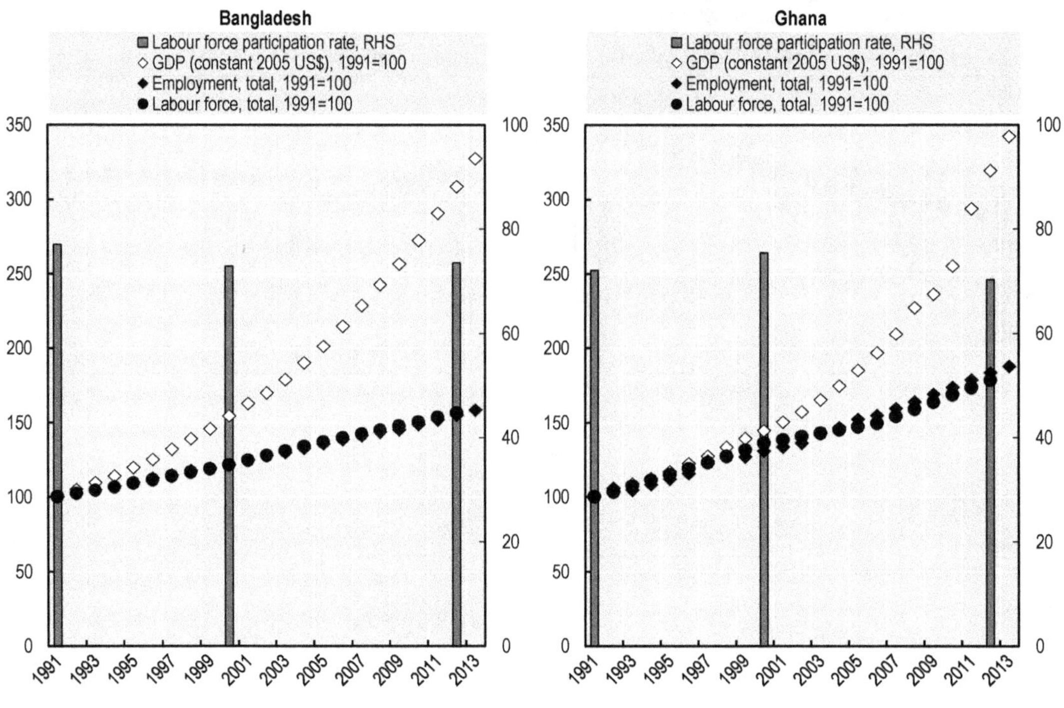


*Notes:* Total employment figures in 2013 are based on preliminary estimates. The labour force is the actual number of people available for work. The labour force of a country includes both the employed and the unemployed (that is those looking for a job).

*Source*: World Bank (2014), *World Development Indicators* (database) http://data.worldbank.org/data-catalog/world-development-indicators (accessed on 3 February 2015) and ILO (2015), *Employment Trends*, www.ilo.org/empelm/units/employment-trends/lang--en/index.htm.

These statistics from a diverse range of high, middle and low-income countries clearly demonstrate that the world economy is deeply engaged in a long-term growth process that is not generating employment. This trend is of fundamental concern for future livelihoods. Automation is a major factor, along with the out-sourcing of jobs from developed countries to low-income countries, and increases in productivity in the latter. The consequence will be the persistence of unemployment in a number of high-income countries, notably in Europe. The situation will be softened with the gradual retirement of people in a context of ageing societies. In many middle and low-income countries, however, the difficulty of absorbing rapidly growing labour forces will introduce increasing tensions in labour markets and society.

### *Inequality is on the rise*

Chapter 2 has already outlined how the past two centuries of global economic growth have been accompanied by rising inequalities. At the country level, economic growth has also not been shared inclusively. Although many economies have reduced poverty over recent decades, inequality in income per capita is increasing among and within countries (see Figure 2.2 in Chapter 2). Today, the poorest 66% of the world's people are estimated to receive less than 13% of world income, while the richest 1% receive nearly 15%. Beyond income, about 50% of the world's wealth is owned by the richest 1% of the population (UNDP, 2014).

Across regions, the gap between rich and poor countries remains high. Inequality between richer and poorer countries is more pronounced and location appears to be a decisive indicator of inequality (Oxford Martin School, 2013). Inequalities across regions tend to be relatively high and often persistent, locking poor regions such as Asia-Pacific and Africa into relative income stagnation. Around 70% of the world's poorest 10%, in terms of per capita incomes, live in Africa and Asia (not including China) (Figure 3.7).

**Figure 3.7. Percentage of global income declines by different countries/regions**

Global income distribution by decile versus income share of each region/country at a given global income decile, 2014

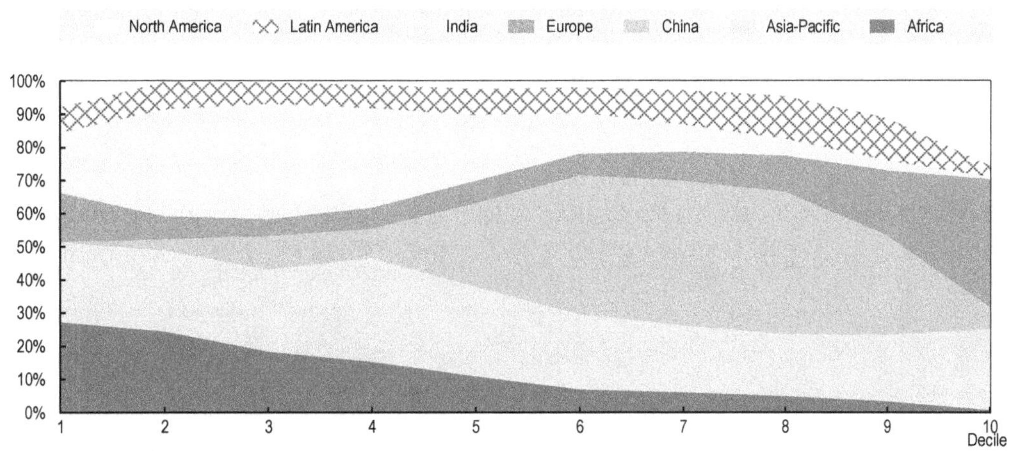


*Notes:* The horizontal axis represents the deciles of the global income distribution. The vertical axis represents the shares of each region/country of global incomes at a given decile. For example, among the 10% poorest people globally (decile=1), almost 30% live in Africa.

*Source*: Credit Suisse (2014), *Global Wealth Databook 2014*, Research Institute, Credit Suisse, Zurich, p. 110.

In Western Europe and North America, inequality was improving until the 1970s (van Zanden, 2014), but has been on the rise ever since. In OECD, top gross earnings, measured as the 90th percentile of the earnings distribution, have risen 0.5% faster every year than those at the bottom (10th percentile) (OECD, 2014b). Inequality is also increasing within many emerging and developing economies. In China and India, income groups in the upper brackets have increased their incomes proportionately more than those in the lower brackets (OECD, 2014a). China's Gini coefficient for disposable income has risen by at least 50% to 0.42 (The Economist, 2012a). The biggest exception to this upward trend is Latin America and the Caribbean (Table 3.1), due, among other things, to the expansion of education, public transfers to the poor (UNDP, 2014) and labour force participation (as in Brazil). Many emerging economies managed to significantly reduce poverty and to expand the middle class (whose lower threshold can be defined as people living at USD 10 a day) over the last decade (Figure 3.8). Nonetheless, the share of people at vulnerable incomes (here regarded as those individuals with incomes or consumption spending between USD 2 and 10) remains significant and sometimes increased.[1]

**Table 3.1. Inequality trends vary across regions**

Number of countries with rising or falling income inequality by region, 1990-2012

| Region | Rising inequality | Falling inequality | No trend* | Total |
|---|---|---|---|---|
| Africa | 13 | 19 | 3 | 35 |
| Asia | 18 | 10 | 3 | 31 |
| Latin America and the Caribbean | 4 | 14 | 2 | 20 |
| Europe, North America, Oceania and Japan | 30 | 8 | 6 | 44 |
| Total | 65 | 51 | 14 | 130 |
| Percentage of countries | 50 | 39.2 | 10.8 | 100 |
| Percentage of total population | 70.6 | 25.3 | 4.1 | 100 |

*Note:* * Inequality remained relatively constant or fluctuated without a clear upward or downward trend during the period.

*Source:* UNDP (2014), *The 2014 Human Development Report – Sustaining Human Progress: Reducing Vulnerabilities and Building Resilience*, Human Development Report Office, United Nations, New York, http://hdr.undp.org/sites/default/files/hdr14-report-en-1.pdf.

**Figure 3.8. The BRIICS reduced poverty and expanded their middle class over the last decade but many people remain at vulnerable income/consumption levels**

GDP per capita (in USD, 2005 PPPs), by income/consumption decile

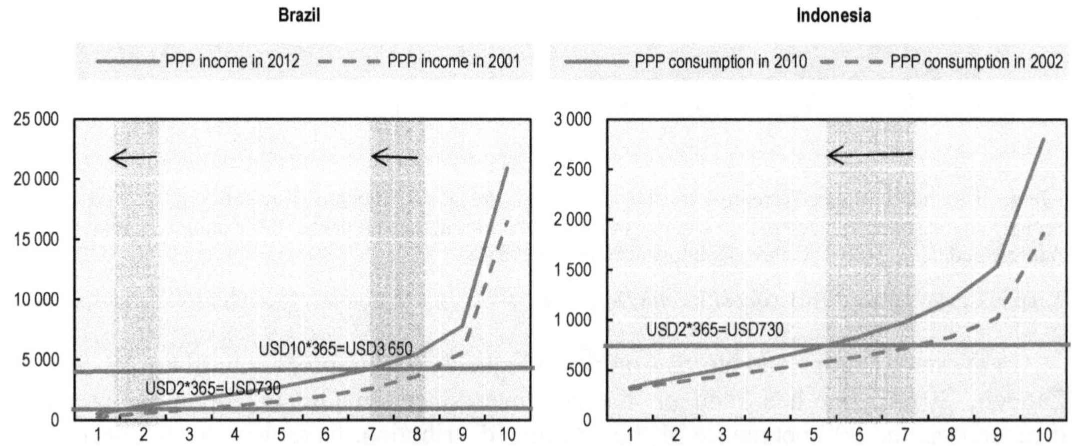

**Figure 3.8. The BRIICS reduced poverty and expanded their middle class over the last decade but many people remain at vulnerable income/consumption levels** (*cont.*)

GDP per capita (in USD, 2005 PPPs), by income/consumption decile

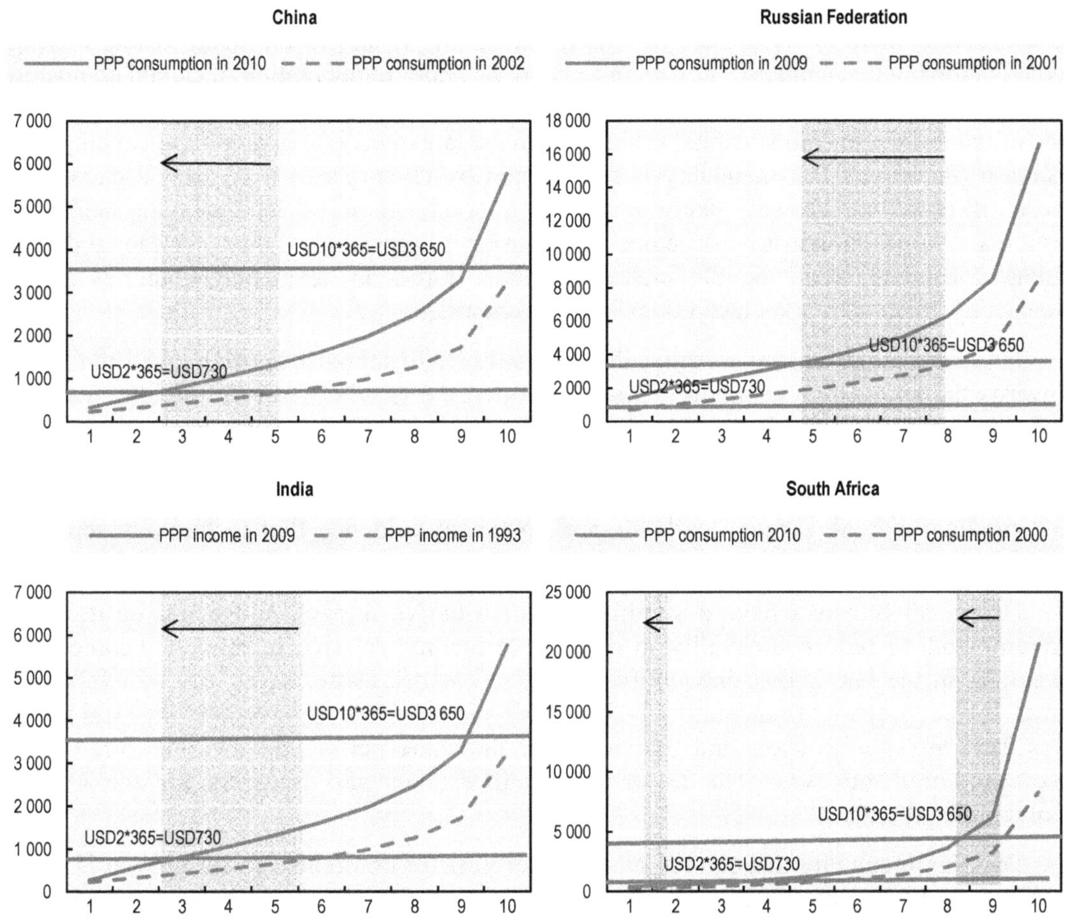


*Notes:* The horizontal axis represents the deciles of each country's income/consumption distribution. For all countries, the analysis is based on consumption data, except for Brazil where it is income data. Horizontal lines for USD 2*365 = USD 730 and for USD 10*365 = USD 3650 represent the USD 2 a day poverty line as well as the USD 10 a day which can be regarded as the lower level of the middle class. The width of the light grey bar represents the reduction of the share of people living at USD 2 a day. For example in India, the light grey bar cuts the horizontal axis at the 5th decile and 3rd decile. Thus, around 20% of the population moved beyond the USD 2 a day poverty line between 1993 and 2009. The width of the light blue bar represents the increase of the middle class. For example in South Africa, the light blue bar cuts the horizontal axis at the 9th and 8th decile. Thus, around 10% of the population moved from a vulnerable consumption/income situation to the lower level of the middle class 2000 and 2010.

*Source:* World Bank (2015a), PovcalNet (database), http://iresearch.worldbank.org/PovcalNet/index.htm (accessed on 4 February 2015).

The impact of the financial crisis was uneven. The largest increases in the Gini index were seen in countries hit hardest by the crisis, such as Spain and Greece, where disposable income inequality increased by four points between 2007 and 2011, despite increases in taxes and social transfers to cushion the impact (OECD, 2014b). Lower-income households either lost more during the crisis or benefited less from the recovery.

On average across OECD countries, the income of the bottom 10% of the population has dropped twice more than that of the top 10% since 2007 (OECD, 2014b).

The increase in inequality observed in many parts of the world contradicts Kuznets' theory, which predicted that inequality would decline as GDP grows, after an initial increase as the development process takes off (Kuznets, 1955). What are the main factors driving today's growing inequalities? They seem to lie in the better remuneration of capital compared to labour in the long term – a trend observed over centuries (Piketty, 2014). As long as the rate of interest remunerating capital is higher than the rate of economic growth, inequality will increase (Piketty, 2014). Inequality is accentuated by rates of return on capital exceeding those of economic growth, likely reflecting a combination of labour-saving technical progress, changes in industrial structure, and a stronger bargaining position for capital due to rising global integration, rapidly increasing labour forces in developing countries and a weakening of labour market institutions in many countries.

There are good reasons to think that inequality will increase further given the trend towards the knowledge economy. This will widen the gap between the highly educated and the lower-skilled. Skills-biased technological change has outpaced educational attainment and per capita income growth, both of which have an equalising effect and tend to lower earnings dispersion. Moreover, greater disparity in earnings among high and medium-income earners lends support to recent evidence that technology replaces medium-skilled jobs, leading to polarisation of earnings (see technology section below).

Taxes and transfers have a significant redistributive impact, and could be used by governments to reduce inequality in disposable income relative to market income. For example, in the late 2000s, inequality in OECD countries after taxes and transfers was much lower compared to inequality before taxes and transfers. On average, the Gini index was 25% lower after taxes and transfers. For the same period, poverty measured after taxes and transfers was 55% lower than before taxes and transfers for the OECD (Joumard et al., 2013).

Tackling inequality through tax and transfer policies could also foster growth if well-implemented (Cingano, 2014). Reducing income disparities at the bottom of the income distribution seems to have a greater positive impact on economic performance than if the focus is on reducing top inequality. Yet, policy makers can ensure that wealthier individuals contribute their fair share of the tax burden – notably by improving tax compliance, eliminating or scaling back tax deductions which tend to benefit high earners disproportionally, reassessing the role of taxes on all forms of property and wealth, including the taxation of capital income, and broadening the tax base by closing loopholes in the current tax system.

Finally, economic growth remains important to cut poverty and inequality, but sustained efforts for redistribution are needed. The World Bank, for example, has developed simulations to show that significant reductions of poverty and inequality cannot be achieved without explicit efforts to redistribute income and to encourage inclusive growth through shared prosperity (Box 3.1).

**Box 3.1. How economic growth and shared prosperity can cut poverty in the developing world**

In 2014 the World Bank announced the goal of reducing global extreme poverty (those living on less than USD 1.25 a day) to 3% of the world population by 2030. The World Bank has recently made simulations around this goal, which found that the 3% objective would be extremely difficult to achieve without growth rates in emerging and developing economies as high as those of the 2000s (up to 2008). However, even in the absence of high growth rates, reducing poverty to 3% may be facilitated by serious efforts towards greater inclusion and reduced inequality. This "shared prosperity" approach aims to increase the income and consumption of the poorest 40% in each country. The choice of the 40% at the bottom of the pyramid is justified by the fact that it encompasses the part of the population that is generally vulnerable to a decline in economic activity. The impact of serious inclusion efforts could be significant. Strategies would include major social transfers (see below) to reduce inequality, as well as strong actions to ensure that the poor get decent returns on their assets (especially their labour, but also other assets, such as land holdings). Improved access to education, health, and capital are critical factors in enhancing these returns. However, these objectives assume that there are no major unpredictable events, such as conflicts or natural disasters (although their potential impacts are also simulated in the World Bank study).

*Source*: World Bank (2015), *A Measured Approach to Ending Poverty and Boosting Shared Prosperity: Concepts, Data, and the Twin Goals,* policy research report, World Bank, Washington DC, https://openknowledge.worldbank.org/bitstream/handle/10986/20384/9781464803611.pdf.

### *Social, health and welfare expenditures are mounting*

Social protection – welfare support in the form of pensions, health insurance, and compensation for unemployment – ensures the sustainability of basic livelihoods. It can protect the poor and vulnerable, as well as those affected by disasters. Yet globally, only 20% of the world's population has adequate social security coverage, and more than half lack any coverage at all (UNDP, 2014). Social protection systems are most developed in high-income economies, although government budgets are now under stress. Middle-income countries are developing national systems covering between 20 to 60% of workers (UNDP, 2014). This is especially the case for pensions and health insurance in Asia, and social programmes that encourage education and nutrition for the poor in Latin America. In low-income countries, social protection covers only 10% of workers (UNDP, 2014), and those individuals with poor or non-existent pension and health insurance coverage. Often people have to count on traditional forms of community support.

In developed economies, the cost of social protection and welfare systems has been steadily increasing (see Figure 3.9 for health). Today, average spending on health and pensions by OECD countries stands at 7.8% and 6.6% of GDP respectively (OECD, 2014c). In continental Europe, the state shoulders a significant share of these expenses, whereas in North America it is individuals who shoulder many of the costs. In the US, 47 million people still lack health insurance of any kind.

**Figure 3.9. The growing cost of health expenditures, 1995-2012**

Expenditures as a share of GDP in %

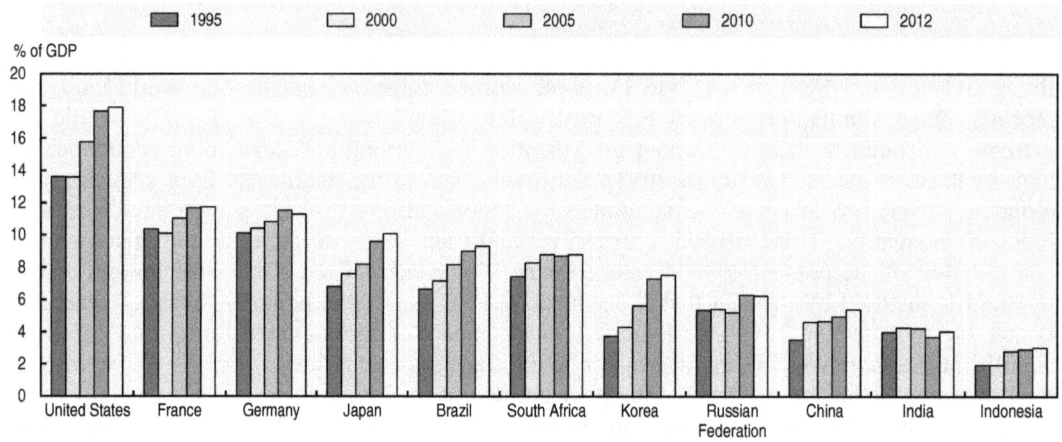


*Note:* Total health expenditure is the sum of public and private health expenditure. It covers the provision of health services (preventive and curative), family planning activities, nutrition activities, and emergency aid designated for health but does not include provision of water and sanitation.

*Source*: World Bank (2014), *World Development Indicators* (database), http://data.worldbank.org/data-catalog/world-development-indicators (accessed on 4 February 2015).

Most Asian countries kept social spending low while their economies grew very rapidly. This helped to maintain a high rate of savings and investment. The Asian welfare system still looks lean compared to Western standards – public health spending is still at only 2.5% of GDP, compared to roughly 7% in OECD countries. However, with a steep decline in fertility rates and rapidly ageing societies – particularly in Singapore, Korea and Hong Kong, China – new forms of welfare state systems are being put in place. Inspired by Western approaches, these involve the state taking charge of most welfare expenses. For example, prior to the Asian financial crisis of 1997/98, none of Chine Taipei's unemployed received state benefits. By 2001, they all did. China is following the same path in line with their "harmonious society" slogan. As a result, China's rural health insurance scheme, which in 2003 covered 3% of the eligible population, now covers 97.5% (The Economist, 2012b).

In Latin America and other emerging countries, social protection programmes have significantly helped reduce poverty. These take the form of cash transfer programmes linking family payments to education and health care for the young. For instance, Brazil's *Bolsa Familia* programme is estimated to have accounted for 20-25% of poverty reduction. South Africa's child support grant has reduced child poverty from 43% to 34% (UNDP. 2014). Similar programmes have had also noticeable impacts in developing countries (see Table 5.1 in Chapter 5).

The past century's extraordinary progress in health has been a major factor in the world's economic and social progress. Most of this progress has been in the eradication of infectious, communicable diseases. Today it is non-communicable diseases (mainly cancer, cardiovascular and neurodegenerative diseases) which pose considerable challenges to societies, including in economic terms. These have become the principal causes of death, responsible for 63% of all deaths in 2008, or 36 million people (Oxford Martin School, 2013). Eighty per cent of these deaths were in low and middle-income countries. Each 10% rise in deaths from non-communicable diseases is associated with a

0.5% lower rate of annual growth (WHO, 2011, cited in Oxford Martin School, 2013). As populations grow larger and live longer, the total cost of treating non-communicable diseases over the next two decades is estimated at about USD 30 trillion; adding in the cost of lost productivity makes the bill even higher. Globally, it would mean a cumulative output loss of USD 47 trillion over the next two decades – "enough money to eradicate USD 2-a-day poverty among the 2.5 billion people in that state for more than a century" (Bloom et al., 2011, cited in Oxford Martin School, 2013).

However, infectious diseases remain a significant threat, particularly in today's highly mobile, interconnected world. Among them, HIV (which has infected 75 million people and killed 36 million worldwide) and various types of influenza continue to thrive. Some, like SARS, which emerged in East Asia in 2008, have been rapidly subjugated. However, the recent outbreak of Ebola in West Africa shows the devastating impact of uncontrolled epidemics. While the number of deaths (more than 7 500 at the end of 2014) is dwarfed by some natural disasters such as earthquakes, the outbreak has caused multiple problems in the three countries affected (Sierra Leone, Guinea and Liberia): emigration from infected areas, declining agricultural production, rising food prices, and reduction of foreign investment (including cancelling of major projects). It is estimated that the GDP of those countries could be reduced by between 3 and 5% as a result (World Bank, 2014).

### *Financial fragilities persist*

Financial fragilities were at the root of today's "great recession". Such crises are not new. The subprime crisis and its subsequent "replicas" have been preceded by hundreds of other financial and monetary crises in previous decades – though many of lower magnitude or confined to a specific country (e.g. Mexico, Russia) or region (East Asia) (Figure 3.10). However, the most recent crisis, caused by the enormous and unregulated speculative search for profits throughout the global financial system, was of a much greater magnitude. More than USD 20 000 billion were needed to rescue the system from the knock-on effects of the subprime-induced crisis (Rischard, 2014). The second major shock was the euro crisis, caused by the "mis-design" of the euro area – principally the absence of mechanism forcing fiscal convergences between EU members. The euro crisis rescue bill has been lower than that of the global financial crisis, but nevertheless significant at USD 6 000 billion (Rischard, 2014).

Policy measures taken in recent years by governments to reduce the overall fragility of the financial and banking systems have been considerable (e.g. separating investment banking from credit banking), but more will be necessary to make the system truly robust (Rischard, 2014; Wolf, 2014). Part of the problem lies in the strong interdependence of economies, which means that shocks reverberate more widely.

The next major shocks may well come from the emerging countries, whose growing corporate sector has benefited from massive lending by the global financial system. Some of these countries, such as Russia, have recently been affected by the fall in oil and natural resources prices, as well as a slowdown in economic activity. This could make it difficult for a number of big businesses to repay their loans, and may eventually create panic in financial markets. China represents another major financial risk. The nation faces a difficult policy dilemma since sustaining its robust growth momentum may require policy measures that could heighten financial instability and risk a public finance crisis. The regular commercial banking sector in China has become large, with total assets exceeding 200% of GDP by the end of 2012. This has been associated with a rapid expansion of domestic claims of depository institutions between 2008 and 2012, when they reached 155% of GDP (OECD, 2014d). Such fast growth raises concerns about credit quality and financial stability. The consequence of a serious financial crisis in China would be considerable for the world economy because the Chinese economy is now so globally integrated through trade and finance.

**Figure 3.10. Financial crises since 1800**

Percentage of countries in default or restructuring: 1800-2006

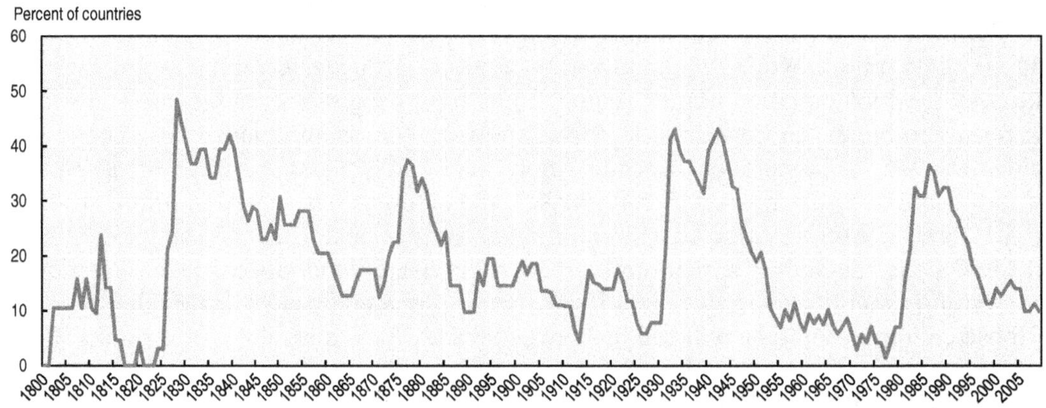


*Source*: Reinhart, C. M. and K. S. Rogoff (2011), "From financial crash to debt crisis", *American Economic Review*, Vol. 101(5), August, 2011, Pittsburgh PA, pp. 1676-1706, www.aeaweb.org/articles.php?doi=10.1257/aer.101.5.1676.

## Technology promises both risk and opportunity

Throughout mankind's history technology has been a game changer. It offers a host of opportunities and solutions. Not only does it directly influence individual well-being, such as medical or communication devices, but it can also have an indirect effect on many of the issues described so far. Yet technology is not without its downsides. We have already presented the worrying global trend towards jobless growth – increasing automation may well accelerate this trend. Other risks include the ability to create weapons of mass destruction, as well as unintended risks from technological development such as pollution and carbon dioxide emissions, nuclear accidents, and the effect on natural biological balances of new genetically manipulated lifeforms and materials such as nano-particles.

### *Jobs are increasingly threatened by automation*

Technology brings about loss of jobs. With the rise of processing power and digital information, computers are increasingly able to perform complicated tasks more cheaply and effectively than people. According to Frey and Osborne (2013), 47% of jobs are at high risk of being automated in the United States over some unspecified number of years, perhaps a decade or two (Figure 3.11). The most vulnerable jobs are those that involve routine, repetitive tasks. However, white-collar occupations such as accountancy, legal work and technical writing may also be phased out. The wealth generated by the digital revolution has gone overwhelmingly to the owners of capital and the highest-skilled workers. Over the past three decades, labour's share in output has shrunk globally from 64% to 59% (The Economist, 2014a).

New jobs are concentrating at both the upper and lower end of the skills distribution, creating competition among global companies for the highly skilled, reducing prospects for those at the bottom to progress, and generating a bleak outcome for those in the middle. The portfolio of basic skills required to function effectively in highly connected societies has changed. Some 6% of the total employment in OECD countries now consists of ICT specialists; ICT-intensive occupations account for more than 20% of all employment (OECD, 2014e).

If technology developments are such that they dramatically transform employment conditions, the future of work needs to be approached from a new perspective: for instance, more time and resources should be given to lifelong learning, and possibly more time for leisure or family care, etc. Also, since wealth could be increasingly generated by highly automated manufacturing and service activities, some futurist experts are even proposing that robots be taxed (discussions at Bellagio workshop, see Box 1.1 in Chapter 1).

**Figure 3.11. Risks of US job losses through computerisation, 2012**

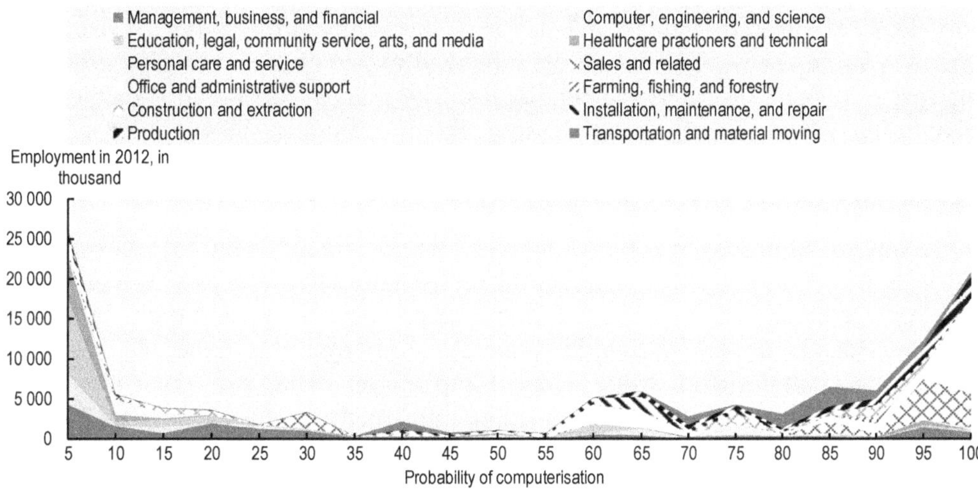


*Notes:* The probability of computerisation is based on 2010 data. The employment figures are based on 2012 data.

*Source*: Adapted from Frey, C.B. and M.A. Osborne (2013), *The Future of Employment: How Susceptible are Jobs to Computerisation?* Oxford Martin Programme on the Impacts of Future Technology, Oxford Martin School, Oxford, www.oxfordmartin.ox.ac.uk/downloads/academic/The_Future_of_Employment.pdf.

## *Living conditions are transformed by new technologies*

Digital technologies can have a dramatic effect on our daily lives. There are now 2.5 billion Internet users and 6 billion people have access to mobile phones (when only 4.5 billion have access to working toilets) (UN, 2013, cited in Oxford Martin School, 2013). This has major implications for our lifestyles, offering the potential to enhance livelihoods through education opportunities, improved health, and access to global markets. It can even influence civil movements through free speech and democracy, as we have seen during the Arab Spring. Low-income countries have especially benefited from such opportunities. Africa has been particularly fast in absorbing this trend, and is now home to twice as many mobile phones as the United States. It is the also most advanced in the world when it comes to "mobile money" (Oxford Martin School, 2013), facilitating people's access to markets and financial services, thus contributing to their standards of living.

Digital technologies, combined with advances in bio and nanotechnologies, will also have tremendous impacts on medical treatments and health care. Some techniques are already spreading rapidly, such as cheap self-diagnosis equipment (e.g. for diabetes monitoring and treatment) and non-invasive surgery. Other techniques with longer-term applications include advances in organ transplants and the development of bio-genetics medicine to treat or prevent health problems, including cancer, neurodegenerative and other illnesses of genetic origin.

### *Managed well, technological innovations can enable inclusive development*

While new technologies can have major, positive impacts on the livelihoods of low-income people, this depends on attention being paid to inclusive development (OECD, 2013b). Developing and emerging countries can be the loci of very dynamic innovation hotspots, so-called "islands of excellence", such as Bangalore for information technology, or Brazil for agriculture and aeronautics. Yet the performance of these specific areas or sectors does not generally benefit a wider area; the highly skilled firms, research labs or universities at the centre of these innovations tend to be connected to global players and counterparts working on frontier technologies. The greater performance of these sectors relative to the wider economy can increase inequality, although the whole economy could benefit by redistributing the profits generated through state budgets for better basic services, improved social protection and so on.

One way to insert low-income economies into the global technology and production world is to establish and grow manufacturing activities that are part of a global value chain. Some convincing developments have taken place in East Africa, in Kenya for instance, to create a competitive IT industry (Kimenye and Kibe, 2014). Plugging advantageously into global value chains implies an improved investment climate, provision of good training structures, adequate infrastructure, etc.

A second type of innovation is specifically developed for, or by, low-income groups. Known as "inclusive innovations" (OECD, 2013b), they might appear technically modest, but they can have considerable impacts on people's lives. Examples include eye care in India, computer-based functional literacy, and agricultural devices such as irrigation pumps, solar power, etc. Where low-income groups are the target consumers, one approach is to provide cheaper, simplified and possibly lower quality versions of more sophisticated goods and services. Pricing and financing strategies are essential to reach a large set of people through micro-credit, micro-leasing, etc.

"Grassroots innovations" are developed by lower income groups themselves, often using indigenous or traditional knowledge. They are directed towards local development, empowering local communities to find solutions that meet their needs. Various forms of support can be provided for such innovators, such as "business incubators", dedicated technical networks, etc. For example, the Honey Bee Network in India acts as a business incubator, helping innovators by documenting and developing their knowledge, ideas and products, such as the pedal-powered washing machine (Paunov, 2013). To date, the impacts of these inclusive and grassroots innovations have not been well evaluated (OECD, 2013b).

Complementing these approaches, social innovators or social entrepreneurs bring new types of services to people in need or in difficulties: poor children in deprived schools, slum inhabitants, old people, etc. (OECD, 2014h). These business models can ensure the survival, and preferably the development, of initiatives without subsidies or any form of government support, although philanthropic investments are generally welcome. This movement is spreading worldwide, supported by powerful international networks such as Ashoka. This network, launched in the US 20 years ago, has supported some 3 000 social entrepreneurs in developed and developing countries through personal grants and managerial assistance. A number of them have become efficient change makers through their demonstrative, piloting effects, leading sometimes to change in national legislations, or to national programmes modelled on their initiatives.[2]

### *The future impact of technology can be considerable*

Despite the surge in automation, uncertainties around future developments of long-term productivity growth remain huge. While some view the current economic slowdown as cyclical, others argue that it is largely structural, reflecting diminishing contributions by ICTs, with no other major new general-purpose technology in sight to provide a lasting resurgence in growth (The Economist, 2014a). However, the IT revolution in its most recent developments seems to be bringing significant change to how economies function: the marginal cost of production for a number of goods has declined to almost zero, while making very cheap goods and services accessible to a mass of people – as illustrated by 3D printing technology and MOOCs (massive on line open courses). The "Internet of things", coupled with the development of "big data", transforms the conditions of exchanges between people, as well as the monitoring of all types of activities, energy and resource consumptions, transport and logistics, etc. Some analysts consider that these transformations are giving rise not only to a new "Industrial Revolution", but also to new forms of economies based on collaborative approaches, illustrated by the so-called "share economy", that could even possibly replace traditional capitalism founded on profit and property accumulation (Rifkin, 2014).

Others predict an intelligence explosion in which artificial intelligence takes over human intelligence, but the extent to which this could affect our livelihoods is unclear (Kurzweil, 2005). Whatever the trends, they will be tempered by significant regional differences over the acceptability of new technologies – witness the anti-stem cell research movement in the US and the resistance to genetically modified food within the European Union, versus the strong pro-robotics culture in Japan.

## Massive demographic changes will affect livelihoods

The next 50 years will see massive demographic transitions. Most high and middle-income countries will experience an ageing process in which their population sizes will either stagnate or a gradually decline. For example, working-age populations will continue to grow in low-income countries, particularly in Africa and South Asia (Figure 3.12). All regions except Europe are likely to see a working-age population increase until 2025; beyond that year China's population is also predicted to start to decline.

**Figure 3.12. Working-age populations are projected to grow substantially in low-income countries**

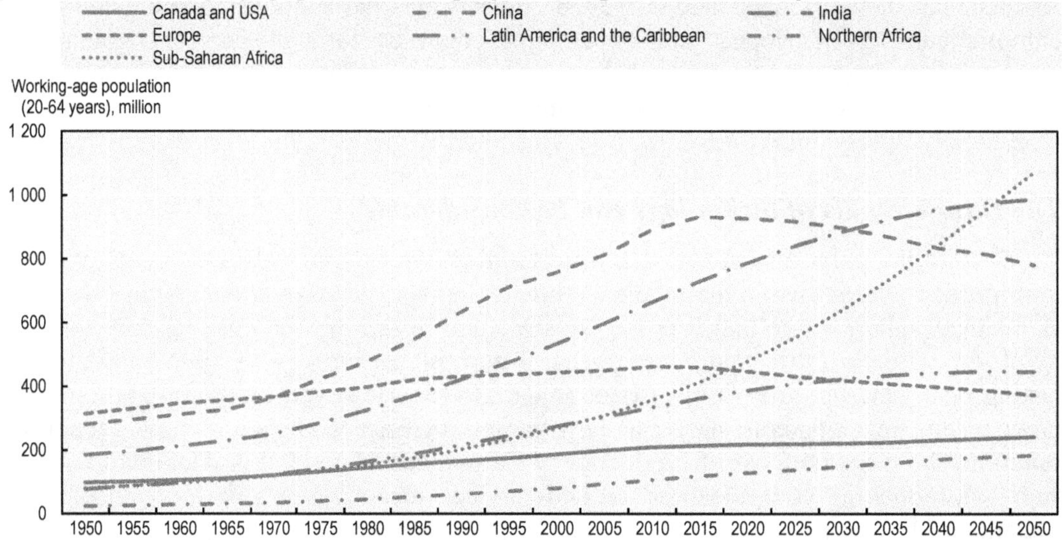


*Source:* UN-DESA (2012a), *World Population Prospects: The 2012 Revision* (database), Department of Economic and Social Affairs, United Nations, New York, http://esa.un.org/wpp (accessed on 4 February 2015).

### *Ageing populations will increase costs*

The rich-country trend of living longer and having fewer children is now appearing in lower-income countries (Figure 3.13). Since the 1950s, world's average life expectancy has risen by 20 years while the average fertility rate has halved. The increasing trend towards older populations could mean even greater costs in terms of pensions and health spending.

According to some estimates, the additional global economic burden of this ageing trend could amount to USD 200 000 billion (Rischard, 2014) – 10 times the cost of the financial crisis. However, these costs would be spread over several decades, making the process more manageable than the more immediate financial crisis. Tackling such pension and health pressures requires reforms that increase resources (through private funding or taxes) and decrease the dependency ratio of non-working populations to working age populations. This could involve increasing the retirement age, increasing labour force participation (especially by women) or turning to immigration. Openness to migration is a key factor for maintaining the growth rate of economically advanced but ageing countries (OECD, 2014e).

**Figure 3.13. Populations are getting older in many middle-income countries**

Median age 2010, 2025, 2050

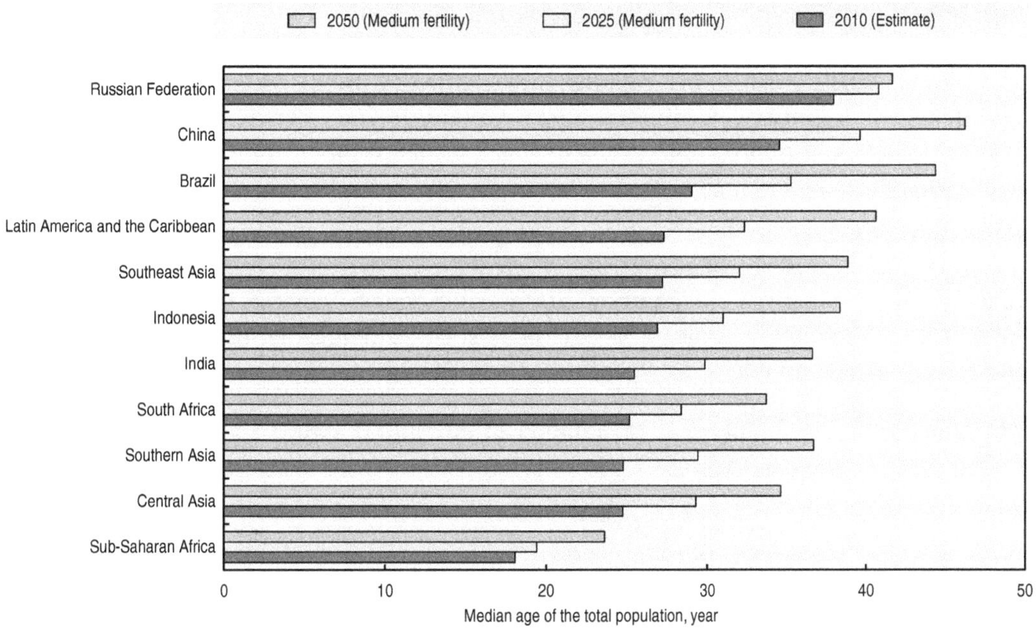


*Note:* Median ages estimated for 2010 and projected for 2025 and 2050 assuming medium fertility.

*Source*: OECD (2014), *Perspectives on Global Development 2014: Boosting Productivity to Meet the MiddleIncome Challenge*, OECD Publishing, Paris, http://dx.doi.org/10.1787/persp_glob_dev-2014-en, based on UN-DESA (2013), *World Population Prospects* (database), http://esa.un.org/unpd/wpp/unpp/panel_population.htm (accessed on 4 February 2015).

## *Absorbing the "youth bulge" is a challenge for developing countries*

While many developed countries are experiencing negative birth rates and even a gradual reduction of their population size, considerable increases are foreseen in developing countries, and notably in Africa and South Asia (Figure 3.11, above). Africa has seen a decrease in mortality combined with high fertility rates, contributing to a population explosion.

Countries with a large ratio of active to non-active population can enjoy a "demographic dividend". The ability to reap this demographic dividend, however, depends on a country's capacity to absorb its large share of young people into the labour force and employ them in productive activities. India's demographic dividend, for example, could add about 2% every year to India's per capita GDP growth over the next two decades.

Sub-Saharan Africa's labour force is growing by about 8 million people a year; South Asia's by 12 million a year (World Bank, 2012). How will these enormous contingents of young people be absorbed by the economy? What will be the consequences if they are not? Chronic poverty and unemployment among young people tend to lead to social revolts, as the Arab revolutions of 2011 demonstrated.

The World Bank estimates that in 2020 there should be around 600 million more jobs than in 2005 in order to keep the world's ratio of employment to working age population constant (World Bank, 2012). More than 175 million of these jobs, or nearly 1 million a month, would need to be created in Asia and the Pacific. Between 2015 and 2020, 60 million jobs would have to be generated in South Asia; 42 million in sub-Saharan Africa and 30 million in the Middle East and North Africa. On the other hand, Eastern Europe and Central Asia would require only 2.4 million new jobs over the same period (World Bank, 2012). For some regions, the challenge might be achievable. As noted above (Chapter 2, Figure 2.8), the last five years (2008-2013) have seen the net creation of 42 million jobs in South Asia, i.e. two-thirds of the number required according to the World Bank projections.

However, the gap between actual employment and the working age population is huge and will be growing in some regions, reaching large proportions in the long term (Figure 3.14). The gap may reach about 200 million in sub-Saharan Africa in 2030. Such a large mass of young people who are unable to find jobs could be a considerable contributor to social and political instability.

**Figure 3.14. The gap is growing between the number of jobs and the working-age population, 1991-2030**

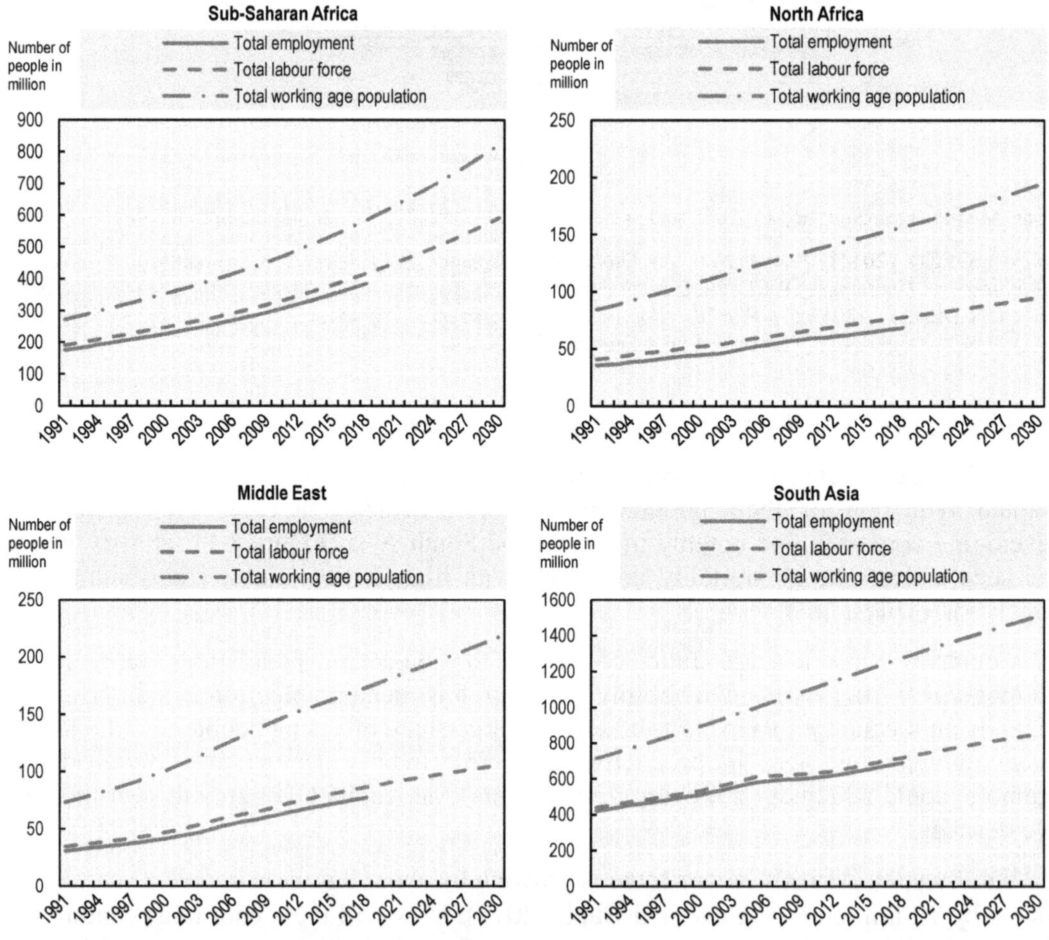


*Note:* Projections start in 2014. The labour force is the actual number of people available for work. The labour force of a country includes both the employed and the unemployed (those looking for a job).

*Source:* Adapted from ILO (2015), *Employment Trends*, www.ilo.org/empelm/units/employment-trends/lang--en/index.htm.

More generally, the main challenge in low-income countries is to expand productive jobs and reduce the vulnerability of many working poor. As we saw in Chapter 2, nearly half the people at work in developing countries are farmers or self-employed and so are outside formal labour markets. Therefore labour policies and institutions may not be central to job creation. Catalysts may be policies that address several targets simultaneously: they should make cities work better for rural migrants, help farmers access and apply appropriate agriculture techniques, or allow firms to develop new exports and related jobs. Jobs are the cornerstone of development, and development policies are needed for jobs (World Bank, 2012).

Some regions, like the Middle East and North Africa (MENA), continue to suffer from high levels of structural unemployment, requiring deep economic reforms (World Bank et al., 2013). Fundamental problems include uncompetitive economic structures, inefficient education systems, investment climates affected by bureaucratic governments, corruption and social tensions. All together, the result is a limited provision of quality jobs.

### *Urbanisation goes with "slumification"*

The growing urbanisation of the planet is another emerging trend with implications for livelihoods. Nearly half of the world's population lives in urban areas – a share which is expected to grow to 60% by 2030 (Figure 3.15). The trend towards urbanisation is especially notable in low-income countries. Today there are 35 megacities across the world;[3] only 10 are in OECD countries. Cities provide job opportunities and access to services such as education and healthcare. Many cities contribute to a large share of the country's GDP relative to their population and land area. Cities also play a key role as transport hubs.

However, in many countries, rapid urbanisation has gone hand-in-hand with "slumification". In the late 2000s, slum dwellers represented more than 30% of the world's urban population, with the greatest shares in sub-Saharan Africa (more than 70% of the sub-continent's population), and South Asia (about 60% of the region's population; Baker, 2008). In both regions, cities have had difficulties absorbing such large contingents of rural migrants.

Urbanisation also poses significant challenges to people's health. In some Asian cities, air pollution has already reached levels that far exceed World Health Organization safe levels, with serious implications for people's health and for mortality rates (OECD, 2012b). On a more global level, cities have expanded in surface area by 171%; their physical size has more than tripled in the BRIC countries since 1950 (Baker, 2008), while the urban population over that time has almost doubled in this group of countries. Although urbanisation is often accompanied by the more productive use of arable land, the loss of natural land has considerable implications for ecosystems and food security for future generations.

Chapter 5 outlines some ideas for preventing the concentration of populations in large urban centres and for building green and resilient cities.

**Figure 3.15. The world will become increasingly urban, 1955-2050**

People living in urban areas (in % of total population), by region

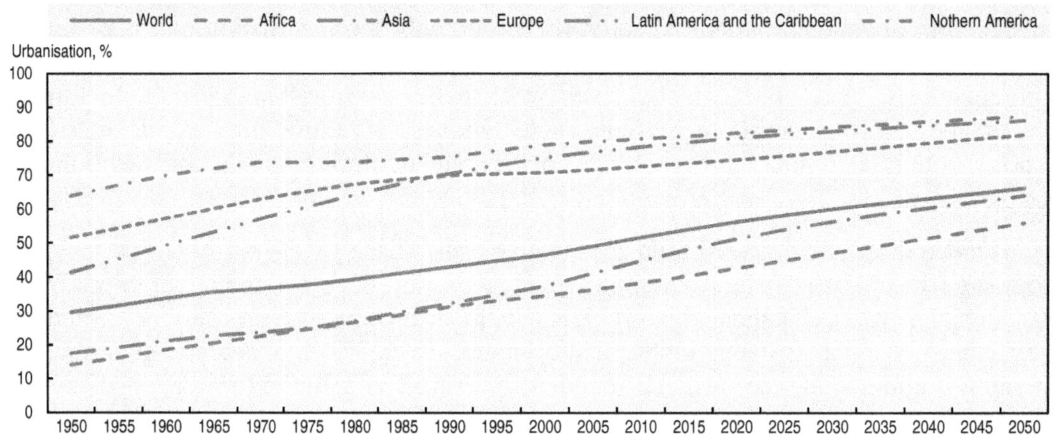


*Source:* UN-DESA (2012b), *World Urbanisation Prospects: The 2011 Revision*, Department of Economic and Social Affairs, United Nations, New York, www.un.org/en/development/desa/publications/world-urbanization-prospects-the-2011-revision.html.

## Environmental degradation has long-term consequences for livelihoods

There is a clear negative correlation between growth in GDP per capita and the quality of the environment (van Zanden, 2014). Climate change, accelerated by rising global greenhouse gas (GHG) emissions, will affect people's lives through higher average global temperatures, causing more extreme weather events, glaciers and permafrost to melt, and the sea level to rise. Global average temperature is projected to be 3 to 6 degrees Celsius higher by the end of the century (OECD, 2011). The impact on economic growth is predicted to be severe. The various effects of climate change are projected to lower GDP in East and South Asia by more than 5% in 2060 (OECD, 2014f). Impacts and costs will be diverse and wide-ranging, affecting sectors from health to agriculture, transport and beyond (Figure 3.16).

In addition to climate change, and partially driven by it, the loss of biodiversity will deeply transform living conditions on the planet. Biodiversity has declined worldwide as land use has changed dramatically. Since 1820, cropland has increased in global coverage from 2% to 11% of all ice-free land areas (15 million square kilometres), while the share of pasture grew from 2% in 1700 to 24% in 2000 (34 million km$^2$) (van Zanden, 2014).

The costs of inaction on climate change, including economic and social burdens, will increase with time (World Bank, 2012; OECD, 2012b). Continued disturbances to ecosystems could pass a tipping point beyond which damage is irreversible. Today, many policy makers seem to consider that it is too late for costly mitigation efforts, and are turning their attention towards adaptation efforts. Some analysts think, however, that it would be possible to put in place efficient financial mechanisms to reduce carbon dioxide emissions (The Global Commission on the Economy and Climate, 2014). Some policy options are outlined in Chapter 5.

**Figure 3.16. Climate change will reduce economic growth in most regions and sectors**

A. OECD projection of regional economic impact (in % of GDP) due to climate change

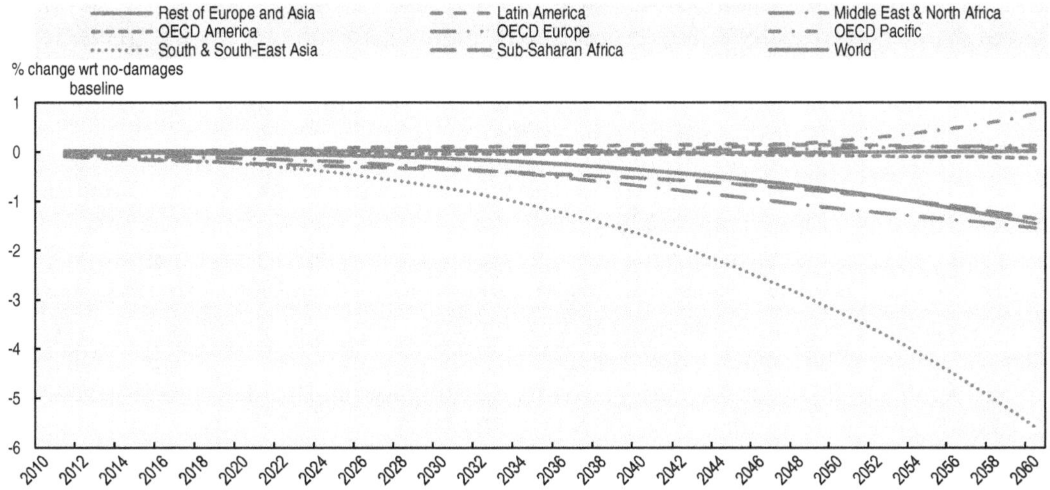


B. Shares of global impact on GDP due to climate change based on OECD projections

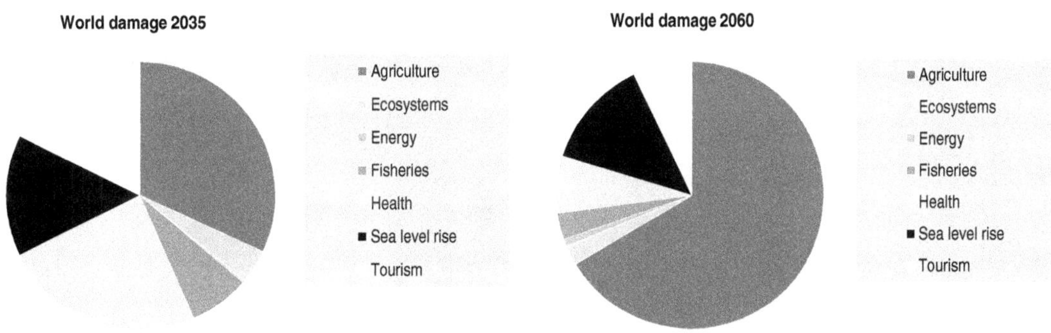


*Notes:* Panel B: Agriculture refers to changes in crop yields. Ecosystems relate to willingness to pay to avoid impact, while energy shows estimated changes in demand for cooling and heating. Fisheries refer to changes in catch, while health captures changes in labour productivity and in demand for healthcare due to certain illnesses or pathologies. Sea level rise denotes damages related to coastal land losses and damages to capital.

*Source*: OECD (2014f), *Policy Challenges for the next 50 Years*, OECD Economic Policy Paper, July 2014, OECD, Paris.

## *Extreme weather events and natural disasters are increasing*

Extreme weather events are increasing in magnitude and frequency, driven largely by climate change. We see, year after year, an increasing number of extreme weather events such as floods and hurricanes, directly caused by the global warming process (Figure 3.17). Sea level rise is another threat, affecting agriculture productivity, creating health hazards and generating large migrations. Coastal zones are particularly exposed to climate change impacts, especially those that are densely populated. The human impact is worsening as populations increase. Hundreds of millions of people are now exposed to dramatic situations caused by climate change.

Between 1901 and 1910 there were 82 recorded natural disasters, but between 2003 and 2012 there were more than 4 000 (UNDP, 2014). Every year between 2000 and 2012, more than 200 million people, most of them in developing countries, were hit by natural disasters, especially droughts and floods. Figure 3.17 summarises the frequency of natural disasters (earthquakes, droughts, floods, storms) and the economic losses they caused between 1980 and 2010. Particularly worrying is the much greater incidence of hydrological and meteorological disasters (UNDP, 2014).

Risk management or disaster preparedness initiatives could do much to diminish the impact of natural disasters on people's livelihoods, but country efforts have been mixed due to the high cost of such approaches. Failure to act implies the need for costly post-disaster reconstruction to restore the infrastructure of the affected area. This entails costs to individuals, insurance companies and governments. Important progress, however, has been made since the tsunami that killed hundreds of thousands of people around the Indian Ocean in 2004. An international early warning system has been established, and has already proven its usefulness (see UNDP, 2014).

**Figure 3.17. Natural disasters are more frequent than 30 years ago – and are costing us more**

A: Number of natural disasters and extreme weather events, 1980-2014

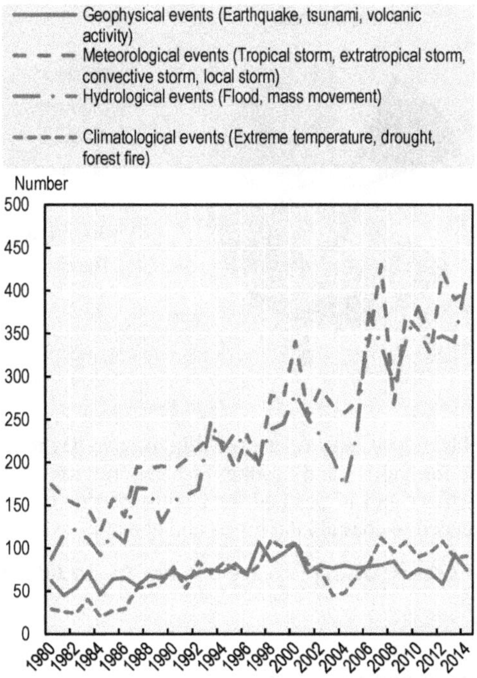


B: Costs of natural disasters and extreme weather events (in USD million), 1980-2014

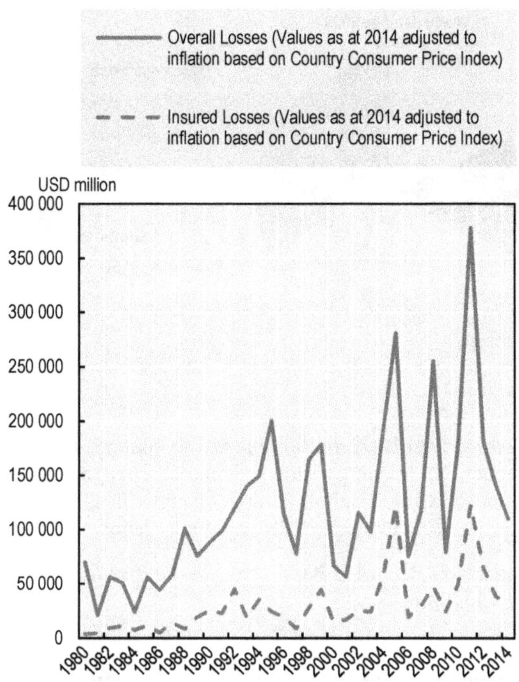


*Source*: Munich Re (2015), NatCatSERVICE (database), Geo Risks Research, Munich Re, www.munichre.com/natcatservice (accessed 28 January 2015).

**Figure 3.18. The increasing incidence of droughts, 1975-2039**

1975-1984

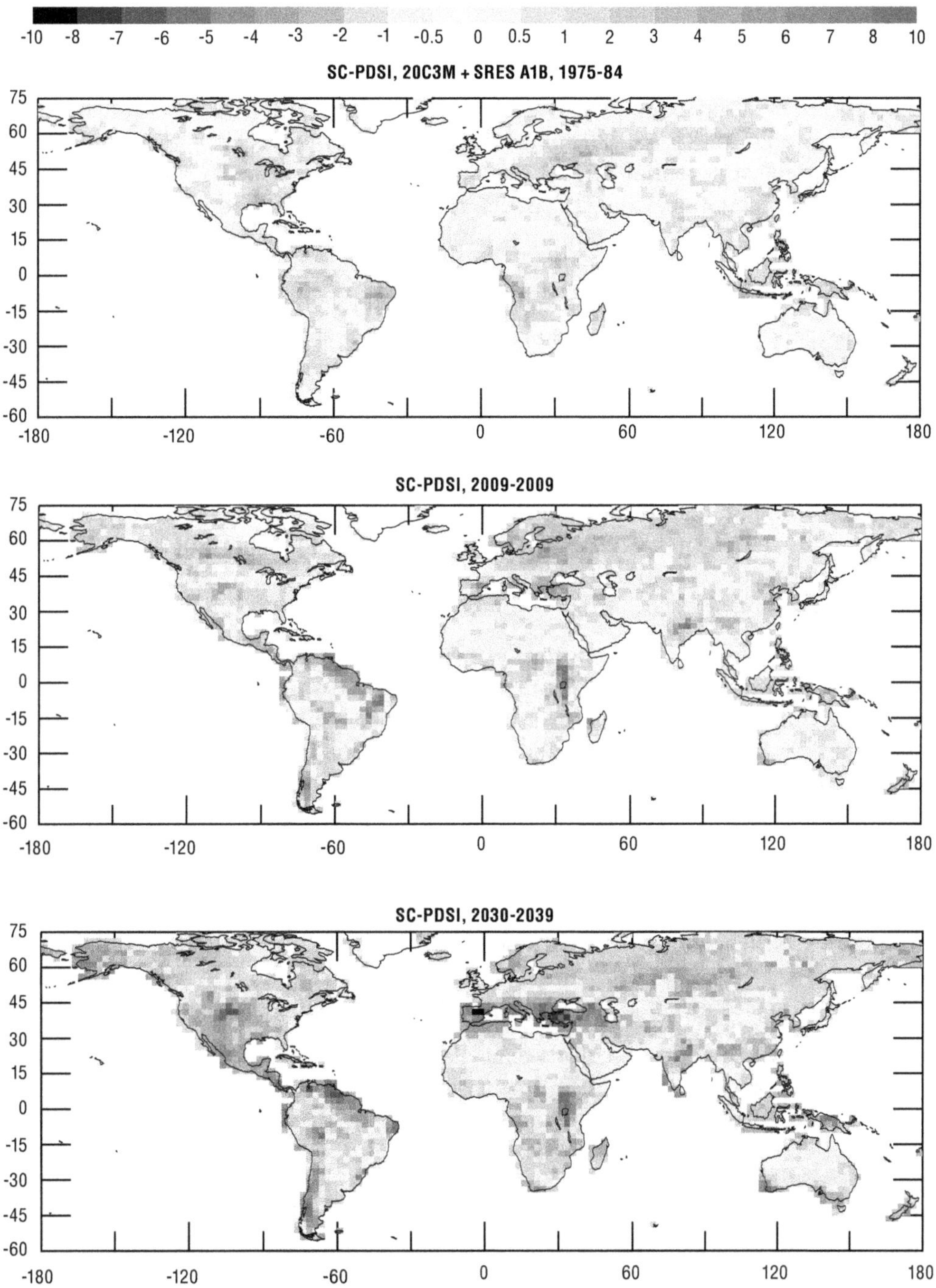


*Notes*: Black to grey areas are extremely dry (severe drought) conditions while blue colours indicate wet areas relative to the 1950-1979 mean. Figures are based on Palmer Drought Severity Index. For technical details on the calculations see Dai (2011). More recent (forthcoming) calculations using a revised method yielded similar drought change patterns but with substantially reduced magnitude.

*Source*: Dai, A. (2011), "Drought under global warming: A review", *WIREs Climate Change*, John Wiley & Sons, New Jersey, Vol. 2, pp. 45-65, www.cgd.ucar.edu/cas/adai/papers/Dai-drought_WIRES2010.pdf.

One of the most problematic climate change impact in the coming decades will probably be the multiplication of droughts (Figure 3.18). Droughts can contribute to higher food prices, famine and social unrest, with strong destabilising effects for the countries involved.

By 2050, more than 40% of the world's population will live under severe water stress, while nearly 20% could be exposed to floods (OECD, 2013f). A recent survey by the World Economic Forum (WEF, 2015) revealed that water crises are judged to be a global risk with the greatest potential impact, and that this risk will be even more acute in 10 years' time. The economic value of assets at risk from floods is expected to be about USD 45 trillion by 2050. Water pollution is also increasing, adding to uncertainty about future water availability. These water risks are exacerbated by climate change. A recent OECD report (2013c) reviews countries' initiatives to adapt water management to climate change. It reveals that nearly all countries project increasing water risks due to climate change. Extreme events (floods and/or droughts) were cited as a primary concern by 32 countries, while 23 cited water shortages as a key issue.

### *Increased growth means greater demands on energy and natural resources*

Evolving living standards and consumption are projected to increase global energy demand by 37% to 2040 (IEA, 2014). While new finds, such as shale gas energy in the US, can reduce local or regional shortages, the question of how to satisfy the global energy demand in the long term remains unresolved.

Global water demand is also projected to increase by some 55% between 2000 and 2050, due to growing demand from manufacturing, thermal electricity generation, and domestic use (OECD, 2012b). Water scarcity will worsen due to unsustainable use and management of water resources as well as climate change; the number of people living in areas affected by severe water stress is expected to increase by another 1 billion to over 3.9 billion by 2050. As a result, city dwellers and urban industries will increasingly be competing with other water users for access to water resources. If not properly managed, this competition could have undesirable social, environmental and economic consequences (OECD, 2014g). According to certain projections, by 2025, two in every three countries will become water-stressed, implying that 2.4 billion people will have absolute water scarcity (World Bank, 2015b).[4] North and South Africa and South and Central Asia will be especially affected (Oxford Martin School, 2013).

Poor nutrition and food insecurity can also be exacerbated by climate events (e.g. droughts) or mismanagement of resources (e.g. overfishing). To feed the world in 2050, food production may need to rise by some 70%. This may require 50% more water – which will be a challenge, as explained above. Furthermore, 40% of arable land is already degraded to some degree, a problem that will be exacerbated by global warming (Oxford Martin School, 2013). We are now living in a world of environmental co-dependencies in which energy, water, food, climate, and other trends are closely linked (Oxford Martin School, 2013). Thus, when we consider such trends combined, the future prospects are alarming.

## Crime, conflict and poverty are fuelling each other

Poor livelihood conditions threaten insecurity and insecurity undermines livelihoods. This section explores the interconnections among crime, conflict and livelihoods.

Security and peace are essential for livelihoods. Yet, 1.5 billion people across the world (about one-fifth of the world's population) live in countries affected by conflict. Experts interviewed by the World Economic Forum see inter-state conflict as one of the most important global risks in terms of its high likelihood and probable negative impact (WEF, 2015). Some parts of the world are heavily compromised by conflict, causing them to lag behind in economic and human development. In fact, most of the countries concerned face cycles of repeated violence, weak governance and instability, leading to different forms of violence, often linked to each other. Political movements can obtain financing from criminal activities, as in the Democratic Republic of Congo (DRC) and the Islamic State. Criminal gangs can support political violence, as in Jamaica and Kenya. Ideological movements make common cause with local grievances, as in Afghanistan and Pakistan. Furthermore, rising levels of violence and crime and poor access to justice affect many countries worldwide, not just conflict-affected and "fragile states" (OECD, 2015).

### *Poverty fuels crime*

Rates of violent crime have fallen across developed countries since peaking in the mid to late 1980s, although the reasons for this remain unclear (UNODC, 2012). Population ageing in developed countries is likely to continue this trend. Nonetheless, violent crime is still significant in urban areas in both developed and developing countries. This trend is also increasing alongside the rapid and massive urbanisation process in developing countries. The overall evolution of economies with an increasing number of unqualified young people in a context of jobless growth is also marginalising more and more people. Economic recessions can contribute to higher crime rates (ibid., 2012).

Drug trafficking and other criminal activities, supported by international networks, provide a living to large contingents of unemployed young people. In a number of high-income countries, urban areas heavily influenced by gangs are increasingly pushing wealthier people out in search of safety in more segregated quarters (e.g. gated residences). In these urban areas, informal activities linked to drugs and other trafficking are the main source of income for large segments of jobless young people. In low-income countries often characterised as "fragile states", the direct and indirect costs of insecurity caused by crime, robbery and other social disturbances have considerable consequences, not only for people's living conditions, but also for overall economic growth and social progress (World Bank, 2011).

The challenge is that the causes and effects of violence are often interlinked, feeding each other and creating vicious cycles. Inequality, poverty and poor education are viewed as common drivers of conflicts by citizens (Figure 3.19). Similarly, unemployment is a predominant motive for young people to join rebel movements and urban gangs (Figure 3.20).

Risks increase when internal pressures from unemployment and inequality meet weak governance. Weak governance makes a country particularly vulnerable, easily resulting in breakdowns of social cohesion. Weak governance also explains why countries become trapped in recurring conflicts.

**Figure 3.19. Inequality, poverty and poor education are viewed as common drivers of conflicts by citizens**

Citizens' views on the drivers of conflict, in % of survey respondents choosing a given driver

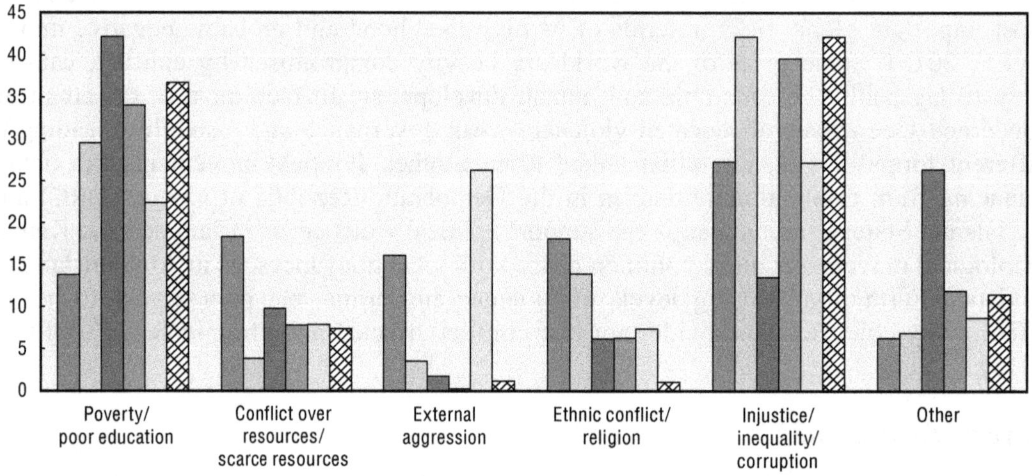


*Notes:* Surveys were conducted in six countries (Colombia, Côte d'Ivoire, DR Congo, Mali, Sierra Leone and West Bank and Gaza Strip) in 2010 (Bøås, Tiltnes and Flatø). Bars represent countries. The purpose of the figure is to identify trends without highlighting any specific countries.

*Source*: World Bank (2011), *World Development Report 2011: Conflict, Security and Development*, The World Bank Group, Washington DC, http://siteresources.worldbank.org/INTWDRS/Resources/WDR2011_Full_Text.pdf.

**Figure 3.20. Unemployment is a predominant motive to join rebel movements or gangs**

Citizens' views on what drives people to join rebel movements and gangs, in % of survey respondents choosing a given driver

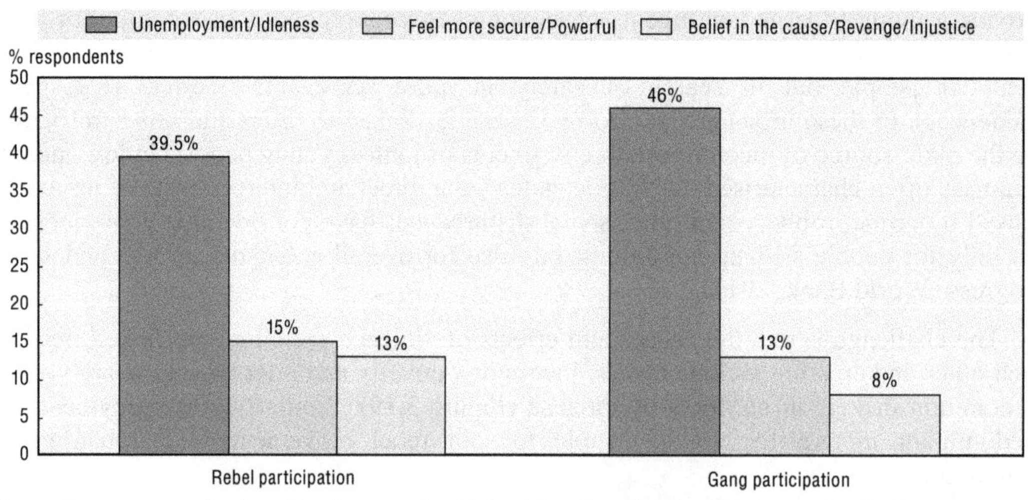


*Notes:* Surveys were conducted in six countries (Colombia, Côte d'Ivoire, DR Congo, Mali, Sierra Leone and West Bank and Gaza Strip) in 2010 (Bøås, Tiltnes and Flatø). Bars represent countries. The purpose of the figure is to identify trends without highlighting any specific countries.

*Source*: World Bank (2011), *World Development Report 2011: Conflict, Security and Development*, The World Bank Group, Washington DC, http://siteresources.worldbank.org/INTWDRS/Resources/WDR2011_Full_Text.pdf.

### *Conflict undermines development*

Conflict has serious consequences for people's safety and living conditions. Recent political instability has had an enormous human cost: about 45 million people were forcibly displaced due to conflict or persecution by the end of 2012 – the highest in 18 years – more than 15 million of them refugees (UNDP, 2014). Armed conflicts within countries account for the vast majority of conflicts worldwide (Figure 3.21).

Persistent conflicts in some low-income countries have considerable negative impacts on development, as shown by the strong rise of poverty in such countries (World Bank, 2011) (Figure 3.22). For example, countries that experienced major violence between 1981 and 2005 had on average a poverty rate 21 percent points higher than countries that saw no violence (Figure 3.22; OECD 2014i; OECD 2013e).

Conflicts do not only affect livelihoods in the countries in which they occur, but also in surrounding countries. 75% of refugees are hosted by neighbouring countries. For example, Tanzania is making development progress, but each neighbouring conflict accounts for a loss of 0.7% loss in GDP (World Bank, 2011).

**Figure 3.21. Armed conflicts within countries account for the vast majority of conflicts worldwide**

Number of armed conflicts by type, 1946-2013

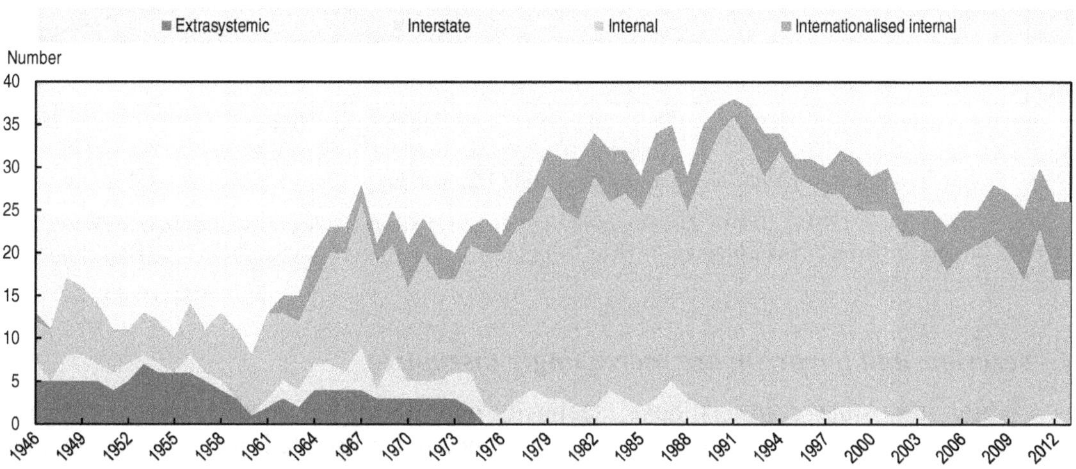


*Notes:*

1. Extra systemic armed conflict occurs between a state and a non-state group outside its own territory. (In the COW project, extra systemic war is subdivided into colonial war and imperial war, but this distinction is not used here.) These conflicts are by definition territorial, since the government side is fighting to retain control of a territory outside the state system.

2. Interstate armed conflict occurs between two or more states.

3. Internal armed conflict occurs between the government of a state and one or more internal opposition group(s) without intervention from other states.

4. Internationalised internal armed conflict occurs between the government of a state and one or more internal opposition group(s) with intervention from other states (secondary parties) on one or both sides.

*Source*: Adapted from UCDP/PRIO (2014), *Armed Conflict Dataset v.4-2014, 1946-2013*, Department of Peace and Conflict Research, Uppsala University, Sweden, www.pcr.uu.se/research/ucdp/datasets/ucdp_prio_armed_conflict_dataset.

On the other hand, significant progress can be made for livelihoods if a country can recover from conflict and re-establish stable security. This has been the case in Ethiopia, which more than quadrupled access to improved water between 1990 and 2010: from 13% to 66% of the population. Mozambique tripled its primary school completion rate from 14% in 1999 to 46% in 2007, and under-nutrition fell from 56% of the population in 1997 to 40% in 2005. Bosnia and Herzegovina increased measles immunisation for children aged 12-23 months from 53% in 1995 to 96% in 2007 (World Bank, 2011).

**Figure 3.22. The poverty gap is widening between peaceful and conflict-ridden countries**

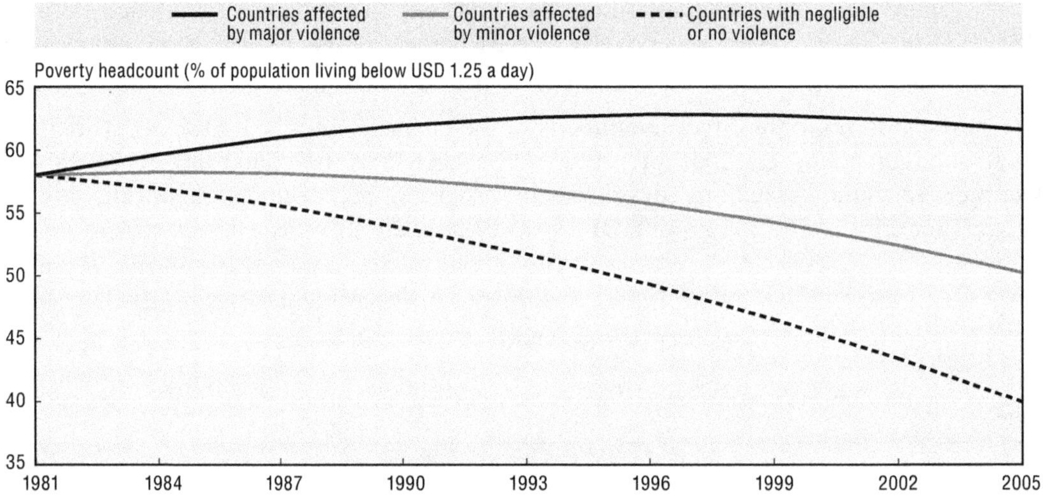


*Note:* Poverty is defined by people living at less than USD 1.25 per day.

*Source:* World Bank (2011), *World Development Report 2011: Conflict, Security and Development*, The World Bank Group, Washington DC, http://siteresources.worldbank.org/INTWDRS/Resources/WDR2011_Full_Text.pdf.

## *Cybercrime and terrorism are increasingly disruptive*

While inter-state conflicts have declined, new forms of threats have emerged. Terrorism has become a permanent source of concern for populations and governments around the world since 9/11. Revolutions against dictatorial or repressive regimes, as in the Arab world, have sparked conflict. And unexpected tensions in Eastern Europe – notably the Ukrainian conflict – have considerable implications for commercial, financial and other exchanges with Russia, creating another major source of uncertainties for the world economy and politics.

Criminal networks exploiting opportunities offered by ICT developments (see below), and all forms of Internet-based delinquency affect the lives of millions of people. The Internet and social networks are being increasingly used by terrorist networks. Furthermore, there is an increasing number of cyber-attacks on selected targets (e.g. banking systems, nuclear weapons, electricity networks) in some countries. According to the Norton cybercrime report, "The cost of cybercrime in just 24 countries is estimated to cost the world economy USD 274 billion per year" (Norton, 2011, cited in Oxford Martin School, 2013). Counteracting and preventing the negative effects of these cyber developments require strongly co-ordinated international measures.

## Governments are ill-equipped to deal with the various challenges to livelihoods

While the problems faced by individual countries vary considerably depending on their level of development and the regions in which they are located, there are a few common weaknesses inherent in policy-making processes. These are undermining governments' ability to tackle head-on the trends identified in this chapter. They include resistance to change; poor trust in government; institutional "silo" mentality; weakness of sub-national entities; and the challenges of global governance.

### *Resistance to change is a serious obstacle*

They are many forms of resistance to change. In many countries, political leaders and policy makers are too often biased by short-term views and interests rather than long-term perspectives, and tend to delay significant reforms (Attali, 2014; Oxford Martin School, 2013). Other sources of resistance to change come from protected professions (such as bankers) that have strong vested interests in the status quo, as well as industrial lobbies that defend established trades or technologies in which they hold monopolistic positions.

### *Trust in government is low*

Since the beginning of the economic crisis, trust in public institutions has received heightened political attention. Today, only 4 out of 10 citizens worldwide have trust in their government (Figure 3.23). Significant erosion in trust in a number of OECD countries (Figure 3.24) has implications for the effectiveness of policy making and the successful implementation of reforms. Rebuilding trust requires more efficient and more reactive public action, greater transparency and a sustained fight against political misconduct and corruption.

**Figure 3.23. People increasingly trust business more than government to do what is right**

Global trust in government and business since 2009

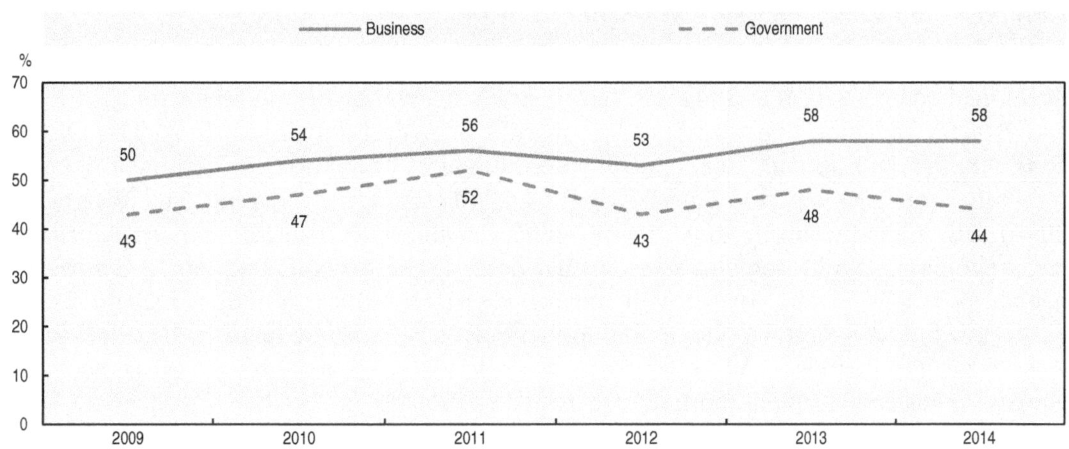


*Source:* Edelman Berland (2014), "2014 Edelman Trust Barometer", webpage, www.edelman.com/insights/intellectual-property/trust-2014 (accessed on 3 February 2015).

**Figure 3.24. Confidence in government is eroding in OECD countries and some major emerging economies**

Confidence in national government in 2012

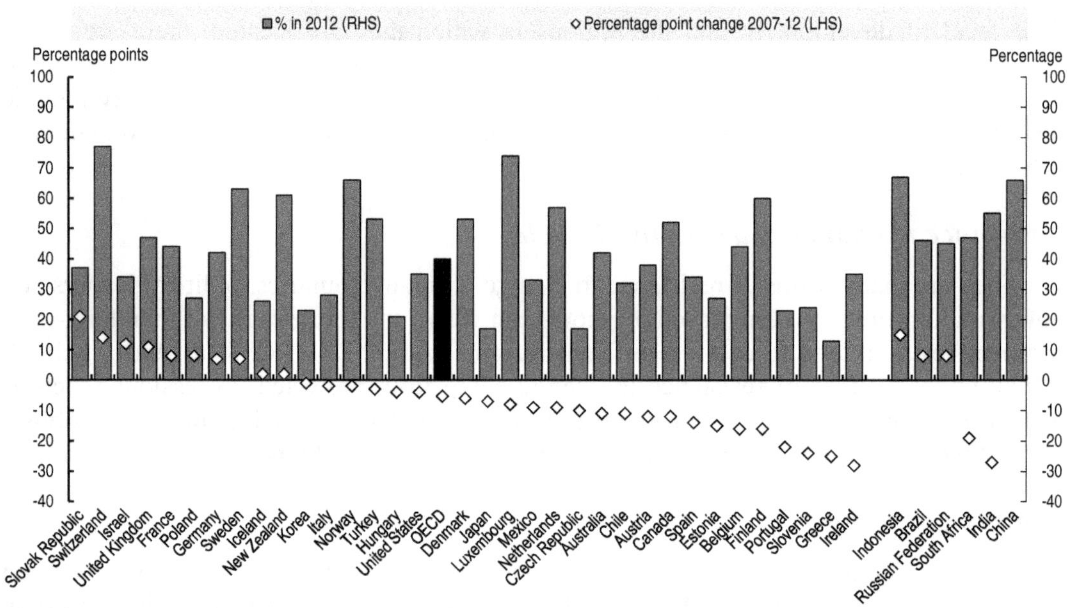


*Notes:* Data for Chile, Germany and the United Kingdom are for 2011 rather than 2012. Data for Iceland and Luxembourg are for 2008 rather than 2007. Data for Austria, Finland, Ireland, Norway, Portugal, Slovakia, Slovenia and Switzerland are for 2006 rather than 2007. Data refer to the percentage who answered 'yes' to the question: "Do you have confidence in national government?" Data arranged in descending order according to percentage point change between 2007 and 2012.

*Source:* OECD (2013d), *Government at a Glance 2013*, OECD Publishing, Paris, http://dx.doi.org/10.1787/gov_glance-2013-en.

## *Indebted states are constrained in their action*

A major consequence of the crisis has been to jeopardise state budgets in a number of developed countries (US and France; see Figure 3.25) and emerging countries (e.g. India and Brazil), reducing considerably their margin of action and investment. The OECD considers that appropriate fiscal consolidation measures could bring government debts in individual countries down to 60% of GDP by 2030 (Braconier, Nicoletti and Westmore, 2014). But in the meantime some major threats remain, with financial markets punishing weak economies with problematic sovereign debt. These tensions take place against the backdrop of long-lasting low growth, raising a serious risk of deflation. Debate on the best ways to re-boost economies is raging between advocates of large budget deficits (a Keynesian perspective) and advocates of austerity (a more orthodox perspective). However, austerity implies the need for major savings in government budgets and will reduce room for essential expenditures for maintaining livelihoods, e.g. social protection.

**Figure 3.25. Government debt is growing in selected OECD countries**

Government debt to GDP ratios, in % of GDP, 1970-2012

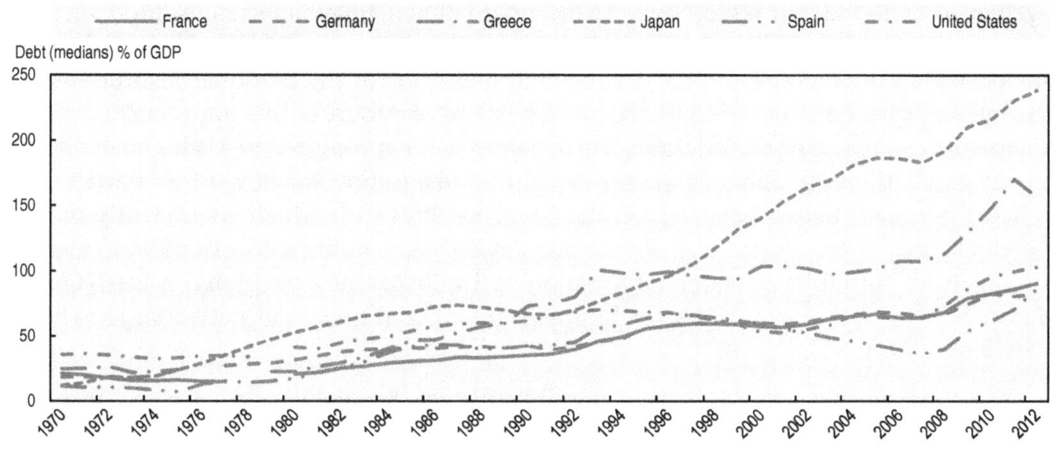


*Source:* Mauro P. et al. (2013), "A modern history of fiscal prudence and profligacy", IMF Working Paper No. 13/5, International Monetary Fund, Washington DC, www.imf.org/external/pubs/cat/longres.aspx?sk=40222.0. Created using IMF Data Mapper: www.imf.org/external/datamapper/ index.php?db=FM.

## *Institutional silos reduce efficiency*

Policy initiatives that can make real differences to livelihoods, such as green growth (see Chapter 5), require integrated, holistic approaches on many fronts: infrastructure, financial incentives, procurement policies, training and education, technology, land reform, etc. The problem, however, is that policy domains tend to be managed with a silo mentality by governments, making it very difficult to overcome interdepartmental barriers when implementing holistic policies. It is generally necessary to have pilot programmes with high political visibility to remove related inertia and obstacles. Beyond such national, highly visible initiatives, on a more routine basis, – e.g. relations between education and employment – it is of utmost importance to find ways and means for governments and other responsible actors to influence factors that together shape "positive spirals".

## *Over-centralisation is undermining local adaptation capacity*

Many of the actions needed for increasing adaptation and resilience capabilities of populations should be implemented at the local level. This is especially true of developing countries. When local communities have the right skills and capacity, they can make significant economic and social progress (Wong, 2012). In the same vein, efficient decentralisation mechanisms in developed countries, such as in Switzerland or Italy, increase local resilience to crises while stemming rural-urban migration. Meanwhile, on a global level, megacities have increasing influence within the scope of the global economy (Oxford Martin School, 2013). Furthermore, a number of countries are facing demands from local regions for more autonomy and even full independence. All these factors militate for reconsidering, in many countries, conditions in which power is devolved to the different sub-national levels of governments. The question of sustainability and resilience of livelihood should be central in this perspective.

### *Global governance is failing*

A major problem is the extraordinary difficulty governments have in working together to tackle global issues such as the international financial system, food security, climate change and cyber-security. Reasons range from nationalistic attitudes and uncoordinated interventions to the fragmented mandates of international institutions and inadequate representation (UNDP, 2014). The lack of progress in improving the global governance system has considerable consequences for a number of issues that directly impact populations' livelihoods across the globe. Inspiration for how to proceed can be gained from past success stories (e.g. the Montreal Protocol, which successfully banned chemicals that were destroying the ozone layer). A number of actions can also be envisaged for introducing better information and transparency on global issues (Oxford Martin School, 2013) as well as for building global coalitions and networks for change (Rischard, 2002).

The next chapter envisages five possible futures for livelihoods derived from the various trends explored in this chapter.

## Notes

1. See also Annex 3.A1, which shows GDP per capita per consumption/income deciles for selected developed and income countries over the last decade. For example, Germany appears to have been remarkably stable over the period, with no change in wealth distribution. The US curves show an increase in inequality benefiting the richest 10% of people. In Bangladesh and Nigeria, inequality remains similar at the end of the 2000s as compared to around a decade ago, with some reduction of poverty.

2. See www.ashoka.org.

3. A megacity is usually defined as a metropolitan area with a total population in excess of 10 million people (Wikipedia, 2015).

4. "Water scarcity" refers to the volumetric abundance, or lack thereof, of water supply. According to the 'Falkenmark indicator' or 'water stress index' (Falkenmark, Lundquist and Widstrand, 1989), water scarcity is defined in terms of the total water resources that are available to the population of a region; measuring scarcity as the amount of renewable freshwater that is available for each person each year. If the amount of renewable water in a country is below 1 700 $M^3$ per person per year, that country is said to be experiencing water stress; below 1 000 $M^3$ it is said to be experiencing water scarcity; and below 500 $M^3$, absolute water scarcity.

# *References*

Attali, J. (ed.) (2014), *Pour une économie positive*, La Documentation française, Paris.

Baker, J. L. (2008), *Urban Poverty: A Global View,* Urban Papers UP-5, January 2008, The World Bank, Washington DC, http://documents.worldbank.org/curated/en/2008/01/9112288/urban-poverty-global-view.

Bloom, D. et al. (2011), *The Global Economic Burden of Noncommunicable Diseases*, World Economic Forum, Geneva.

Braconier, H. and, G. Nicoletti (2014), "OECD@100: Policies for a Shifting World", Working Party No. 1 on Macroeconomic and Structural Policy Analysis, Economics Department,; 69th Meeting of the Economic Policy Committee, Paris, 7 February 2014 - ECO/CPE/WP1(2014)2, OECD, Paris.

Braconier, H., G. Nicoletti and B. Westmore (2014), "Policy Challenges for the Next 50 Years", OECD Economic Policy Papers, No. 9, OECD Publishing, Paris, http://dx.doi.org/10.1787/5jz18gs5fckf-en.

Cingano, F. (2014), "Trends in Income Inequality and its Impact on Economic Growth", *OECD Social, Employment and Migration Working Papers*, No. 163, OECD Publishing, Paris, http://dx.doi.org/10.1787/5jxrjncwxv6j-en

Credit Suisse (2014), *Global Wealth Databook 2014*, Research Institute, Credit Suisse, Zurich, p. 110.

Dai, A. (2011), "Drought under global warming: A review", *WIREs Climate Change*, John Wiley & Sons, New Jersey, Vol 2, pp. 45-65, www.cgd.ucar.edu/cas/adai/papers/Dai-drought_WIRES2010.pdf.

The Economist (2014a), "Coming to an office near you", The Economist website, 16 January 2014, www.economist.com/news/leaders/21594298-effect-todays-technology-tomorrows-jobs-will-be-immenseand-no-country-ready.

The Economist (2014b), *Securing Livelihoods*, special edition printed for the Bellagio workshop, The Economist, London, www.visionariesunbound.com/events/securing-livelihoods/the-economist-securing-livelihoods-magazine.

The Economist (2012a), "For richer, for poorer", special report: The World Economy, The Economist website, October 13th 2012, www.economist.com/node/21564414.

The Economist (2012b), "New cradles to graves", The Economist website, 6 September 2012, www.economist.com/node/21562210.

Edelman Berland (2014), "2014 Edelman Trust Barometer", webpage, www.edelman.com/insights/intellectual-property/trust-2014 (accessed on 3 February 2015).

Falkenmark, M., J. Lundquist and C. Widstrand (1989), "Macro-scale water scarcity requires micro-scale approaches: Aspects of vulnerability in semi-arid development", *Natural Resources Forum*, Vol. 13, No. 4, pp. 258-267, http://onlinelibrary.wiley.com/doi/10.1111/j.1477-8947.1989.tb00348.x/abstract.

Frey, C.B. and M.A. Osborne (2013), *The Future of Employment: How Susceptible are Jobs to Computerisation?* Oxford Martin Programme on the Impacts of Future Technology, Oxford Martin School, Oxford, www.oxfordmartin.ox.ac.uk/downloads/academic/The_Future_of_Employment.pdf.

The Global Commission on the Economy and Climate (2014), *The New Climate Economy*, The Global Commission on the Economy and the Climate, http://newclimateeconomy.report.

Human Security Report Project (2013), *Human Security Report 2013: The Decline in Global Violence: Evidence, Explanation, and Contestation*, Human Security Press, Vancouver, www.hsrgroup.org/our-work/security-stats/State-Based-Armed-Conflicts-By-Type.aspx.

IEA (2014), *World Energy Outlook 2014*, International Energy Agency, Paris.

ILO (2015), *Employment Trends*, www.ilo.org/empelm/units/employment-trends/lang--en/index.htm.

Joumard I., M. Pisu and D. Bloch (2013), "Tackling income inequality: The role of taxes and transfers", *OECD Journal: Economic Studies*, Vol. 2012/1, http://dx.doi.org/10.1787/eco_studies-2012-5k95xd6l65lt

Kimenyi, M.S and J. Kibe (2014), "Africa's powerhouse", Brookings website, 6 January 2014, www.brookings.edu/research/opinions/2013/12/30-kenya-economy-kimenyi.

Kurzweil, R. (2005), *The Singularity Is Near: When Humans Transcend Biology,* Viking, New York, www.kurzweilai.net/the-singularity-is-near.

Kuznets, S. (1955), "Economic growth and income inequality", *The American Economic Review*, New York, Vol. 45, No. 1, www.aeaweb.org/aer/top20/45.1.1-28.pdf.

Mauro P. et al. (2013), "A modern history of fiscal prudence and profligacy", IMF Working Paper No. 13/5, International Monetary Fund, Washington DC, www.imf.org/external/pubs/cat/longres.aspx?sk=40222.0.

Munich Re (2015), NatCatSERVICE (database), Geo Risks Research, Munich Re, www.munichre.com/natcatservice (28 January 2015).

Norton (2011), "Norton Cybercrime Report", Norton website, http://uk.norton.com/cybercrimereport (accessed 22 January 2015).

OECD (2015), *States of Fragility 2015: Meeting Post-2015 Ambitions*, OECD Publishing, Paris, http://dx.doi.org/10.1787/9789264227699-en

OECD (2014a), *Perspectives on Global Development 2014: Boosting Productivity to Meet the Middle Income Challenge,* OECD Publishing, Paris, http://dx.doi.org/10.1787/persp_glob_dev-2014-en.

OECD (2014b), *Income Inequality Update, June 2014,* OECD, Paris, www.oecd.org/els/soc/OECD2014-Income-Inequality-Update.pdf.

OECD (2014c), *Society at a Glance 2014: OECD Social Indicators*, OECD Publishing, Paris, http://dx.doi.org/10.1787/soc_glance-2014-en.

OECD (2014d), *OECD Economic Outlook*, Vol. 2014/2, OECD Publishing, Paris, http://dx.doi.org/10.1787/eco_outlook-v2014-2-en.

OECD (2014e), *Megatrends: Policies for a Shifting World,* Global Strategy Group, discussion notes for the second meeting of the OECD Global Strategy Group on 25-26 November 2014, OECD, Paris.

OECD (2014f), *Policy Challenges for the next 50 years,* OECD Economic Policy Paper, July 2014, OECD, Paris.

OECD (2014g), *Managing Water for Future Cities,* Policy Perspectives, OECD, Paris, www.oecd.org/environment/resources/Policy-Perspectives-Managing-Water-For-Future-Cities.pdf.

OECD (2014h), *Development Co-operation Report 2014: Mobilising Resources for Sustainable Development*, OECD Publishing, Paris, http://dx.doi.org/10.1787/dcr-2014-en.

OECD (2014i), *Fragile States: Domestic Revenue Mobilisation in Fragile States*, OECD Publishing, Paris, www.oecd.org/dac/governance-peace/conflictandfragility/docs/FSR-2014.pdf.

OECD (2013a), *How's Life? 2013: Measuring Well-being*, OECD Publishing, Paris, http://dx.doi.org/10.1787/9789264201392-en.

OECD (2013b), "Innovation and inclusive development", conference discussion report, Conference on Innovation for Inclusive Development, Cape Town, 21 November 2012, www.oecd.org/sti/inno/oecd-inclusive-innovation.pdf.

OECD (2013c), *Water and Climate Change Adaptation: Policies to Navigate Uncharted Waters*, OECD Studies on Water, OECD Publishing, Paris, http://dx.doi.org/10.1787/9789264200449-en.

OECD (2013d), *Government at a Glance 2013*, OECD Publishing, Paris, http://dx.doi.org/10.1787/gov_glance-2013-en.

OECD (2013e), *Fragile States: Resource Flows and Trends, Conflict and Fragility*, OECD Publishing, Paris, http://dx.doi.org/10.1787/9789264190399-en.

OECD (2013f), *Water Security for Better Lives*, OECD Studies on Water, OECD Publishing, Paris, http://dx.doi.org/10.1787/9789264202405-en.

OECD (2012a), *OECD Science, Technology and Industry Outlook 2012*, OECD Publishing, Paris, http://dx.doi.org/10.1787/sti_outlook-2012-en.

OECD (2012b), *OECD Environmental Outlook to 2050: The Consequences of Inaction*, OECD Publishing, Paris, http://dx.doi.org/10.1787/9789264122246-en.

OECD (2011), *OECD Environmental Outlook to 2050*, OECD Publishing, http://dx.doi.org/10.1787/9789264122246-en.

OECD (2010), *The OECD Innovation Strategy: Getting a Head Start on Tomorrow*, OECD Publishing, Paris, http://dx.doi.org/10.1787/9789264083479-en.

Oxford Martin School (2013), *Now for the Long Term: The Report of the Oxford Martin Commission for Future Generations*, Oxford University Press, Oxford, www.oxfordmartin.ox.ac.uk/downloads/commission/Oxford_Martin_Now_for_the_Long_Term.pdf.

Paunov, C. (2013), *Innovation and Inclusive Development: A Discussion of the Main Policy Issues*, OECD Science, Technology and Industry Working Papers, No. 2013/01, OECD Publishing, Paris, http://dx.doi.org/10.1787/5k4dd1rvsnjj-en.

Piketty, T. (2014), *Capital in the Twenty-First Century*, Belknap Press, Cambridge MA, www.hup.harvard.edu/catalog.php?isbn=9780674430006.

Reinhart, C. M. and K. S. Rogoff, (2011), "From financial crash to debt crisis," *American Economic Review*, Vol. 101(5), August 2011, Pittsburgh PA, pp. 1676-1706, www.aeaweb.org/articles.php?doi=10.1257/aer.101.5.1676.

Rifkin, J. (2014), *The Zero Marginal Cost Society*, Macmillan, London.

Rischard, J-F. (2014), "Visionaries unbound: Securing livelihoods", presentation, Securing Livelihoods workshop, Bellagio, Italy, 4-8 August 2014.

Rischard, J-F. (2002), *High Noon: Twenty Global Problems, Twenty Years to Solve Them*, Basic Books, New York, http://books.google.fr/books/about/High_Noon.html?id=7gl_AAAAMAAJ&redir_esc=y.

UCDP/PRIO (2014), *Armed Conflict Dataset v.4-2014, 1946-2013*, Department of Peace and Conflict Research, Uppsala University, Sweden, www.pcr.uu.se/research/ucdp/datasets/ucdp_prio_armed_conflict_dataset.

UN (21 March 2013), "Deputy UN chief calls for urgent action to tackle global sanitation crisis", UN News Centre, United Nations, Washington DC, www.un.org/apps/news/story.asp?ewsID=44452-VMZu1vnF9ik.

UN-DESA (2013), *World Population Prospects* (database), Department of Economic and Social Affairs, United Nations, New York, http://esa.un.org/unpd/wpp/unpp/panel_population.htm.

UN-DESA (2012a), *World Population Prospects: The 2012 Revision* (database), Department of Economic and Social Affairs, United Nations, New York, http://esa.un.org/wpp .

UN-DESA (2012b), *World Urbanisation Prospects: The 2011 Revision*, Department of Economic and Social Affairs, United Nations, New York, www.un.org/en/development/desa/publications/world-urbanization-prospects-the-2011-revision.html.

UNDP (2014), *The 2014 Human Development Report – Sustaining Human Progress: Reducing Vulnerabilities and Building Resilience*, Human Development Report Office, United Nations, New York, http://hdr.undp.org/sites/default/files/hdr14-report-en-1.pdf.

UNODC (2012), *Monitoring the Impact of Economic Crisis on Crime*, Statistics and Surveys Section, United Nations Office on Drugs and Crime, Vienna, www.unodc.org/documents/data-and-analysis/statistics/crime/GIVAS_Final_Report.pdf.

van Zanden, J., et al. (eds.) (2014), *How Was Life? Global Well-Being Since 1820*, OECD Publishing, Paris, http://dx.doi.org/10.1787/9789264214262-en.

WEF (2015), *Global Risks 2015: Insight Report, 10th Edition*, World Economic Forum, Geneva.

WHO (2011), *Global Status Report on NonCommunicable Diseases*, World Health Organization, Geneva.

Wikipedia (2015), "Megacity", Wikipedia website, http://en.wikipedia.org/wiki/Megacity (accessed 26 January 2015).

Wolf, M. (2014), *The Shifts and the Shocks: What We've Learned—and Have Still to Learn—from the Financial Crisis,* Penguin Press, New York.

Wong, Susan (2012), *What have been the impacts of World Bank Community-Driven Development Programs? CDD impact evaluation review and operational and research implications*, World Bank, Washington DC, http://documents.worldbank.org/curated/en/2012/03/16374801/impacts-world-bank-community-driven-development-programs-cdd-impact-evaluation-review-operational-research-implications.

World Bank (2015a), *PovcalNet* (database), http://iresearch.worldbank.org/PovcalNet/index.htm.

World Bank (2015b), "Water," World Bank Group website, http://water.worldbank.org/node/84122 (accessed 27 January 2015).

World Bank (2014), *The Economic Impact of the 2014 Ebola Epidemic: Short and Medium Term Estimates for West Africa*, Working Paper No. 91219, The World Bank Group, Washington DC, http://documents.worldbank.org/curated/en/2014/10/20270083/economic-impact-2014-ebola-epidemic-short-medium-term-estimates-west-africa.

World Bank (2012), *World Development Report 2013: Jobs*, The World Bank Group, Washington DC, http://siteresources.worldbank.org/EXTNWDR2013/Resources/8258024-1320950747192/8260293-1322665883147/WDR_2013_Report.pdf.

World Bank (2011), *World Development Report 2011: Conflict, Security and Development*, The World Bank Group, Washington DC, http://siteresources.worldbank.org/INTWDRS/Resources/WDR2011_Full_Text.pdf.

World Bank (2010) *Innovation Policy: A Guide for Developing Countries*, The World Bank Group, Washington DC, https://openknowledge.worldbank.org/handle/10986/2460.

World Bank et al. (2013), *Transforming Arab Economies: Travelling the Knowledge and Innovation Road, The* World Bank Group, *Washington DC,* http://beta.cmimarseille.org/featured/transforming-arab-economies-traveling-knowledge-and-innovation-road.

# Annex 3.A1. Income/consumption inequality in selected countries

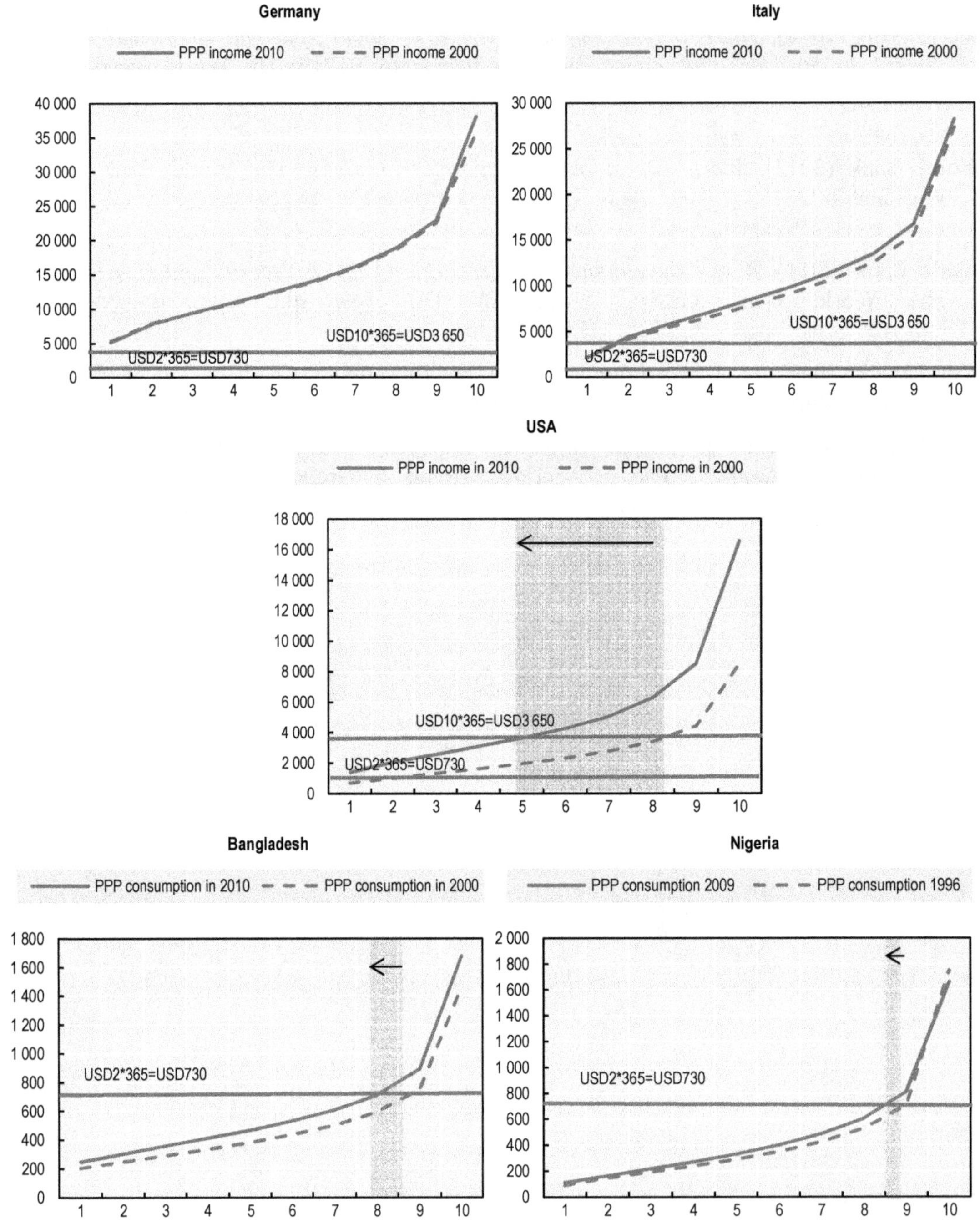


*Notes:* The horizontal axis represents the deciles of each country's income/consumption distribution. The analysis is based on consumption data for Bangladesh and Nigeria. For Germany, Italy and the United States the analysis is based on income data. Horizontal lines for USD 2*365 = USD 730 and for USD 10*365 = USD 3 650 represent the USD 2 a day poverty line as well as the USD 10 a day which can be regarded as the lower level of the middle-class. The width of the light grey bar represents the reduction of the share of people living at USD 2 a day. For example in Bangladesh, the light grey bar cuts the horizontal axis at the 9th and 8rd deciles. Thus, around 10% of the population moved beyond the USD 2 a day poverty line between 2000 and 2010. The width of the light blue bar represents the increase of the middle class. For example in the United States, the light blue bar cuts the horizontal axis at the 8th and 5th deciles. Thus, around 30% of the population moved from a vulnerable consumption/income situation to the lower level of the middle class between 2000 and 2010.

*Source:* World Bank (2015a), *PovcalNet* (database), http://iresearch.worldbank.org/PovcalNet/index.htm.

# Chapter 4
# Scenarios for future livelihoods

*This chapter explores a range of possible futures for livelihoods. It uses a foresight approach to develop five alternative scenarios for the future which build on some of the trends outlined in Chapter 3. The five scenario storylines look forward to 2030: three are crisis scenarios, while two are more positive; all are possible based on current trends. Scenario 1 describes a world in which rapid automation and ageing populations in the developed world lead to dramatic jobless growth. Scenario 2 imagines the impact of widespread drought in those developing regions already struggling to employ a large share of young people. Scenario 3 envisages the impact on livelihoods of another major global financial crisis. Scenario 4 takes a more optimistic perspective to describe a world in which technology is a positive force for jobs, education and solutions to cope with environmental challenges. Scenario 5 explores a world in which jobless growth encourages people to value social well-being over economic growth and to develop creative ways of making a living. All the scenarios raise a wealth of policy options and possibilities for building inclusiveness and resilience into future livelihoods.*

**Key messages**

- Imagining alternative scenarios can help widen the perspective on possible futures for livelihoods and related policy implications.
- Several emerging trends threaten to challenge progress on livelihoods (outlined in Chapter 3). Envisaging five alternative scenarios for the interaction among some of these trends reveals a range of actions required to create resilience in the face of potential crises.
- Of the five possible futures developed, three are dire – involving massive population movements, inequality, poverty and citizen unrest – while two involve vibrant societies that possess the skills, creativity and flexibility to thrive and stave off global crises. Which scenario triumphs depends on the building blocks laid down today.
- The visioning exercises underline the need to work towards more inclusive and resilient livelihoods. This will require bold action:
  - to do more at the global level to try to prevent some of these scenarios from occurring
  - to rethink how education and skills building are delivered
  - to develop more effective taxation policies and income redistribution approaches to combat inequality and invest in social inclusion
  - to create more flexible and adaptive labour approaches to respond to technical change, to capitalise on people's mobility and other forces that reflect the dynamism of societies
  - to build resilience and adaptability from the ground up – from individuals up to entire societies.

The outlook for livelihoods will continue to be shaped by an increasingly diverse array of actors; by the interplay of the various trends discussed in the previous chapter, plus some new ones; and by the effectiveness and coherence of domestic and international policy intervention.

In this context of complexity, pluralism and unpredictability, conventional policy approaches involving quantitative forecast-based planning can result in uncertainty, which in turn can be used to justify inaction. Forecasting cannot anticipate disruption or novel situations and does little to help develop or explore longer-term developments that might be fundamentally different from the business-as-usual outlook.

This chapter instead uses a scenario approach to develop five possible livelihood landscapes for the world in 2030. The scenarios are based on OECD economic forecasts, but include some of the emerging trends outlined in Chapter 3. The chapter explains first why scenarios can be a powerful approach for policy makers. It then outlines the five scenarios in turn, along with their policy implications.

## Scenarios can help anticipate the future in an unpredictable world

Stories of the future can be developed using a variety of methods. In this chapter, a scenario is not the same as a baseline projection developed in econometric forecasting. Scenario-based approaches involve more open thinking to develop stories about the future and then use these to make sense of a puzzling and messy situation. Scenarios differ from forecasts in three ways (Figure 4.1):

1. While scenarios often use data-based research for their content, they are not constructed by extrapolating present trends into the future. Instead they explore how and why "bends" might bend or break and redirect attention to weak signals emanating from new and emerging trends.
2. Scenarios always come in sets of two, three or more plausible stories. This encourages and enables thinking outside the box. This helps avoid delaying action until there is enough evidence to predict the next crisis. Scenarios are designed to encourage constructive engagement with uncertainty in order to avoid missed opportunities and blind spots.
3. Scenarios are user and use-specific. Scenario work is not an end but a means within a wider intervention. The power of scenarios is realised in the depth and quality of the strategic conversation enabled in the development and use of the scenarios.

**Figure 4.1. Scenarios are not forecasts**

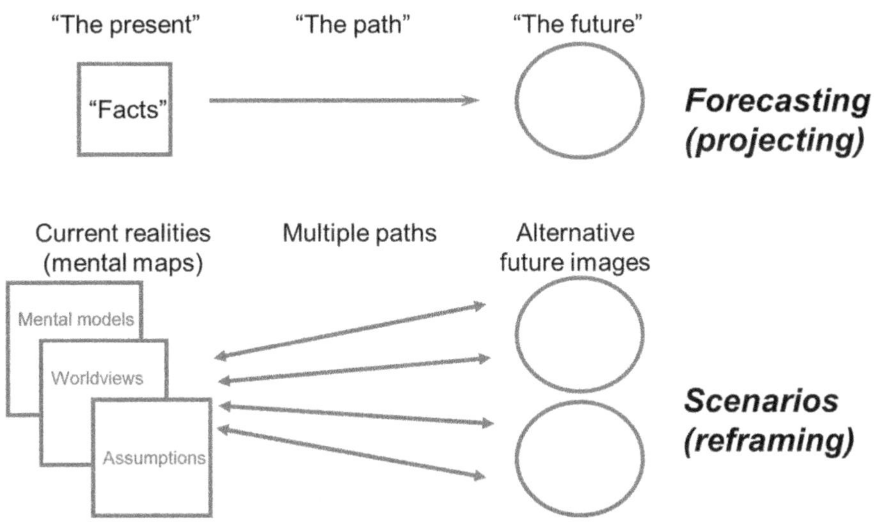


Among the many subtle by-products of engaging with scenarios is a greater sense of confidence about an uncertain future. This confidence is quite different from the feeling of security that arises from accepting a single predicted future as "true". It is related, instead, to a faster, more flexible and reflective sense of the future that contributes, in turn, to a capacity for agility and resilience – getting ahead of connected challenges by imagining different potential paths.

### *Thinking about scenarios can help people talk to each other*

Scenarios enable and enhance the quality of strategic dialogue on extremely complex, contentious issues. Where there is deep disagreement, a wide-ranging, open, and honest discussion is almost impossible under normal circumstances. However, a team of people from many different perspectives can create scenarios together in a neutral and safe future space. This enables disagreement to be managed as an asset and promotes collaboration even when there is no easy agreement on policy positions. Often, in the process of sharing and co-creating stories, those who hold an opposing position begin to understand the other point of view and to see possible opportunities for collaboration. A well-known example of a fruitful collaboration occurred in a scenario project undertaken during the post-apartheid transition in South Africa in the early 1990s (Box 4.1).

In a research setting or culture of experts, scenario-based dialogues can be an effective way of enabling interesting, interdisciplinary insights and identifying assumptions that have become so engrained that they are no longer questioned. As in any discipline-based culture or professional field, experts can become blind to their own mental models. To enable more interdisciplinary and collaborative work, scenarios offer a method of research that encourages thinking outside the accepted model.

**Box 4.1. How scenarios helped to shape the political transition in South Africa**

The South African scenarios were developed to help the country transition from apartheid. At the time there was intense pressure for rapid land reform and other profound changes in the economic life of the country. The scenario team brought together representatives from all parts of the deeply divided South African political spectrum. The team came up with four scenarios, none of which represented a future anyone initially wanted. One of the scenarios represented a rapid reorganisation of the economy, including extensive financial system reforms – but the team agreed that the most plausible outcome of such rapid reforms would be a fiscal crisis. The scenario was called "Icarus" after the mythological boy with wings who flew too close to the sun. Another scenario – which eventually emerged as a desired future – was a measured approach to reforming the economic system to allow the government to be sustainable. This scenario was called "Flight of the Flamingos", because while flamingos take off slowly, they take off together.

In the decades following this exercise, the two scenarios that generated the most discussion – "Icarus" and "Flight of the Flamingos" – were alluded to in national news media, sermons, and government discussions. The scenario exercise had helped provide a common language for a transformative vision of the future. And in creating the four scenarios, the diverse team established a level of trust.

*Source*: Kahane, A. (2012), *Transformative Scenario Planning: Working Together to Change the Future*, Berrett-Koehler Publishers, California, www.bkconnection.com/books/title/transformative-scenario-planning.

## There are various ways of envisaging the future

For developing the scenarios in this book, the first step was to select a baseline. We chose the OECD's baseline projection for long-term growth and development to 2060 (Braconier, Nicoletti and Westmore, 2014). This sets the stage for five variants, but with the shorter time horizon of 2030. The OECD projection predicts continued, although slower, economic growth around the globe (Box 4.2 and for more detail see Annex 4.A1).

The implications of these projections include that countries can improve growth prospects by implementing policies with four goals: (1) accelerating global integration (including encouraging migration flows); (2) making institutions more resilient to shocks (e.g. demographic ones); (3) curbing pollution and mitigating (or adapting to) climate change; and (4) making the most of the knowledge economy, which will be the main driver of growth in the future (Braconier, Nicoletti and Westmore, 2014).

**Box 4.2. OECD economic projections to 2060**

Analysis in *Policy Challenges for the Next 50 Years* (Braconier, Nicoletti and Westmore, 2014) suggests that there will be a gradual convergence of per capita incomes between developed and developing economies, while the economic balance will continue to shift towards emerging economies. However, the growth outlook for the global economy is mediocre compared to the past, with large uncertainties surrounding productivity. While growth will be more sustained in emerging economies than in the OECD, it will slow as countries catch up with higher-income countries. Ageing will depress growth everywhere, and in OECD countries a reduction in immigration may further harm growth. It may also be curbed by the worsening impact of environmental degradation, especially in Asia, largely due to the effects of climate change, which are likely to affect these countries earlier than expected (see Annex 4.A1).

### *Alternative pathways of the future can be considered*

In light of the discussions in Chapter 3 about emerging trends affecting livelihoods, a set of alternative pathways of the future can be considered. Incorporating these emerging trends in the analysis will complement OECD's baseline projection and help to enhance the anticipation capability and to develop possible policy actions. These include another major financial crisis or medium-term environmental impacts such as longer droughts. Additionally, the uncertainty about the outcomes of trends and their interactions suggests complementing the baseline projections with alternative, possible outcomes. These include:

- The chance of other major financial crises is possible. Recent discussions and literature clearly point to this continued risk (for example, see Wolf, 2014).
- Possible social disruptions at the national or regional level are likely, in reaction to increased inequality around the world and cuts in government social programmes.
- Major geopolitical disturbances or global conflicts can be envisaged. Recent tensions surrounding the Ukraine crisis and continued conflicts in the Middle-East clearly point to this threat.
- Protectionist tendencies during the last crisis indicate that fragmentation remains a possibility.
- Political economy dynamics – such as resistance to reforms and reluctance of governments to press for them –make the reduction of expenditures to balance budgets in some OECD countries unlikely.
- Some of the recent literature shows that productivity around the world could get another boost and increased automation may challenge the future of jobs (Brynjolfsson and McAfee, 2014).
- Increased competition for talent may lead to very different future migration trends. For example, emerging youth bulges in some regions, such as sub-Saharan Africa or South Asia, may be taken into account when thinking about future migration trends.
- Local and regional impacts of climate change, such as droughts or floods, are may affect livelihoods in the coming decades.

## Five possible scenarios to broaden the policy dialogue

By developing new scenarios which reflect some of the trends identified in Chapter 3, we can obtain a broader perspective on relevant policy areas. The key trends considered are:[1]

1. The ageing trends in developed and some emerging economies; and youth bulges in Africa, South Asia as well as the MENA region.
2. The trend towards automation and jobless growth, as well as technological advances that underpin new forms of growth e.g. green growth, self-generated work and the shared economy.
3. The increasing occurrence of droughts induced by climate change.
4. Persistent financial fragilities that trigger a new global financial crisis.

We have developed five partial alternative variants (three negative or dystopian scenarios and two utopian) by focusing on these trends.[2] The scenarios are not fully developed; they are simply suggestions for how the future might look. They are partial for the following reasons:

- Each scenario only combines a couple of emerging trends; they ignore some other relevant trends. They do so in order to highlight specific aspects, and to avoid getting lost in too many unmanageable possible interactions.
- Some of the emerging trends are particularly relevant for some regions (e.g. youth bulges in sub-Saharan Arica, Middle East and South Asia). Therefore, the storylines developed do not always have the same relevance in other geographic regions.
- Several different scenarios may occur in parallel in different parts of the world.

For each scenario we also identify some policy actions which may be needed to either avoid the worst effects (for the three crisis/dystopian scenarios) or else to bring about the positive utopian outcomes. They offer an opportunity for further dialogue among key stakeholders involving public and private entities. They also help develop the policy priorities discussed in the next chapter.

### *Scenario 1: "Automated North"*

#### *Automation proceeds faster than expected and affects ageing societies in particular*

This scenario is particularly relevant for all countries with ageing populations: mainly the advanced economies and some emerging economies (especially China).

Automation in advanced economies and some emerging countries becomes omnipresent; jobs in most sectors are increasingly taken over by robots and artificial intelligence systems. Economic growth in those economies is largely jobless. Automation does not only replace lower-skilled jobs (in transportation/logistics, production and administration), but also high-skilled activities (including jobs in management, science and engineering, the arts, and the legal and medical fields).[3] For example, solving a legal case or diagnosis based on a patient's symptoms can increasingly be done using "big data" – applying powerful computer programmes to very large data sets.

The process of automation is very fast; faster than previous technological revolutions which have also altered the jobs landscape. Therefore, most people whose jobs are replaced by robots or artificial intelligence fail to adapt fast enough and find it difficult to secure their livelihoods. Some new jobs do emerge for people with new ideas, but there are not enough new jobs to allow everyone to be employed. New demand for traditionally produced goods and services emerges (e.g. traditionally produced agricultural goods or restaurants where dishes are cooked by a human), which leads to a re-emergence of some jobs even for mid-level skills. But again, many people are left without jobs even if they are highly skilled.

Inequality increases faster than expected. People whose livelihoods are under pressure will increasingly protest against the government. Social tensions and disruptions increase. Tensions are particularly strong in those countries with high structural unemployment (as in Greece and Spain after the global economic crisis of 2008/09). Increased automation makes these tensions even more fundamental.

Automation is fastest in ageing societies, where economic growth remains possible even despite the smaller working age population. The need for massive immigration inflows to secure growth is fading quickly. In fact, with fewer jobs available to nationals, pressure is growing to increase barriers to immigration in developed countries.

The problem of financing pension and other social security systems becomes a yet more fundamental challenge for all these economies. With less fiscal revenue due to fewer people with waged income and at the same time more people in need of social security support (both old and working age people), government debt accumulates unabated and becomes unmanageable.

In many developing countries, the automation process is much slower, meaning that these countries are no longer competitive, even in low-cost, low-value added sectors. Many activities that had been off-shored are now taken back to developed country firms (in all sectors: agriculture, manufacturing and services). Nevertheless, there might still be room for traditional economic activities conducted by humans in developing countries. Goods and services produced by people in these economies will be used to serve the emerging domestic consumer markets as well as those in neighbouring countries.

Only a few talented persons from developing countries can seek a better life in advanced countries because of those countries' tightened migration regimes in response to changing trends of public opinion.[4] Larger-scale migration occurs mainly within regional blocs of developing countries.

### *Key policy implications*

How realistic is this scenario? It is certainly not pure fiction; Chapter 3 demonstrates that some of these trends are already in play.

The policy implications of this scenario are about adaptation rather than prevention, given that automation and ageing are already occurring. What policies at the global, regional, national and local level are needed to help individuals secure their livelihoods?

- *A new form of redistribution is needed.* In a jobless world, income redistribution becomes crucial. People need to have income to buy goods and services. Otherwise, even the robots and artificial intelligence systems come to a standstill. Jobless growth without appropriate redistribution will lead to rising inequality and increasing social disruption. A system of guaranteed income for all requires serious consideration. At the very least, a social protection system is needed which compensates all those people without jobs. Yet pension and other social security systems in those countries most affected by jobless growth are already under pressure. Current systems are largely based on taxing wage incomes. In a context of jobless growth, extending social security systems without a drastic paradigm change for generating more state revenues is not viable.

- *Globally co-ordinated capital taxation policies could be necessary.* The dilemmas of income redistribution raised above suggest that countries may need to tax capital income (both profits and property) more strongly. However, capital is mobile and can soon be shifted to other countries where capital income taxes are lower or inexistent. To address this challenge, taxation policies would need to be co-ordinated globally.
- *The pressure on the free movement of goods, services and labour may increase rapidly.* Under this scenario, the continued free movement of goods and services becomes less likely. Developing countries, which are losing economic opportunities due to increased re-shoring of international firms with their origins in developed countries, may try to secure their domestic and regional markets by an introduction of new protectionist barriers and securing business opportunities by participating in regional blocs. Developed countries, on the other hand – where the automation process is fastest – may increase barriers to international migration. Policy makers around the globe must think carefully about how to avoid a global economic slowdown due to increased barriers to trade and migration. What would be an appropriate global trading system under these circumstances?
- *Adaptability and flexibility in skills and interests will need to be fostered.* Such an approach would allow people to cope with the rapid changes. Education systems must accommodate these emerging needs and life-long learning systems will need to be developed. Continuous ICT-enabled learning remains highly important. Much of this knowledge can be acquired individually. Communities and countries need to provide the infrastructure and space for this type of learning, including virtual interactions.
- *Communities need to develop new social norms.* As available jobs decline, people will increasingly engage in unpaid activities (leisure, social media, sharing economy, voluntary work, etc.). Communities will be challenged to develop new social norms, in which being in paid work is no longer a requirement for social respect.

## *Scenario 2: "Droughts and joblessness in the South"*

### *Droughts become widespread and challenge the resilience of livelihoods, particularly in regions with a large share of young people*

This scenario is particularly relevant for regions with emerging youth bulges such as sub-Saharan Africa, North Africa, Middle East and South Asia. Many of these regions are already struggling to create productive employment opportunities for their people. In some of these countries, many livelihoods are still based on subsistence farming.

Securing livelihoods in these regions becomes yet more challenging in this scenario as climate change leads to more frequent and longer droughts (already occurring – see

Chapter 3). Subsistence livelihoods that are already threatened will be challenged yet more fundamentally. Subsistence farming becomes almost impossible. Larger scale farming is also seriously challenged. Famines become the norm, not only for small-scale farmers but also for poor people in urban areas, as food prices skyrocket.

While droughts also become more widespread in many developed regions (including the United States and Southern Europe), these regions are expected to manage the situation through new technologies such as desalination of seawater and infrastructure to transport water over long distances. By 2030, other environmental challenges such as rising sea levels are not expected to challenge livelihoods yet on a large scale, but this is likely to become a more serious problem some decades later.

Droughts combined with a large share of jobless young people increase migration. Migration initially takes place within countries as many rural people whose livelihoods are threatened seek a better life in the cities. However, international migration also increases once cities' absorption limits are reached.

The outcome of this scenario is greater inequality. Guaranteeing equal opportunities for all becomes more challenging. Social disruption increases. The pace of change – including the emerging youth bulges as well as longer and stronger periods of droughts – is very fast. Countries, communities and individuals are unlikely to be able to adapt livelihoods or support mechanisms fast enough.

### *Key policy implications*

How realistic is this scenario? Youth bulges are already an issue in many countries, and as little action has been taken to mitigate climate change, current trends indicate that widespread droughts will occur in the next 15 years (Chapter 3). It is unclear, however, how devastating or long the droughts will actually be and how often they will occur. It is also an open question as to what extent countries will be able to adapt to these fast-changing environmental challenges. Can countries, communities and individuals in these developing countries find new ways to create jobs for their youthful populations and make a living, despite the added burden of drought?

As for Scenario 1, the policy implications of this scenario are more about adaptation than prevention. What policies at the global, regional, national and local level will help individuals secure their livelihood in the future?

- *International agreements on water sharing need to be strengthened.* Currently, agreements on water sharing (e.g. between China, which has headwaters for major river systems in Asia, and the countries downstream) are neither sufficient nor sustainable enough to ensure more balanced water management during drought periods (Ambec, Dinar and McKinney, 2013). This increases the risk that countries will hoard water, which may become a source of major conflicts.
- *Strategies for water access need to be developed.* Developing countries with coastlines should tap into global knowledge on water desalination and attract investors to help develop desalination parks. Increasingly, international financial institutions such as the World Bank and the Asian Development Bank may support developing countries in such initiatives (World Bank, 2012). The situation for land-locked countries is more challenging. These countries need to urgently develop alliances with countries with access to the sea so that they are ready to meet future water challenges.

- *Developing countries need to adapt to drought.* Developing countries with large youth bulges and at risk of drought need to develop and implement plans for the large-scale relocation of people and for more drought-resistant agriculture. Recent agricultural research and support could help farmers adapt to the new local climatic conditions. New drought-resilient crops and agricultural methods may also help to sustain livelihoods in those places.
- *Internal and international migration needs to be managed to avoid "slumification".* Urban policies which promote "secondary cities" or "eco-cities" could help to better manage internal migration pressures. Such cities can absorb people who can no longer make a living as small-scale farmers, but would need to create a niche for new jobs, potentially in service sector industries. For international migration, resettlement agreements between countries and within regions and states could be envisaged (e.g. 2001 agreement between New Zealand and Tuvalu to resettle islanders – see Shen and Binns, 2010). However, such agreements are unlikely to be viable for the expected large-scale population movements likely under this scenario.

### *Scenario 3: "Global financial crash"*

#### *A major new financial crisis triggers the collapse of the global trading system and a shift to protectionism*

This scenario would affect the entire world, although the origin of the global financial crisis is assumed to be in the emerging economies, meaning especially big challenges for them.

A housing bubble in China and some other emerging countries bursts. Commodity prices continue to fall rapidly, creating significant challenges for currency stability in countries reliant on commodity exports, such as the Russian Federation, Brazil, many African countries, and Australia and Canada. Alternatively high levels of corporate debt in the developing world become unsustainable and lead to a large financial crisis and capital outflows from developing countries which create problems for their balance of payments and debt repayments.

Even though the crisis starts in the developing world it has strong effects on financial markets in developed countries because of their great exposure in these countries and because of their fragile and overleveraged financial markets (Wolf, 2014).

The financial disruptions trigger a major global economic crisis, affecting trade, investment and consumption around the globe. Protectionist pressure re-emerges, as during the 2008 crisis. This time, however, governments face more difficulty in bailing out financial institutions and investors because of their still weak fiscal positions. They are therefore unable to protect domestic jobs and sectors.

Regional blocs and new geopolitical alliances emerge and the global trading system becomes more fragmented. The Arab world unites to help countries in particular difficulty, such as Egypt, with high rates of poverty and no oil resources. Resource-rich countries (notably the United Arab Emirates) are particularly badly hit by the global economic depression and the break-up of the global trade regime.

The European Union experiences increasing tensions, with disagreements among countries on the best way to react to the financial crisis, and panic that affects several banking systems. The European Central Bank does not have sufficient reserves to counteract the problems in the EU financial sector. Some countries leave the euro, creating a division within the European system and exacerbating the financial crisis.

Protectionism does not help to avoid social disruption and governments fail to address increasing inequality. Expectations of the emerging middle classes remain unmet. In developed and developing countries alike, many people's livelihoods come under pressure. Opposition to government and social riots increase, along with poverty rates. A large share of the billion people living just above the USD 1.25 a day poverty line falls back in poverty, and many vulnerable low-income households in developed countries are also badly affected. Developed countries find it difficult to deal with the new fiscal costs of bailing out their financial sectors as well as providing social protection to the most vulnerable citizens.

### *Key policy implications*

How realistic is this scenario? Existing signs of financial sector imbalances in the emerging world and the continued fragility of the developed country financial system make this a very plausible scenario – one which could become a reality much earlier than 2030.

Policy implications involve both prevention and adaptation. While a detailed discussion of the necessary preventive financial measures is beyond the scope of this book, key actions include:

- *Strengthening global and regional framework conditions* and avoiding unhealthy financial activities.
- *Increasing co-ordination among the global financial institutions* so that they can respond to a crisis decisively. Greater mobility of financial resources among the central banks, the IMF, the World Bank and regional development banks would be an important outcome.
- *Agreements across countries* to focus on international reserve currencies, exchange rate management, and printing of money.
- *Ensuring a proper place for emerging countries* within the global financial system, which will almost certainly include the BRIICS by 2030.

While some preventive measures have been put in place since the last financial crisis, more are needed and they need to be adopted globally. The urgency with which governments must address these issues cannot be underestimated. The sustainability of government operations depends on citizens' trust in government. Another global financial crisis which affects people's livelihoods and increases inequality would damage trust in government even more fundamentally.

However, as the major global financial reform issues are unlikely to be addressed in time, it is important to focus on those policies that help cushion individuals and communities from major financial and economic crises, such as:

- *Banking structures that disconnect local banks from the global financial system.*
- *The development of local currencies* that also disconnect local economies from the global economy. This would be both an important adaptive and preventive measure (see Chapter 5).

- *The organisation of sound economic barter systems.* Barter involves the direct exchange of goods or services for other goods or services without the use of money. It is usually bilateral, but may be multilateral (i.e., mediated through barter organisations). Such systems usually exist in parallel to monetary systems in most developed countries, though to a very limited extent. Barter usually replaces money as the method of exchange in times of monetary crisis, such as when the currency may be either unstable (e.g. hyperinflation or a deflationary spiral) or simply unavailable for conducting commerce.
- *The establishment of self-financing community-based groups* (peer-to-peer lending groups) to make participants more resilient to major disruptions in the interconnected global financial system.
- *Improving technology to improve the assessment of financial risks.* Technological advancements give small investors many more choices, and data transparency allows pension funds to assess risk and the underlying soundness of countries and companies in which they might invest.

## *Scenario 4: "Regenerative economies"*

### *Technological innovations create enough new jobs for most people and economic activity becomes sustainable based on renewable energy*

This utopian scenario could apply to all regions of the world. However, the speed of change is faster in advanced and emerging countries than in low-income countries. The main attributes of this scenario are fast technological advancement creating many new jobs and solutions for today's biggest challenges to humanity, particularly the greening of economic activity.

Innovative technology creates new products and services at a rapid pace. Many new fields flourish, including renewable energy, cyber-security, environmental resilient engineering, robot-enhanced service jobs, and jobs requiring high skills in nanotechnology and biotechnology. One of the most lucrative and innovative new technological applications may be 3D food printing from chemicals that allows nourishment to be delivered on demand anywhere. Productivity in the world's knowledge economies continues to increase at a fast pace.

As the real economy becomes a virtual economy, many sectors undergo a transformation. Technological innovation in agriculture, for example, results in a rural-to-urban migration in many developing countries. To avoid this migration resulting in overcrowded city slums, developing countries follow China's lead in creating planned, medium-sized cities with energy-efficient infrastructure, allowing for sustainable urbanisation.

The greening of economic activity happens in many ways and in many forms. A circular economy develops through the systematic recycling of natural resources used in production and consumption processes. Green cities with retrofitted energy-efficient buildings, low-energy transport modes (such as bus rapid transit), etc. allow significant energy savings. Solar energy becomes a major power source, thanks to advances in fuel-cell technology and capacitor storage. Water use is much better managed, thanks to IT-based monitoring techniques. Agriculture is transformed through genetic modification, new nutrients matched to local soil conditions, hydroponic cultures, satellite and drone monitoring, etc. Local small-scale farming flourishes, reducing long-distance transport of goods and carbon emissions.

Improved ICTs mean that national borders and distances become less relevant. Markets become more international than ever before. State measures to avoid international competition become obsolete because they cannot be introduced fast enough to cope with the pace of technological change. Geographical and cultural differences begin to only be expressed in arts and crafts. By 2030, the world has one single integrated economy.

There will be many more high-tech jobs for highly skilled people than there are skilled people to fill them. Countries reshape their education systems so that people can perform in this fast developing knowledge economy. Training is available freely (online) or at low costs for all age groups under this scenario.

The challenge is not the existence of jobs, but the availability of educated people to fill them. The competition for skilled workers intensifies. Human capital becomes a critical asset. Rapidly developing countries need human capital, which many cannot build up fast enough internally through conventional brick and mortar universities. They have to rely more on information technology enhanced learning such as massive open online courses, cyber learning, and virtual universities where the challenge will be to assure quality. The competition for talent becomes a race for researchers and students – the ability to attract international talent becomes a key asset.

Most young people do not invest in one field in which they will work the rest of their lives; instead they move from specialisation to specialisation, learning narrowly focused skill sets for application in larger, computer-designed contexts. The old paradigm of education followed by a career is replaced by a series of individualised lifelong certification training programmes.

With such an intense focus on high-tech skills training, educational inequality becomes more important than income inequality. Avoiding greater educational inequality is a challenge, as not all people are suited to become workers in a purely knowledge economy. Unskilled workers without up-to-date technological training may find fewer opportunities. And older workers may lose their jobs when they do not keep up to date with new technology. On the other hand, older workers can choose to be retrained because educational programmes are offered at low cost and regardless of age.

For certain people, social security systems are still needed. But such systems are more affordable for nation states under this scenario. The core reason is that more people choose to work rather than to live on benefits as job opportunities are exciting and financially more attractive. Also, people choose to work until they are older because pensions are less attractive than working longer.

### *Key policy implications*

How realistic is this scenario? The signs are already there in parts of Asia (China and Korea), Europe (particularly in Northern European countries) and North America (several US states), in the form of very proactive technology and green growth strategies. The increasing pace at which the world is becoming integrated would, thanks to improved ICTs, make this scenario relevant for all countries in the world. However, it is very uncertain whether technology will really create enough new jobs.

The policies to support a shift in this direction are not about securing livelihoods, but about improving livelihoods around the globe sustainably. While they can be accelerated by global or national state initiatives, the importance of technology in this scenario means that many of the actions can also be taken by private actors, foundations and public-private partnerships:

- *Reshaping education systems around the globe to build flexible technological skills.* Beyond the basic education, the most crucial assets will be cognitive, flexible skills with a very strong focus on the latest technologies. People of all ages will need to have the opportunity and incentives for continuous retraining.
- *Matching skills to the global labour market.* A new global system is required which can match the skills needed by the labour market with those available anywhere in the world. Big data analytics can help create such a system, which could be developed by private or public initiatives.
- *Ensuring the right conditions to attract and retain talent.* Countries that have traditionally benefitted from the immigration of highly skilled workers, mainly OECD countries, will likely need more proactive policies to attract and retain them because of intense competition for talent driven by rising demand and opportunities in emerging economies. Governments, but also companies, will be challenged by the fact that it is no longer enough to attract or retain talent by providing good salaries. Other quality of life factors will become more relevant, such as quality of social institutions and schools, networks, infrastructure, air quality and congestion; for instance, many multinationals are finding it harder to get staff to work in Beijing because of the city's pollution levels (Douglass and Edelstein, 2009). Also, foreign talent may increasingly be encouraged to work for firms through tax incentives, opportunities to develop skills and careers within or outside companies or even an arrival bonus (Saez, 2014; Florida, 2006; Fishman, 1998). Governments or companies themselves can initiate such incentives.
- *Ensuring equality:* In the very fast changing technology world of this scenario, education becomes the main driver of inequalities and a significant number of people risk being left behind, if they do not adapt quickly and deeply enough. It is therefore key to provide efficient social security systems offering systematic guarantee support to all who are temporarily unemployed, in the form of financial aid coupled with intense training facilities. This applies in particularly to the young people entering the labour markets. In developing countries with emerging youth bulges, the transitions into a knowledge economy are even more challenging, particularly as ICT infrastructure development may not be fast enough to make sure that all people have access to online platforms, allowing them to become knowledge workers. In those countries, a priority may therefore be to establish equal opportunities in access to modern educational systems and tools.

### *Scenario 5: "Creative societies"*

#### *Diverse local experiments and initiatives focus on individual resilience and social well-being.*

This is a world in which technology-induced joblessness increases in developed and developing economies alike. Big projects – including big environmental projects – are beyond the reach of most governments, leaving individual communities to make a virtue of necessity by becoming more resilient. Societies evolve towards new ways of living and working, in which individuals and communities are the key actors of change.

Meanwhile, the IT revolution changes the way the economy functions, via phenomena such as 3D printing technology, the "Internet of things" and massive online open courses (MOOCs). This transforms exchanges between people, transport, logistics, consumption of energy, and reduces the cost of production, ushering in a new form of economy based on collaborative approaches – and undermining traditional capitalism (Rifkin 2014).

In this entrepreneurial economy, individuals are much more autonomous and independent of institutions and organisations. Young people do not follow a career-ladder job path, focusing instead on meaningful work and work-life balance, with income supplements in rich countries to assure at least minimal levels of livelihoods for all. These supplements are made possible because governments have stopped increasing transfer payments – funding for health, welfare, and pensions remains relatively static.

In this scenario everyone is an entrepreneur because in the absence of secure full-time employment, it is individuals who must put together a portfolio of work made up of part-time jobs, shared work with colleagues, and other innovative approaches. Companies outsource work in discrete projects, so workers may sometimes be engaged in several projects at one time followed by a period during which they have no paid employment. This flexibility is not so easy for older workers, however, but they are helped to adjust through income support and online training, which is available to all. In addition, flexible retirement-age policies encourage older people to continue to engage in occasional projects. Community-based, multigenerational work projects become increasingly popular.

This portfolio lifestyle is made possible by three important factors:

1. technology, which allows work from anywhere at any time
2. the adoption of minimum incomes in most developed countries, paid for by higher taxes on capital, rather than labour
3. new social attitudes in which young people are not so much interested in the consumer culture, but contribute to what might be called "the experience economy."

In many ways, the world of creative societies is one of local experiments in well-being. And even at the national level, much more attention is paid to inclusive growth – growth plus well-being – rather than mere economic growth. In developed economies, city-corporate partnerships flourish and help finance green infrastructure. Most multinationals are active in communities – corporate reputation is tied closely to social responsibility.

Cities attempt circular economies and many other green initiatives, especially retrofitting of buildings and water conservation. A robust urban food movement develops with many urban community gardens. And public-private livelihood incubators flourish in most cities, providing job counselling, the matching of skills and opportunities, start-up financing, and individually tailored aid packages for young and old.

A great deal of technology-enabled creativity occurs in the service sector. In countries with ageing populations, new sensor technology and other devices enable young people to monitor older people in their own homes. A rising interest in high quality care takes place in communities, which have become centres of new social experiments and locally focused agriculture, crafts, and work centres. Barter economies flourish as cash-strapped workers trade skills and services on a one-to-one basis. In this "Uber" world,[5] people do odd jobs or offer "restaurants for a night" in their homes or take any number of other informal economy approaches to their livelihoods – all made easier through social media and proliferating mobile phone applications. People sell their services virtually – everyone is a "producer."

The patchwork nature of support – grants for specific projects rather than policy initiatives for all – means that inequality emerges at the community level as well as at the individual and national levels. Positive feedback loops lead to the rich getting richer. Successful communities are like magnets, attracting people to live there because of the high quality of life.

In a world in which travel and leisure activities are valued above possessions, and "work-life" balance tilts towards the "life" side of the scale, rising inequality does not seem so burdensome. A livelihood means having the capacities to meet your needs and the context to exercise that capacity. In creative societies, the growing numbers of young people who are less consumer-oriented see work as an opportunity to contribute to society, not as an onerous necessity.

### *Key policy implications*

How realistic is this scenario? At first glance, this scenario seems to be more plausible in richer countries, where most people have moved beyond basic subsistence. In low-income, developing countries people may not have the luxury to focus on anything other than immediate survival needs. However, this community-based, low-wage kind of living is already familiar to people in developing economies. To some extent, developed countries learn from developing and emerging economies, which, in many cases, have succeeded with experiments in social inclusiveness and adaptive, frugal innovation. Innovations can be "disruptive", such as those developed in India in the late 2000s, aiming at "getting more from less for more people" (Mashelkar, 2009): fuel-efficient small cars like the Tata Nano; or new drugs based on traditional medicine. These innovations respond directly to the needs of the poorest people (and are known as "disruptive" because they can render industries and occupations obsolete).

While creative societies would take different paths in the developed and developing worlds, there are some similarities, some of which are already present: the rise of social entrepreneurs and the "social economy"; the rise of innovative finance and money in forms of micro credit, social impact bonds (see Chapter 5), or local currencies; investments in the "bottom of the pyramid" in the developing world; the diffusion of "frugal innovations", etc. So while the scenario is already plausible, it is occurring on a small scale. A much wider scaling up would be necessary for it to have a significant impact.

Through their "frugal" ways of living, people in this scenario help to prevent major crises and tensions, as well as reduce their potential impacts. Key policy implications for achieving it include:

- *Transforming education*: In order to operate in a creative society, life skills in a broad sense are fundamental. Skills-for-life rather than jobs-for-life hold the key to the future of livelihoods. Individuals need a strong technical culture in order to get by; they also need an entrepreneurial spirit with a grounding in management, commerce and finance; they need good interpersonal skills, and to understand that happiness can be achieved through frugality and creation rather than increased income, etc.

- *Overhauling legal, administrative and institutional frameworks* to create the necessary flexibility across many domains. Labour markets should be fully open, with no barriers to entrepreneurship, changing jobs, etc. Pension schemes should allow the easy accumulation and transfer of rights. Minimal social security systems should be accessible to all. Relations between central and local governments need to shift fundamentally towards greater decentralisation. Government policies should shift from social services for individuals to intermittent support to communities on a project-by-project basis. The economic and social strengths of communities need to be carefully monitored by governments, who have to ensure that their project-based funding goes to city initiatives that are likely to succeed.
- *Installing proactive and imaginative innovation and technology policies.* A stimulating culture of experimentation needs to be fostered. Research should focus on making the best use of technology for frugal and inclusive innovations, and ultra low-cost products for poor people. As governments will have limited funds and will not be able to engage in large-scale programmes, efficient schemes will be needed that mobilise the creativity and resources of the private sector, along with public and university research teams. This would not only be needed nationally, but also at the global level.
- *Compensating disadvantaged communities will be necessary.* Some communities will lack the social capital necessary to come together to solve problems and combat joblessness. Some budget transfers will probably be necessary from more resilient communities to those less well endowed in social and other capital, or to those particularly challenged by climate, economic or other trends. Which communities succeed and which fail is not necessarily a function of development – some poorer communities have more highly developed social capital than many of the old, industrialised communities.
- *Rising inequality will have to be tackled.* A minimum basic income is likely to be needed to allow everyone to survive even if they lack the creative skills required, to avoid deep inequalities.
- *Developing new ways of measuring progress.* In these creative and diverse societies, it is difficult to benchmark progress using average GDP, especially as multidimensional well-being is the goal. Boundaries between education, work, and retirement are blurred. Social needs vary, and labour market priorities and structures vary across regions, driving new patterns of technology adoption and new models of governance.

## The scenarios translate into a wealth of policy options for secure livelihoods

This chapter set out to demonstrate that other approaches to analysing forward-looking policies are available to policy makers and other stakeholders. Pushing some hypotheses or stories to their extreme, even dramatic, limits helps open up the policy space to discuss new ideas, and more and different possibilities.

The scenarios described in this chapter imply that the future outlook for livelihoods can either be dire, or vibrant. Which one triumphs will largely depend on how prepared we are to face up to emerging trends and tackle them now through bold initiatives and innovative approaches. The scenarios reveal a range of opportunities: from rethinking how education and skills-building are delivered; to how more effective taxation policies and income redistribution approaches can combat inequality and invest in social inclusion; to how a more flexible and adaptive labour approach to technical change, to people's mobility and to other forces can reflect the dynamism of societies; and to how resilience and adaptability can be built from the ground up – from individuals up to entire societies.

Two key outcomes are common to all these policy options: the need to build inclusiveness and resilience. The next and final chapter focuses in on some priority actions at a range of levels for building inclusiveness and resilience into future livelihoods.

## Notes

1. The scenarios do not include the possibilities of pandemics, terrorism and global conflicts. However, these risks are as relevant and real as others, as illustrated by the recent Ebola crisis in Africa; the recurrent terrorist attacks around the globe and recently in France; and the risk of a global geopolitical conflict emerging from the Ukraine crisis. They should be considered in future scenario work.
2. The scenario design emerged from the Bellagio meeting (see Box 1.1 in Chapter 1), as well as an OECD-wide workshop and discussions among this report's team of authors.
3. A possibility outlined by Frey and Osborne (2013).
4. Even now in several developed countries, such as Switzerland and France, public opinion has moved towards more restrictive migration policies (including for higher skilled workers), as people feel at risk of losing their jobs.
5. Uber is an app-based transportation network and taxi company headquartered in San Francisco, California, which operates in cities in many countries. The company uses a smartphone application to receive ride requests, and then sends these trip requests to their drivers. Customers use the app to request rides and track their reserved vehicle's location. Today the service is available in 53 countries and more than 200 cities worldwide. Since Uber's launch several other companies have emulated its business model, in a trend that has come to be referred to as "Uberification" (Wikipedia, 2015).

# *References*


Ambec, S., A. Dinar, and D. McKinney (2013), "Water sharing agreements sustainable to reduced flows", *Journal of Environmental Economics and Management*, Vol. 66, Issue 3, November 2013, Elsevier, Amsterdam, pp. 639–655, www.sciencedirect.com/science/article/pii/S0095069613000429.

Braconier, H., G. Nicoletti and B. Westmore (2014), *Policy Challenges for the Next 50 Years*, OECD Economic Policy Papers, No. 9, OECD Publishing, Paris, http://dx.doi.org/10.1787/5jz18gs5fckf-en.

Brynjolfsson, E. and A. McAfee (2014), *The Second Machine Age: Work, Progress, and Prosperity in a Time of Brilliant Technologies*, W. W. Norton & Company, New York, www.secondmachineage.com.

Douglass, J.A. and R. Edelstein (2009), *The Global Competition for Talent: The Rapidly Changing Market for International Students and the Need for a Strategic Approach in the US*, Berkeley Center for Studies in Higher Education, Berkeley, CA, www.cshe.berkeley.edu/publications/global-competition-talentthe-rapidly-changing-market-internationalstudents-and-need.

Fishman, C. (1998), "The war for talent", Fast Company magazine website, August 1998, www.fastcompany.com/34512/war-talent.

Florida, R. (2006), "The flight of the creative class: The new global competition for talent", *Liberal Education*, Summer 2006, Vol. 92, No. 3, Association of American Universities and Colleges, Washington DC, www.aacu.org/publications-research/periodicals/flight-creative-class-new-global-competition-talent.

Frey, C.B. and M.A. Osborne (2013), *The Future of Employment: How Susceptible are Jobs to Computerisation?* Oxford Martin Programme on the Impacts of Future Technology, Oxford, www.oxfordmartin.ox.ac.uk/downloads/academic/The_Future_of_Employment.pdf.

Kahane, A. (2012), *Transformative Scenario Planning: Working Together to Change the Future*, Berrett-Koehler Publishers, California, www.bkconnection.com/books/title/transformative-scenario-planning.

Mashelkar, R.A. (November 2009), "Breakthrough designs for ultra-low-cost products", video, TED Talks, www.ted.com/talks/r_a_mashelkar_breakthrough_designs_for_ultra_low_cost_products.

Rifkin, J. (2014), *The Zero Marginal Cost Society*, Macmillan, London.

Saez, E. (2014), "Taxes and international mobility of talent", *NBER Reporter,* 2014, No. 2, National Bureau of Economic Research, Cambridge MA, www.nber.org/reporter/2014number2/saez.html.

Shen, S. and T. Binns (2010), "Pathways, motivations and challenges: Contemporary Tuvaluan migration to New Zealand", *GeoJournal 77*, Springer Netherlands, Dordrecht, pp. 63-82.

Wikipedia (2015), "Uber (company)", Wikipedia website, http://en.wikipedia.org/wiki/Uber_%28company%29 (accessed 26 January 2015).

Wolf, M. (2014), *The Shifts and the Shocks: What We've Learned – and Have Still to Learn – from the Financial Crisis,* Penguin Press, New York.

World Bank (2015), *A Measured Approach to Ending Poverty and Boosting Shared Prosperity: Concepts, Data, and the Twin Goals,* policy research report, World Bank, Washington DC, https://openknowledge.worldbank.org/bitstream/handle/10986/20384/9781464803611.pdf.

World Bank (2012), *Renewable Energy Desalination: An Emerging Solution to Close the Water Gap in the Middle East and North Africa*, World Bank, Washington DC, http://water.worldbank.org/sites/water.worldbank.org/files/publication/water-wpp-Sun-Powered-Desal-Gateway-Meeting-MENAs-Water-Needs_2.pdf.

# Annex 4.A1.
# OECD's forecasts to 2060 suggest a mediocre outlook for economic growth

Important elements of OECD's recent long-term projections concern the shift of the world economic balance, productivity growth, trade and integration, climate change and environmental degradation, inequalities, education, ageing societies, migration and fiscal pressures. Key conclusions for these areas are summarised below:

A major **shift of economic balance** occurs towards emerging economies in general, and Asia in particular, from 37% of global GDP in 2012 to 61% in 2060. Economic growth continues to lift masses of people out of poverty, integrating them into the world economy. However, the growth outlook for the global economy is mediocre compared to the past, with large uncertainties surrounding productivity. While growth is more sustained in emerging economies than in the OECD, it is slowing down due as countries catch up with each other.

**Productivity growth slows in countries that were previously growing rapidly,** as productivity and GDP per capita converge with those of developed countries. Improvements in efficiency and innovation will become a major factor of growth in GDP per capita in all types of economies, whatever their development level. Productivity improvements reflect innovation, propelled by rising investments in knowledge-based capital assets such as R&D, employee skills, organisational know-how, databases, design, brands and various forms of intellectual property.

**Global integration continues** as transport costs keep falling and trade barriers are lowered in line with existing trade agreements. The pace of integration slows, however, due to possible new trade barriers, transaction costs and regulatory obstacles. While world exports in relation to GDP tripled between 1950 and 1998, increases are now expected to be around 60% between 2010 and 2060, although regional variations are large.

**Trade, like the economy, becomes concentrated in Asia**. OECD countries' share of world trade is estimated to fall from 50% in 2012 to 25% in 2060. Specialisation patterns continue to evolve and global value added chains develop further. China and other Asian countries continue to specialise in electronics and increasingly in services, while manufacturing shrinks in the OECD. Increased trade integration accelerates the pace of international technology diffusion, further improving efficiency and innovation. This is particularly important for countries that are technologically underdeveloped. Furthermore, increased cross-country interdependence will help spread the impacts of shocks, but will also make the global economy more vulnerable to imbalances.

**The impact of climate change is expected to lower world GDP** between 0.7% and 2.3% by 2060. Impacts will vary, but will be greatest in South and Southeast Asia, at 5% of GDP. Some other regions may actually benefit from higher agricultural productivity, improved terms of trade and in some cases stronger net demand for tourism. Falling agricultural productivity, and capital and land losses from sea level rise, are the main reasons for GDP losses.

**Inequalities** continue to worsen, reaching current US levels across the OECD. Rising capital incomes drive rising disparities in household income, reflecting the replacement of medium-skilled jobs by technology and increase polarisation. Global current account imbalances start to build up again and fiscal and structural reforms need to be pursued.

**Average levels of educational attainment improve**, but progress slows as countries catch up with the leaders. With growing inequality between low and high-income earners, incentives for tertiary education are increased. However, funding constraints, rising costs and insufficient abilities of the stock of potential entrants into tertiary education is holding back the number of people with tertiary education.

**Ageing depresses growth** in advanced and large emerging countries including China, Brazil, and Russia. The share of population has already peaked in the OECD, will reach a turning point in 2025 in China, and is expected to rise until 2060 in India.

As emerging economies catch up with OECD countries, **the economic incentives for immigration to the OECD are reduced. Net emigration of economic migrants from OECD countries is expected between 2010 and 2060.** Slower inflows of high-skilled immigration, due to rapid wage growth in traditional "source" countries, will combine with outflows of low-skilled migrants to have a significant impact on the labour force and GDP across the OECD. For example, the expected decline in migrants could lower potential labour by as much as 20% in the euro area and 15% in the US by 2060.

**Fiscal pressures build up, driven by high debt levels,** unsustainable pension systems, and rising costs of health and education. Fiscal gaps are more than 10% of GDP for the majority of OECD countries. Emerging countries like China and Brazil also face similar fiscal pressures, which combine with demographic pressures. In the BRIICS, total health and long-term care expenditures are expected to double to 5% by 2060. Fiscal pressures will widen account imbalances. It is, however, expected that governments will be able to reduce government debts to 60% of GDP by 2030.

*Source:* Braconier, H., G. Nicoletti and B. Westmore (2014), *Policy Challenges for the Next 50 Years*, OECD Economic Policy Papers, No. 9, OECD Publishing, Paris, http://dx.doi.org/10.1787/5jz18gs5fckf-en.

# Chapter 5
# Bold action for secure livelihoods

*This final chapter outlines how many economic, social, environmental or technology-driven crises can be avoided – or their effects on livelihoods mitigated – through innovative actions which build more secure livelihoods. Building resilience and inclusion involves two main strands: prevention and adaptation. Global or multinational action will be needed for many of the preventive policies required to avert crises linked to the financial system, to climate change, to pandemics and many other challenges. On the other hand, policies at the national or local level are more appropriate for enhancing individuals' adaptation capabilities. The chapter outlines a range of possible initiatives, and ends with a call for action for all relevant players – international, national, local – to move forward and prepare to ensure a better future for livelihoods.*

## Key messages

- Building secure livelihoods involves two main strands: prevention and adaptation.
- **Global** or multinational preventive action will be needed to avert crises linked to the financial system, to climate change, to pandemics and many other challenges. This includes:
  - reaching an urgent global agreement on climate change
  - stabilising the global financial system
  - entering into appropriate multilateral agreements to prevent tax evasion by multinational enterprises and improving progressiveness of tax system
  - managing international migration as an opportunity for global well-being
  - strengthening disaster and disease response capacity
  - creating the conditions for a livelihood-focused technology revolution.
- **National** policies can promote inclusiveness and enhance individuals' capacity to adapt, by:
  - making education accessible for all, with a myriad of pathways for skill acquisition (including basic livelihood skills) and the opportunity for lifelong learning in open-access virtual classrooms. Access to information technologies is of the utmost importance
  - supporting livelihood portfolios made up of part-time work, paid training, and catch-all social support systems
  - investing in children and young people as an opportunity to enhance human capital
  - using green growth to underpin resilient livelihoods
- While support at the national level is needed, it is increasingly up to **individuals and communities** to take action and experiment with options for making their livelihoods more resilient, such as:
  - organising new local economies – such as bartering, skills and services exchanges and sharing – based on social and solidarity principles rather than capitalism.
  - developing new ways of accessing micro-finance, from the use of ICT platforms (such as M-Pesa), to group lending, micro savings, micro finance, crowdfunding and local currencies.
  - building green and resilient cities to reduce emissions, and boost jobs and growth at the same time.
  - solving local problems through citizen action, in close partnership with government.

The scenario exercise in Chapter 4 alerts us to the urgent need for policy options that promote more inclusive and resilient livelihoods across the world. All three of the crisis scenarios raise the spectre of greater inequalities – in income, education and other public services – and social disruption in both developed and developing countries. Innovative actions may avoid or mitigate the negative effects of economic, social, environmental or technology-driven crises, and build more secure livelihoods. Moreover, the two opportunity-based scenarios give hope for improved livelihoods through actions involving new forms of living and working. Although these partial scenarios are simply illustrative of a range of possibilities, they serve to identify policy options that appear to be relevant for the future of livelihoods under many circumstances.

This final chapter gives a taste of what some of these innovative actions might look like, drawing on insights from the scenario exercise and from ideas that emerged during the meeting in Bellagio (see Chapter 1). The ideas suggested here would need to be fleshed out in more detail, and additional policies would need to be considered for other scenarios.

Building resilience and inclusion involves two main strands: prevention and adaptation. Resilience can be enhanced if crises are prevented in the first place. And by detecting negative trends and taking appropriate adaptation measures before crisis point is reached, the effects can be much less serious. Global or multinational action will be needed for many of the preventive policies required to avert crises linked to the financial system, to climate change, to pandemics and many other challenges. On the other hand, policies at the national or local level are more appropriate for promoting inclusiveness and enhancing individuals' adaptation capabilities.

The following three sections discuss examples of possible actions at the global, national and local level respectively. Independent of the targeted level, policies or programmes may be introduced by public authorities, private entities and non-government organisations such as foundations, and individuals or community groups. The sections also contain some "visionary ideas" in boxes. These ideas emerged during the Bellagio workshop on securing future livelihoods (see Box 5.1); they are deliberately provocative, but illustrate the type of bold thinking needed to generate fresh perspectives.

**Box 5.1. Secure Livelihoods: Visions of a better future**

As indicated in Chapter 1, Box 1.1, this work results from a joint initiative of The Rockefeller Foundation, the Economist Intelligence Unit (EIU) and the OECD Development Centre. A key step was a meeting organised in Bellagio in August 2015, hosted by The Rockefeller Foundation and moderated by the EIU. The meeting gathered 27 high level experts from government, academic and business sectors. In particular, brainstorming sessions were organised to propose bold and concrete initiatives that could help to secure livelihoods in the long term. Some of those ideas are reported in the boxes below, signalled by the label "Visionaries at work". For more information, see the summary of the discussions: *Secure Livelihoods, Visions of a Better Future* (The Rockefeller Foundation, 2014).

## Global problems require global solutions

Sustained global efforts are needed to mitigate negative trends or to reduce the risks of emerging crises which threaten to undermine livelihoods. Although a detailed discussion of the global agreements needed on issues related to finance, the climate and so on is beyond the scope of this book, it is worth pointing to some entry points in which the global community, and notably some of its pivotal actors, can have a significant impact.

### *Climate change requires urgent global agreement*

Chapter 3 has outlined the far-reaching impacts of climate change, while Scenario 2 in Chapter 4 tells how livelihoods could be seriously affected by climate change-induced drought.

Urgent global agreement is the main way forward for limiting the human actions that are contributing to global warming. The Conference of the Parties (COP 21) to the 1992 United Nations Framework Convention on Climate Change (UNFCCC) to be held in Paris in November 2015 will be a key opportunity for bold global action. Recent signs are encouraging, in the form of the US-China deal to reduce $C0_2$ emissions. This agreement aims to see China's emissions peak around 2030, and the US to reduce emissions to between 26 and 28% by 2025 compared to 2005 levels.

Greater progress is also needed to establish a fund for helping developing countries in their efforts towards climate mitigation and adaptation. While it is planned to amount to USD 100 billion per year, to date pledges only total USD 10 billion.

### *The global financial system needs to be stabilised*

The "global financial crash" scenario in Chapter 4 paints a dire picture of the impact of another financial crisis. Often such crises affect poor people more than richer people. Further progress is needed to prevent financial speculation with uneven potential gains and losses on an investment (Wolf, 2014). The OECD has recently proposed new measures to be agreed at the international level to prevent the formation and propagation of financial risks of mismanaged national systems (Box 5.2; and see OECD, 2012a).

**Box 5.2. How has the OECD responded to the 2008 financial crisis?**

In response to the unforeseen character and long-term consequences of the 2008 financial crisis, the OECD has undertaken an organisation-wide reflection on the roots of and lessons from the global crisis, and an exercise to review and update the OECD's analytical framework. Of particular note was the launch of its initiative "New Approaches to Economic Challenges" in 2012.

This analytical effort has led to a number of measures for managing systemic financial risks being proposed for discussion, including: (1) to adopt agent-based models that could make comprehensible the complex behavioural dynamics, information asymmetry and externalities affecting the financial system (OECD, 2012a);[1] (2) to strengthen the capital base of banks and make their business models safer by reducing leverage and making risk-weighting of assets less complex and less open to regulatory arbitrage; (3) to broaden the range of non-bank financing instruments available to small and medium enterprises and entrepreneurs; (4) to allocate long-term funds from institutional investors to illiquid assets such as infrastructure; and (5) to reform the managers' remuneration structure as to foster ethical and socially optimal risk strategies (OECD, 2015).

Other policies proposed include some of the concrete ideas mentioned in Chapter 4 (Scenario 3), in particular the need to separate high-risk activities from conventional banking, to give local communities resilient financing solutions and to improve financial literary and inclusion.

1. An agent-based model (ABM) is one of a class of computational models for simulating the actions and interactions of autonomous agents (both individual or collective entities such as organisations or groups) with a view to assessing their effects on the system as a whole.

## *Shared prosperity can be achieved through tax reforms*

Growing inequality is a worrying emerging trend (Chapter 3). Several of the scenarios in Chapter 4 highlight how inequality may drive social unrest and large economic migrations. How can bold rethinking about the way our global economy functions avoid such risks for livelihoods and increase equality? Three possible actions in the area of taxes include:

1. Actively participate in international negotiations on co-ordinated action to combat tax base erosion and profit shifting by multinational enterprises, including by taking action to prevent double non-taxation, and change domestic laws as necessary (Box 5.3).
2. Enter into appropriate multilateral agreements to prevent tax evasion by multinational enterprises, including by providing more transparency of financial account information through the implementation of Automatic Exchange of Information (Box 5.3).
3. Reform the tax system to make it more progressive and equitable.

**Box 5.3. Coordinated international efforts on tax matters**

Multinational enterprises may avoid taxation by artificially shifting profits to low or no-tax locations where there is little or no economic activity, resulting in little or no overall corporate tax being paid (OECD, 2013a). Known as base erosion and profit shifting (BEPS), this practice is of major significance for the developing countries involved, due to their heavy reliance on corporate income tax – largely from multinational enterprises. The OECD/G20 BEPS Project is developing recommendations on 15 specific action items to ensure that this challenge can be addressed in a coordinated way.

In response to a request by the G20, the OECD developed a Standard for the Automatic Exchange of Financial Information for Tax Matters in 2014 for the different types of accounts and taxpayers covered as well as common due diligence procedures to be followed by financial institutions.

For more details see: www.oecd.org/ctp/beps.htm and http://www.oecd.org/ctp/exchange-of-tax-information/automatic-exchange-of-financial-account-information.htm

## *An inclusive approach to international trade is needed*

Under the right conditions, an open trading system can be fundamental for sustained economic growth and the future of livelihoods (Feenstra, 2003). The global trading system would be particularly challenged by a new global financial crisis (see Scenario 3 in Chapter 4). A slowdown in world trade is already noticeable, with increasing signs of protectionist measures (Evenett, 2014). On the other hand, the good news is that after problems in concluding the Doha negotiations, the World Trade Organisation (WTO) has made progress towards an agreement on trade facilitation, which could reduce trading costs by 14% for developing countries and 10% for developed countries (OECD, 2014). Going forward, the liberalisation of services trade – which represents up to 50% of global trade – should receive more attention in the WTO negotiations.

However, an inclusive approach to trade is necessary. Free global trade could have negative consequences for a number of industries and for the livelihoods of people working in these industries – in both developed and developing economies. This may create pockets of poverty, leading to social resentment and unrest. Possible solutions could include implementing new trade regimes and agreements in developing countries gradually, so as to allow time for new industries and services to develop.

### *Better global and regional co-ordination of policies on international migration is needed*

International migration is increasingly recognised as a central pillar of economic and social development. While it can benefit migrants' livelihoods, it also raises both opportunities and challenges for their countries of origin and destination. Looking ahead, major global trends are likely to shift global migration patterns (see Chapters 3 and Chapter 4). Some of these changing trends may occur rapidly and will force public authorities to adjust policies and governance structures rapidly. In the absence of adequate, globally- or regionally -co-ordinated policies, migration can pose challenges to livelihoods in both sending and receiving countries.

To prepare policies which respond to international migration, an informed discussion of possible trends and their impacts in the future is essential. The importance of migration for livelihoods is recognised internationally, particularly through the Global Forum on Migration and Development (GFMD), the Global Knowledge Partnership on Migration and Development (KNOMAD) as well as the Global Migration Group (GMG). These fora engage with governments, organisations and experts around the globe to address the migration and development interconnections in practical and action-oriented ways and to enhance dialogue towards the inclusion of migration-related issues on the post-2015 development agenda. The 2016 edition of the OECD Development Centre's *Perspectives on Global Development* report will explore what the future of international migration could look like, how it affects livelihoods and what policies are needed to secure them.

### *Disaster response capacity needs to be strengthened*

The impacts of natural disasters on livelihoods can be considerable. Recent dramatic events – the 2004 earthquake in the Indian Ocean, Hurricane Katrina, the earthquake in Haiti in 2010, and the earthquake and tsunami in Japan – all caused appalling losses to life, livelihoods and infrastructure. While the UN and some national governments have stepped up their early warning systems and rapid deployment and intervention systems, these need to be scaled up. As populations increase there are likely to be more people affected by natural disasters, and climate change is likely to increase the frequency and severity of many events. More needs to be done to strengthen disaster response capacity through more funding and capacity building at both international and local levels. The world should also be better prepared for unexpected major disasters, such as sudden, large-scale solar radiation or a complete breakdown in electricity and Internet networks. The global or regional impacts should not be underestimated (OECD, 2011a). A global information campaign is urgently needed to inform people of such risks and measures must be taken to organise back-up energy and communication facilities.

### *Response to global pandemics could be improved*

Disease has fundamental implications for livelihoods. As revealed by the Ebola crisis, there is a need to strengthen international institutions to deal with pandemics. There is also a need for better detection and for quicker vaccine development, production and deployment. The response to Ebola has been very slow – we still lack a tested vaccine and the production and systems for inoculating the millions of people at risk. There are also endemic illnesses, such as malaria and dengue fever, for which we have not yet found a satisfactory response and which continue to kill millions of people every year. However, promising initiatives such as GAVI, the global vaccine alliance, attest to the possibility of engaging in global public partnerships to tackle issues like immunisation. GAVI brings together public and private sectors with the shared goal of creating equal access to new and underused vaccines for children living in the world's poorest countries.[1]

### *Stronger water sharing agreements could avert conflict*

In a future involving more frequent and severe droughts in the developing world, stronger agreements on water sharing (e.g. of river water) will be necessary to avert conflicts over water. For example, the Middle East is already arid, and its river basins are shared by many countries that are already in conflict. In the absence of sturdy mechanisms for sharing water, worsening drought will only exacerbate these conflicts. In Asia, where China alone shares more than 40 watercourses with 16 countries, the water treaty regime in place is rather limited (Chen et al., 2013; Wouters, 2014). Two global instruments – the 1997 UN Watercourses Convention 1 (UNWC) and the 1992 UNECE Transboundary Waters Convention (UNECE TWC) – could be borrowed to improve the international water management regimes in Asia and in the Middle East.

### *Global action is needed on cyber security*

Cyber-attacks on individuals, enterprises, banks, infrastructure and governments increase daily (see Chapter 3; and Norton, 2011). Attacks are often followed by retaliation, drawing the world into a dangerous vicious circle. As Internet networks are increasingly globalised, appropriate solutions are needed at the global level. These might include an international cyber police force, established under international bodies and mandated by governments, but operating independently and within commonly agreed ethical rules on privacy of data, conditions of investigations, among other things.

### *Technology development could focus on livelihoods*

As we have seen from earlier chapters, technology could be a potential game changer for global livelihoods, especially if focused on global "public goods" such as climate, clean energy, environment, health and the needs of people at the margin of subsistence. Yet the global research and development (R&D) system lacks institutions and mechanisms to fund such socially oriented R&D. While global R&D spending was expected to be USD 1.6 trillion in 2014 (Grueber et al., 2014) or roughly 2.1% of global GDP, more than 70% was carried out by the private sector and mostly focused on market opportunities.

There are some government initiatives for research to tackle global public goods such as clean energy and global health. Many governments, particularly in developing countries, have set up special initiatives to encourage inclusive innovation aimed at vulnerable populations. Some private companies, particularly multinationals, are also discovering that there is money to be made by developing goods and services aimed at low-income populations because of the large numbers of potential consumers involved (Prahalad, 2006). In addition, some large foundations are filling the funding gap to encourage private companies to invest in technologies for the poor. A good example is the Gates Foundation's Global Health Initiative (OECD and World Bank, 2014). However, there is no large-scale programme that focuses on correcting the market failures which discourage research to support global public goods. Brainstorming sessions at Bellagio came up with an interesting proposal, outlined in Box 5.4.

**Box 5.4. Visionaries at work: A "white" DARPA? An international innovation agency for global public goods and livelihood improvements**

The Defense Advanced Research Project Agency (DARPA) was created within the US Department of Defense in 1959 "for high-risk, high-payoff research, development and demonstration of new technologies and systems that serve the warfighter and the Nation's defense" (DARPA, n.d.). By co-ordinating specialists in different disciplines, it acts as an intermediary between researchers who create ideas and potential applications, which DARPA then hands over to specialised actors to implement. Some of DARPA's key achievements include what eventually became the Internet, the stealth bomber, the global positioning system (GPS), unmanned air vehicles, precision bombs, and many other technologies which have led to what some call a revolution in military affairs (Van Atta, 2008).

It should be possible to set up an international DARPA-type organisation to create a scientific basis for producing radical game-changing technologies for global social welfare rather than for military applications. International development institutions, foundations, and interested governments could help orchestrate the global funding for such an effort. The main problem would be setting up the appropriate governance and management structure for such an organisation. One of the reasons why DARPA has been successful is that it is very agile organisation that plays a co-ordinating and facilitating role. This requires extremely able managers, strong discipline and the willingness to take risks, all of which are hard to come by in governments or in internationally funded efforts that require a high level of transparency and clear accountability.

However, if appropriate governance arrangements can be developed, a "white DARPA" focusing on global public goods and the livelihoods of at-risk populations could have a very positive impact on the future of livelihoods. It could prioritise those technologies identified in this report as particularly important for livelihoods in some regions, such as desalination and water technologies, farming technology, and renewable energy in the context of a new "green revolution" (see Box 5.8). In this spirit, the so-called ARPA-Energy in the United States, modelled on DARPA, advances high-potential, high-impact energy technologies that are too early for private-sector investment (see www.arpa-e.energy.gov).

## Sustaining livelihoods calls for innovative national policy approaches

Discussions in Bellagio revealed that the control and responsibility for livelihoods is increasingly shifting from governments to communities and individuals themselves (The Rockefeller Foundation, 2014), suggesting a new role for government as backstop and enabler in forming creative and regenerative societies. The scenarios in Chapter 4 also suggest the need to re-think and re-tool the way in which governments and national actors work. Their role should be to fund and create jobs and build social protection programmes that meet livelihood needs, in a socially inclusive way. The potentially devastating impact of uncertain global forces and the shift to a knowledge-based economy demand that governments do more to meet their populations' basic needs. They can do this through guaranteed minimum incomes; safety nets for healthcare, pensions and unemployment; and by funding local job, training and education incubators.

### *Education is vital for both inclusiveness and resilience*

With the evolution towards knowledge-based economies, high quality and gender-neutral education becomes essential and needs constant improvement. Education helps people to break out of poverty and reduces inequality. It allows people to develop vital life skills and to become aware of and adapt to major social, environmental and other challenges. Therefore action on this key foundation of livelihoods can have enormous pay offs, if implemented well. The scenario exercise in Chapter 4 has demonstrated overwhelmingly the crucial importance of overhauling education and training systems to keep up with emerging trends.

However, access to quality education is an issue in many places around the world. In lower income countries, many children, and especially girls, do not even have access to primary education that could potentially be a powerful game changer in their lives, giving them a chance to escape poverty. In higher income countries where educational attainment is no longer an issue, quality is often the problem. Educational systems have not been able to ensure the competitiveness of graduates in the labour market or to keep pace with new social and employment trends. In many developed countries, educational reform is met with resistance from stakeholders such as educational institutions, regulating bodies, or labour unions.

Reforming education is a huge subject in its own right – space does not allow a full exploration here. There are many inspiring examples of reforms and good practices around the world on which to draw.[2] The OECD's skills strategy offers general principles for the best development and use of skills in economies (OECD, 2012b; UNESCO, 2013). Here we confine ourselves to outlining some ideas and principles for educational approaches which specifically target livelihood resilience and inclusiveness:

- Primary education should guarantee the best possible learning to everyone, to support the growth and development of each unique personality in all possible ways, as encouraged for example by Finland (UNESCO, 2007).
- Vocational education and apprenticeships are a good way to integrate young people into the business world and labour market. The principle is to provide dual education in which students who enter the technical education system after secondary school spend half of their time in an enterprise, with their curricula and programmes jointly defined by the relevant trade and business sectors. The German and Swiss models continue to be a source of inspiration for this approach (OECD, 2011b).
- Innovative practices, such as the development of MOOCs (massive online open courses), can bring education to potentially marginalised groups. Other initiatives also aim to reach such groups, for instance The Rockefeller Foundation's Digital Jobs Africa initiative, which aims to give computer-based training to one million disadvantaged young people over seven years in six African countries.[3]
- Moving away from single-subject and single-institution learning can enhance flexibility and resilience in a labour market that is increasingly globally integrated and competitive. There is a growing trend towards receiving training in multiple institutions throughout the world, and to mix disciplines. So for instance business graduates might study engineering, or natural scientists might study anthropology, and so on.
- Education should involve lifelong learning. In a world of high unemployment and fast-evolving technology, people need to constantly renew their skills and keep themselves informed if they are to stay employable. The shift towards a knowledge economy and technological advances increase the need for specific skills, especially as middle-level jobs are increasingly being automated (Chapter 3). These trends increase the demand for specialised tertiary education and lifelong learning.

- Resilient livelihoods require a myriad of pathways for skill acquisition. Access to information technologies is of the utmost importance for livelihoods, with increased mobility of the workforce and opportunities for employers and workers to reach out to the world for the right match. Many ICT-enabled learning platforms are currently being developed through private, public and joint efforts. However, what is lacking is an integrated platform that brings together a variety of education and training systems, as well as career mentoring systems. This would give individuals the opportunity to take personalised training courses, as well as to find out about job markets and the latest career opportunities. Participants at the Bellagio seminar proposed an online tutor and career mentor, "Plato", to create such a resource (Box 5.5).[4]

**Box 5.5. Visionaries at work: Plato – an online tutor and career mentor for everyone?**

Plato would be a worldwide platform offering a personalised tutor that guides and supports the individual in lifelong learning and career development. Enabled by IT, Plato's goal would be to provide all people with knowledge, networks, and skills to make a living throughout their lives in a changing world.

The Plato concept is an attempt to respond to the need for inclusion in education and work opportunities, the need for constant re-skilling to keep up with technological advancement, and the need for career management in an evolving global labour market. It would be an online personal and lifelong tutor and career guide for all. It would serve as an educational tool, but also as a guide on educational and work opportunities worldwide. Plato is not meant to substitute the formal educational system, but rather to supplement it by providing personalised assistance and reaching out to people who do not have access to the formal educational system. It would require, however, access to broadband and some basic training in using the platform. This issue would have to be overcome to ensure access to all.

*Plato for education*

As an educational tool, Plato would only require a tablet and Internet connection. Once online, Plato could offer all kinds of educational courses, ranging from pre-school to senior skills renewal. Plato could be used in schools as an audio-visual aid offering educational games and songs, personalised trial and error exercises, or as a testing device to check and evaluate children's progress. Although there are already many educational games, songs, films, and online tests available, many are dispersed around the Internet. Plato would centralise the best of these resources and help people to find the material that is most adapted to them. Some courses might be free, others would charge a fee.

Instructors and teachers could use Plato as a teaching tool. Although this requires instructors to have a minimum computer literacy and creativity in their teaching methods, access to teaching material and resources through Plato could tremendously improve their educational effectiveness. Where there is a lack of instructors or school coverage, such as in developing countries, children could be given Plato for self-learning. In such cases, Plato could be configured to have basic education courses already installed for children, in this way already ensuring a minimum level of educational material.

*Plato for career management*

Plato could also serve as a global career guidance tool. Depending on interest, competence and ambitions, Plato would offer questionnaires and search engines that lead to suggestions for career and education paths. Plato could provide information on different kinds of jobs that exist, statistics on recruitment and necessary skills or qualifications, and recent trends in different geographical locations. It could also give experienced and senior people information on new skills required to pursue or change their career. This could enhance the mobility of workers who are willing to move overseas.

## *Learning should involve livelihood skills*

There is a pressing need to build awareness of livelihood sustainability, risks and resilience-building strategies among young people across the world. A global effort is necessary at the primary and secondary school levels to make young people more aware of livelihoods-related problems and possible solutions. This will require major media mobilisation across all channels, from traditional ones such as TV and the press to the Internet and social media.

Education should also be reformed to build basic capacity for livelihood maintenance and improvement – to help them meet their basic needs and cope with diverse challenges of a financial, social or environmental nature. This need inspired the idea of a Global Open University for Livelihoods during the Bellagio meeting (Box 5.6). This university would be designed as a virtual open platform to which all participants can contribute and share their experience. The first step in implementing this might be to start with a pilot involving a few key establishments and partners.

**Box 5.6. Visionaries at work: The Global Open University for Livelihoods**

The core idea of a Global Open University for Livelihoods is to diffuse information to anyone in the world on how to secure and improve their livelihoods. It would fundamentally be a virtual university, based on a network of key academic establishments that support its development. The university would revolve around three basic functions: education, research and advice.

Most of the teaching would be through teleconferencing and Internet-based information and courses following a MOOCs approach. Students can be both individuals and communities, although communities are particularly important. Face-to-face programmes and on-site training could also be organised by establishments involved in the network. Key materials are concrete experiences that have proven their efficiency. Topics are organised to meet the needs of different target groups: e.g. the rural poor, inhabitants of urban slums, migrants, and jobless people. For instance it might focus on skills that can reinforce individuals' resilience, such as recycling, home energy efficiency, better nutrition and health habits etc., as well as how to access and benefit from formal and informal jobs and social protection schemes. Both developed and developing countries would be covered. Certificates would be provided to students who have completed a defined cycle.

Participants could develop projects around the courses they attend. They might pay a fee to benefit from some coaching or on-site advice. Partnerships could be established with international (and national) organisations involved in relevant fields, such as Ashoka, the international social entrepreneur network (discussed in Chapter 3). Funding could be sought from foundations and international organisations.

## *Livelihood portfolios can ensure inclusive livelihoods*

As full employment becomes an illusion for an increasing number of people, even in advanced economies, regulations and policies will need to change the way labour markets operate. Flexibility is key for helping people to adapt to rapidly changing job opportunities and conditions. Measures for promoting "livelihood portfolios" (see Scenario 5 in Chapter 4) made up of part-time work, paid training, and unemployment benefits can help individuals cope with fluid job situations. Longer working lives will also be necessary to accommodate ageing trends.

Although labour legislation is strongly influenced by country-specific cultures, values and traditions, there are lessons to be drawn from some Northern European countries.[5] Their experience shows that it is possible to maintain a dynamic labour market which provides enterprises with great flexibility to adapt employment to business cycles, while individuals benefit from broad support, including effective training to adapt their skills to market needs. This so-called "flexicurity" model has been particularly successful in Denmark.

**Table 5.1. The impact of cash transfer programmes in a range of developing countries**

| | |
|---|---|
| Mexico | In 2012, cash transfer beneficiaries (*Opportunidades* programme) spent 26% of transfers on productive investments, especially livestock and micro-enterprises. |
| Brazil | The *Bolsa Familia* cash transfer programme enabled beneficiaries to increase their labour participation by 2.6% compared with non-beneficiaries. |
| Kenya | Income in the local economy increased by KES 1.58 for every KES 1 transferred through the OVC cash transfer programme. |
| South Africa | Recipients of cash transfers increased job seeking efforts and migration and were more successful in finding employment than non-recipients. |
| India | Public works created a multiplier of 1.77 in the wider economy for every dollar transferred. |
| Mozambique | Business was stimulated among the local traders surrounding transfer dispensing offices under the social transfer programme GAPVU. |
| Bangladesh | Cash transfers under BRAC (the Bangladesh Rural Advancement Committee) increased GDP by 1.15%, while its costs were 0.2% of GDP. |

*Note:* KES – Kenyan shilling.

*Source:* Adapted from Slater, R. (2008), *Cash Transfers, Social Protection and Poverty Reduction (Draft)*, working paper, Overseas Development Institute (ODI), London, www.odi.org/publications/2738-cash-transfers-social-protection-poverty-reduction.

To achieve this will require good co-ordination among different government departments: employment and social affairs, education and training, as well as local development. Livelihood portfolios would also be supported through the following actions:

- ***Stepping up social protection.*** The need for the significant adaptation of social protection systems is a feature of all five scenarios in Chapter 4. Social protection needs are increasing all over the world. Yet, in developed countries and highly indebted states, social protection is being cut back because of fiscal constraints and pressures. Action is needed to get the private sector and individuals to share some of the cost burden.
- ***A basic income for all in developed countries.*** This sum would be paid to people regardless of their status or employment situation. This is obviously a very challenging proposal, but it makes sense in more than one scenario explored in Chapter 4 (e.g. Scenario 5: creative societies). The approach might be affordable in high-income countries and in some well-organised middle-income countries. It could be introduced gradually in high-income countries by building on and rationalising existing welfare programmes and expenditures – with the minimum

basic income being part of the livelihood portfolios described above. However, the establishment of social support systems including a basic income for all would require a general reorganisation of tax systems, including the introduction of a negative income tax: a progressive income tax system where people earning below a certain amount receive a supplement from the government instead of paying taxes to the government (Friedman, 2002).[6]

- ***Cash transfer programmes for developing countries.*** An effective approach in medium and low-income countries is the use of large-scale cash transfer programmes. These involve lump sum payments to individuals who meet certain conditions, such as sending their children to school. When well-designed and managed, these cash transfer programmes can have a significant impact on livelihoods and economies (Table 5.1).

## *Investing in key age groups will pay dividends*

It appears of crucial importance to provide support to the entire cohort of certain critical age groups. For example, it is vital that young children receive basic health care, nutrition, and education (Figure 5.1). Deprivation in early childhood has many negative consequences for future well-being. Children who lack basic nutrition and healthcare do poorly in school, and are more likely to drop out. Gaps in skills open early. A study has shown that poor children are already at a vocabulary disadvantage by the age of six. Alleviating the worst effects of poverty and deprivation, and breaking the intergenerational cycle of poverty, gives children a better chance.

**Figure 5.1. When investments in life capabilities occur earlier, future prospects are better**

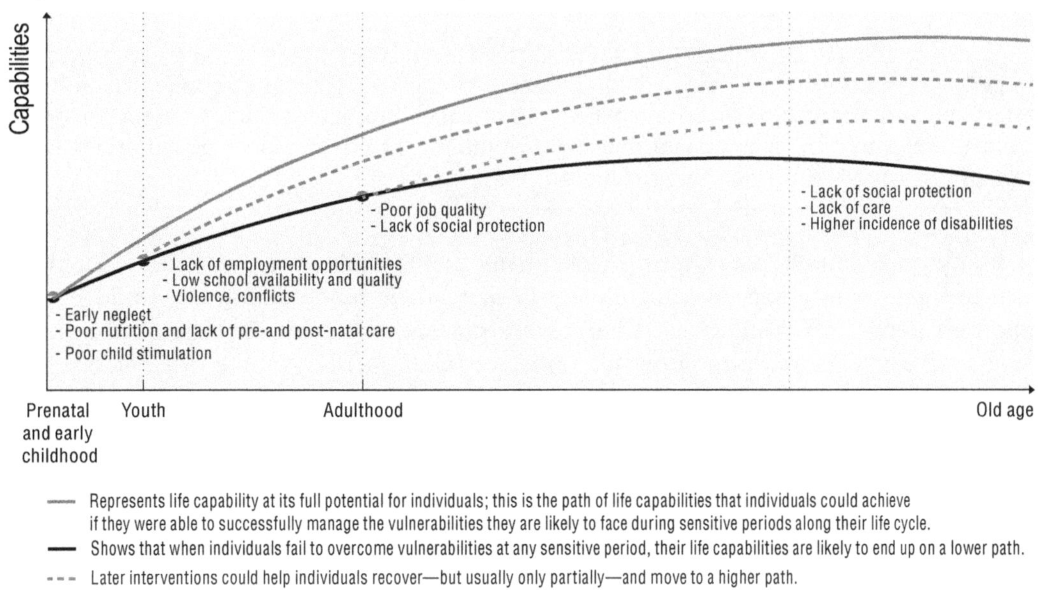


*Source:* UNDP (2014), *The 2014 Human Development Report – Sustaining Human Progress: Reducing Vulnerabilities and Building Resilience*, Human Development Report Office, United Nations Development Programme, New York, http://hdr.undp.org/sites/default/files/hdr14-report-en-1.pdf.

Youth (age 15-24) is another key stage of life which can influence future livelihoods. What young people learn in school and the skills they acquire will have a major impact on their lifelong career. However, the young are particularly affected by unemployment – almost three times the adult rate (Chapter 3).

Investing in young people is critical and brings high returns for social and economic development (UNDP, 2014). The youth bulge in developing countries offers an unprecedented opportunity to enhance human capital to create a large, well-educated and potentially productive labour force. Failing to seize this opportunity represents a considerable loss of potential that not only threatens economic progress, but also raises the risk of social unrest. One controversial scheme, which could – together with other initiatives – help unleash the potential of global youth could involve a universal self-investment grant for young people (Box 5.7). This idea emerged in Bellagio and would need much more thinking through before it could be implemented. However, the core ideas could be adapted for other possible initiatives.

**Box 5.7. Visionaries at work: A universal self-investment grant for young people?**

Personal self-investment grants offered to the entire youth age cohort (ages 15-24) would be a way of investing in young people and at the same time making them more responsible for their own lives. This would enable young people to make their own decisions on the use of these grants.

The grant conditions could vary by a country or locality's characteristics, but might include linking grant payment to school completion. This would function as a non-reimbursable scholarship grant, which imposes the condition of school completion. Alternatively, countries might prefer to apply a completely universal, unconditional grant.

The size of the grant will also depend on each country. Grant amounts could vary depending on per capita income or else they could be fixed amounts. They could also take the form of a lottery in countries with financial constraints. The financial resources needed for such a system could be supported by international financial institutions, or private donor organisations in the form of private-public partnership programmes.

Many other innovative support mechanisms are possible. For example, reducing the costs charged to migrants to send money back to their home countries would have an important impact on livelihoods. Charges are currently as high as 10% of the amount being sent. The G20 is working on this initiative (G20, 2014). Another idea is to provide a kind of "key person insurance" for large family structures that are supported by one person whose death or disability could be financially devastating. More generally, there is a need to develop better non-government insurance and pension mechanisms to support people in the informal economy.

***People's creativity, boosted by new technologies, requires appropriate support***

The new "Industrial Revolution" offers considerable opportunities for the public at large to express its creativity and contribute to the development of new activities and jobs. Today anyone with an innovative idea can download files for services that can manufacture products in various quantities, and people can even manufacture items themselves thanks to 3D printers. A new 'age of makers' has come (Anderson, 2012).

Governments should rethink their innovation policy support accordingly. In addition to the support they traditionally provide to high tech inventions coming from advanced laboratories in universities or industry, there is a need to provide support to a large basis of potential innovators operating in schools, factories, or garages. There is a need to multiply innovation workshops, such as the so-called "FabLabs", along with efficient business incubators in which innovators can find commercial, technical, legal and other forms of assistance. This action should be implemented through close co-operation with local and city authorities (see section below). Some governments in OECD countries have already set up schemes to stimulate and reward bright ideas coming from people and organisations at large, e.g. the UK government with the Nesta foundation.

This trend is supported by the growth of crowd-funding (see Box 5.8), which is dramatically changing the conditions in which individuals and communities can fund the development of their ideas and projects. The crow-funding movement is increasingly spreading in developing countries and may dramatically change the innovation landscape in those countries, along with the rapid expansion of mobile services that are impacting commerce and finance and other sectors, such as health.

**Box 5.8. Crowdfunding is gaining influence**

Crowdfunding was given a boost in the wake of the financial crisis as a way for entrepreneurs to raise capital in a context where banks were less willing to lend. It enables entrepreneurs to raise funds in the form of donations or investments from multiple individuals. Kick-starter, for instance – the market leader in pledge or donation-based crowdfunding – has channelled over USD 815 million from 4.9 million individual donors throughout the world since 2009.

Crowdfunding has so far developed in more advanced economies, as it requires some enabling factors, such as a regulatory environment, social media market penetration and Internet availability, a regulated online marketplace that facilitates capital formation, and collaboration with other entrepreneurial events and hubs including business plan competitions, incubators and academic institutions.

However, crowdfunding could also become a useful tool in those developing countries, particularly emerging economies, where the right conditions are in place. Crowdfunding offers the potential to leapfrog the traditional capital market structures and financial regulatory regimes of developed countries. In China, for instance, crowdfunding could reach USD 50 billion by 2025.

It is estimated that there are now up to 344 million households in the developing world that are able to make small crowdfund investments in community businesses. These households have an income of at least USD 10 000 a year, and at least three months of savings or three months savings in equity holdings. Together, they have the ability to deploy up to USD 96 billion a year by 2025 in crowdfunding investments.

*Source*: infoDev (2013), Crowdfunding's Potential for the Developing World, Information for Development Program, The World Bank, Washington DC, www.infodev.org/infodev-files/wb_crowdfundingreport-v12.pdf.

## *Green growth underpins resilient livelihoods*

While global agreement is needed to create a framework for tackling climate change, it is action at the national and local level that will make much of the difference. The adaptation to, and mitigation of, climate change require large and varied efforts.

The Global Commission on Economy and Climate (2014) lists priorities for action, including:

- *Constructing greener cities:* they would be cheaper to build, and this would be particularly important in the developing world, overwhelmed by rural migrants.

Well-designed eco-cities would offer better quality of life, provide jobs, and help in the fight against climate change (see the next section).

- *Repairing farmland:* feeding a world of 8 billion in 2030 will be a challenge. Increasing the productivity of existing agricultural land will be key. It is estimated that if one eighth of the world's degraded agricultural land were restored using modern techniques, it could feed 200 million more people and reduce greenhouse gas emissions. The proposal for a Green Revolution 2.0 responds to this objective (Box 5.9).
- *Developing renewable energy sources:* the costs of producing renewable energy, especially solar and wind power, have fallen rapidly. Low-carbon energy could account for more than 50% of global electricity generation within the next 15 years. The fall in oil prices, however, driven by the development of shale oil in North America, has disrupted this transition towards a low-carbon economy. It is nevertheless essential to keep moving in this direction. More efforts are also needed in energy saving and efficiency, and improving the energy productivity of economies.
- *Reducing fossil fuel subsidies:* globally, fossil fuel subsidies amount to USD 600 billion, while subsidies for clean energy amount only to USD 100 billion. Subsidies need to be switched from supporting fossil fuels to supporting clean energy. However, at the same time lowering the cost of energy for the poor in the developing world is vital. Subsidy reform must therefore be accompanied by appropriate compensation to avoid damaging livelihoods. Otherwise it could be a source of major social unrest and political disturbance, as already experienced in a number of countries.
- *Funding a low-carbon world through green bonds:* the lack of public financing and support for low-carbon infrastructure means that capital is not allocated to sustainable infrastructure, including low-carbon transport and industries. Financial instruments such as green bonds and risk sharing using public-private partnership programmes could significantly cut the cost of capital for sustainable growth. Green bonds are high-rated and generally tax-exempt bonds, which are issued by public authorities or international financial institutions for the development of low-carbon infrastructure.[7]

### Box 5.9. Visionaries at work: A new livelihood-focused Green Revolution?

The Green Revolution more than doubled cereal production in developing nations between 1960 and 1985, with yields of rice, maize, and wheat rising steadily during that period. At its core was the development by agronomists of novel wheat, maize and rice cultivars generally referred to as HYVs or "high-yielding varieties", which significantly out-perform traditional varieties in the presence of adequate irrigation, pesticides, and fertilisers (especially synthetic nitrogen fertilisers).

The results were impressive, especially in Asia where cereal self-sufficiency was attained at a national level by many countries despite soaring populations. India even became a rice exporter. The Green Revolution was supported by a coalition of foundations, bilateral and multilateral donors, and substantial World Bank funding for fertiliser plants and fertiliser import programmes. It had its own *ad hoc* institutions, such as the Consultative Group on International Agricultural Research (CGIAR), which federated research institutes working on HYVs across the world.

**Box 5.9. Visionaries at work: A new livelihood-focused Green Revolution? (*cont.*)**

Spectacularly successful as it has been in terms of boosting food supplies across the developing world, the Green Revolution did not focus on livelihoods *per se*. In fact, the increased level of mechanisation on larger farms made possible by the Green Revolution removed a significant source of employment from the rural economy. The monocultural system associated with HYVs caused the polycultural system associated with traditional varieties, and smallholder agriculture at large, to recede in many places. Local self-sufficiency decreased, while dependency on energy, purchased seeds and other inputs, and third party logistic services increased – generally accompanied by an increased dependency on credit. This, as well as lower food prices due to the vastly increased production volumes, often led to economic difficulties for smallholder farmers and landless farm workers, leaving many of them with rural-urban migration as their only livelihood alternative.

The major emerging labour market, fiscal, energy, environmental and climate challenges ask for a greater emphasis in agriculture on the concept of livelihoods, including on job creation and greater self-sufficiency as well as livelihood resilience. Could a possible successor to the Green Revolution – in the form of a Green Revolution 2.0 – be the way forward?

New technologies that could have hardly been imagined at the time of the Green Revolution could provide a path towards a Green Revolution 2.0. The new technological factor at the heart of the Green Revolution 2.0 is "information": using information for (1) adapting new agricultural business models to local soil, water, and social conditions; and (2) optimising these models for the highest possible performance and efficiency.

In this respect, a Green Revolution 2.0 would be a logical offspring of the ICT revolution that has changed the world over the last 30 years. What's more, many of these technologies have become, or are rapidly becoming, affordable even at a village or community of villages level, in large part thanks to the zero marginal cost, economy-of-sharing features that many of them display.

These new technologies and approaches could make several contributions towards the objective of improved, more robust and resilient livelihoods by:

- increasing food production on existing farms, using technologies that contribute to drought and disease-resistant crops and adding to the Green Revolution's achievements on the cereal front
- re-developing more localised, self-sufficient and resilient agricultural ecologies, for cereal and non-cereal crops alike. At an extreme, they could mark the return of, or a move towards, smallholder agriculture, garden plots, and more autonomous community agriculture
- creating more local jobs through (1) the more intensive, fine-tuned nature of the type of agricultural production and work involved, and (2) employment in related activities such as renewable energy services, 3D printing, seed management, metering and billing, fertiliser mix optimisation, hydroponic systems maintenance, and drone servicing.

In this sense, the Green Revolution 2.0 would be more intensely livelihoods-focused than its predecessor. It would help individuals, families and communities support themselves by providing scope for new jobs and more food resources now, while increasing their local food self-sufficiency and resilience (including through a wider diversity of crops) over the long haul.

## Local initiatives are central to inclusive and resilient livelihoods

While support at the national level is needed, it is increasingly up to individuals and communities to take action and experiment with options for making their livelihoods more resilient. The scenario exercise in Chapter 4 illustrated how anticipatory and preparatory action may reduce the negative effects of crises on livelihoods. It also showed how creative individuals can evolve societies towards new and potentially more sustainable and inclusive forms of living and working. Some such initiatives are already occurring on a small scale, in both developed and developing countries, as described in this section.

### *New ways of organising the local economy should be encouraged*

Social and solidarity-based forms of economy (as opposed to capitalism) are key in the new and adaptive regimes that are gradually taking shape, as noted in scenarios 4 and 5 in Chapter 4. In France, for instance, it is estimated that the *économie sociale et solidaire* (socially and solidarity-oriented economy) represents 6 to 8% of GDP and about 10% of private sector employment (Le Nouvel Observateur, 2014). Key drivers of this social economy are "social entrepreneurs", who introduce a wealth of services, notably for the poor, the disabled, and the marginalised. But wealthy people can also benefit from creativity and engagement. Governments can do much to facilitate and encourage their activities through fiscal arrangements (including for those who benefit from their activities – their employees as well as their clients). They can also help to scale up their operations when successful.

Another area that deserves particular attention for livelihoods is the development of a "barter, experience or share economy" – described in Scenarios 3, 4 and 5 in Chapter 4. Structuring and regulating these new forms of economy, with clear rules of the game for the demand and offer of services and conditions of transactions, will be important as the market expands. The ageing of populations in the developed world offers opportunities for the development of new, local activities adapted to the needs of older people in health care and leisure (among other things). There are also opportunities to take advantage of knowledge and know how accumulated from people with a life-long professional experience. Transfer of experience can take place in the context of some forms of barter economy, while enterprises and organisations can establish internal mechanisms and incentives to facilitate inter-generational transfers of knowledge and know how. National and local traditions and culture will have important influences on these matters, and this will be reflected in related legislation.

On another front, it is important to promote trade-related innovations such as service marketplaces, which correspond well to aspirations and needs for open and flexible exchanges of work. This is an area that is currently booming for localised services, notably for specialised services such as Uber for taxi services, where rides are matched through a mobile phone application. Partly due to a lack of regulation, Uber can charge lower fees than some traditional taxi services.

A project proposed at Bellagio envisages an international service market place – a kind of eBay for services. It may develop as a global platform which brings together existing local services. It could possibly be developed through a public-private partnership. The public dimension would be useful as a way to introduce quality control and assurance, based on feedback from users.

### *Local financial initiatives can boost livelihoods*

The provision of micro-finance to people who want to develop their own businesses has proven to be a very efficient way of combatting unemployment. It can be much cheaper than the costs of supporting the unemployed through public services (Attali, 2014). New ways of accessing micro-finance range from the use of ICT platforms (such as M-Pesa, a mobile phone-based money transfer and micro financing service)[8] to new styles of group lending, micro savings, micro finance, crowdfunding (see Box 5.8) and local currencies.

Key challenges are to develop mechanisms for funding start-ups that cater to the needs of low-income populations as well as new technology ventures, both of which have trouble attracting traditional finance. Venture philanthropy funds, although still modest in volume, offer interesting possibilities from this viewpoint and could be boosted by appropriate tax incentives. These funds, managed in a professional manner, finance an increasing number of projects in developing countries, with a fair rate of success (IFC, 2013).

The development of local and complementary currencies can also be a useful way to improve the resilience of local economies. Local currencies are used among defined communities (cities, enterprises affiliated to a specific sector, or network, etc.), and complement traditional money for specific uses. Some analysts consider this the best way to stay away from the turbulences and crises inherent to the globalised financial system (Lietaer, 2001). There are currently more than 5 000 such local currencies operating throughout the world. A number of international complementary currencies, such as the "Bitcoin", are also growing in importance.

Some local, complementary currencies have been in operation for almost a century. This is the case of the Swiss WIR, a currency established in the 1930s at the time of the Great Depression, and which is now used by more than 60 000 enterprises. It helps in transactions among various actors involved in the production and delivery chains, facilitating conditions of payment, notably when economic conditions are tense. This system is considered to have played a critical role in smoothing the functioning of the Swiss economy during times of crisis. Some governments have promoted the development of such systems nationwide, e.g. in Uruguay, in order to strengthen the small and medium-sized enterprise sector. Local currencies are particularly adapted to local exchanges between individuals and providers of local products and services.

### *Social impact investments should be scaled up*

When state budgets are tight, efficient public-private partnerships (PPPs) can help mobilise private and business money for better-managed investments, thanks to greater experience in business practices. PPPs have traditionally been used for large infrastructure projects, but are increasingly getting involved in smaller scale operations with social purposes, through "social impact investments". These involve private businesses investing in public interest activities against the promise of being repaid later by high-return social bonds funded by public authorities. They have proved very useful in certain countries, such as the UK for improving public services, including prisons, with a guarantee of efficiency and effectiveness and best value for money. This approach could be encouraged for improving many services and infrastructure that concern basic needs and are crucial to poor and deprived populations, e.g. health care, shelter, sanitation, and possibly education. They can apply also to the environment, in the form of "green bonds" (see discussion in previous section).

## *Cities of the future should be green and resilient*

As noted in Chapter 3, 60% of the world's population is likely to be living in urban areas by 2030, and developing countries will see the greatest urbanisation growth. However, in many cases, urban growth is poorly managed, generating significant economic and social costs in providing infrastructure and basic services, along with problems linked to air pollution, inefficient energy consumption, increasing social exclusion, etc. (see Chapter 3).

Green cities address both issues – economic activity and environmental systems – at the same time. Cities are critical drivers of economic growth, being where most jobs are created. The building of such eco or green cities in the developing world would be of crucial importance, as discussed in Chapter 4. Drawing on the experience accumulated in a number of countries from various parts of the world, it is recommended to draw up plans for renovating cities in developing countries – as well as for building new "eco cities" that would respond to their ecological challenges and create a significant amount of activities and jobs for large contingents of people, particularly youth entering the labour markets and rural migrants.

Some measures can enhance resilience, reduce emissions, and boost jobs and growth at the same time. For example, investment in green space and efficient waste management bolsters climate resilience, absorbs carbon, and enhances the attractiveness of cities to global talent and capital. While the benefits of economic density have to be balanced against the potential risks of increased exposure to shocks such as climate hazards (Rockefeller Foundation and USAID, n.d.), there is evidence that more compact, connected and better co-ordinated cities can also be more resilient (see, for example, OECD, 2013b). In that respect, The Rockefeller Foundation's "100 Resilient Cities" project provides an interesting example of a global network of cities aiming at developing a roadmap to resilience.[9]

With the rising incidence of climate-related hazards impacting urban areas, it is crucial that cities invest in enhancing their resilience to ensure they can withstand the shocks of future extreme events, minimise the damages, and recover quickly. Coastal cities are at particularly great risk. The OECD analysed the climate risks faced by the 136 port cities globally with more than a million residents in 2005, and found they had about US$3 trillion worth of assets at risk in 2005, or about 5% of global GDP that year; by the 2070s, that is expected to rise to US$35 trillion, or 9% of projected global GDP. The most exposed cities as of 2005, the study found, were Mumbai and Kolkata in India; Guangzhou and Shanghai in China; Miami, Greater New York and New Orleans in the US; Ho Chi Minh City in Vietnam; Osaka-Kobe in Japan, and Alexandria in Egypt (OECD, 2013b). Sound urban management can reduce vulnerability to climate hazards – for example, through better planning to restrict development in the most exposed locations. Transport systems, utilities (e.g. energy, water) and buildings also need to be made more resilient, and basic infrastructure such as sewers needs to be well maintained.

Some cities, driven largely by the use of technologies, are already starting to show examples of greener growth. Smart transport systems are developing. Bus Rapid Transit systems, for example, allow for the redistribution of road space in favour of buses through dedicated bus lanes, pre-boarding ticketing and custom-designed stations. They can reduce traffic congestion, carbon emissions and air pollution. They have already been introduced in 160 cities including Bogotá, Guangzhou (China), Ahmedabad (India). Other innovations include electric and hybrid buses, an electric taxi fleet, and car sharing (The Global Commission on the Economy and Climate, 2014).

### *Citizens should be engaged in policy-making processes*

Citizen trust in government action has to be rebuilt in many countries. A good way forward is to engage citizens themselves in game-changing actions. The impressive development of philanthropic activities in which individual donors are actively involved in the targeting and control of the use of their funds, show the potential benefits of such engagement. There are many areas where such mobilisation can take place, as long as people can see tangible results from their engagement.

A key level for this is precisely the city level. By adopting new practices that first demonstrate to citizens the value of their actions and secondly have "contagious" positive effects on the wider community, they can help to solve many local issues, from health care to crime prevention and environmental management. A good example occurred in Bogotá in the late 1990s. Citizens took part very efficiently in coping with water shortages caused by damage to a water tunnel feeding a large part of the city, thanks to diverse water saving practices inspired by creative campaigns launched by the municipal authorities (World Bank, 2014).

Communities can work in close collaboration with a range of government departments, in a well co-ordinated manner. Joint efforts may include income earning and learning centres where individual can collaborate and contribute towards work for all. Volunteer work options, in which individuals receive government subsidies for some social contributions to society, include planting village gardens, improving infrastructure, restoring ecosystems, or tutoring on job creation schemes.

**A call for action**

The challenges ahead are considerable: youth bulges in developing countries, ageing populations in developed countries, rising unemployment in many parts of the world, increasing inequalities, persisting financial fragilities, enduring or new conflicts, accelerating climate change; all these trends will dramatically affect livelihoods in the coming decades. However, at the same time they could also be turned into opportunities for innovation, through attempts and experiments to find better ways of coping with challenges and difficulties. Such innovations or experiments could be technological but also social, implying new modes of consumption and production, and new forms of organisations or institutions.

There is a need for all relevant players – international, national, local – to move forward and prepare to ensure a better future for livelihoods. At policymaking level, foresight and scenario exercises can be a useful and powerful tool to make practitioners more aware of the broader challenges and opportunities, and encourage them to imagine appropriate policy responses and strategies that could be later implemented and scaled up.

Policy experimentation will often be necessary, especially for the bolder and more controversial actions. New schemes can be piloted, new approaches can be tested, and new instruments can be prototyped with specific groups, in "living labs" and other places. Rigorous methods, inspired by behavioural sciences, are available today for conducting economic and social experiments, including some on a large scale, to ensure the appropriateness of policy approaches.

Once experiments have proven the validity and utility of new ideas, it should be easier to scale them up. Success stories should help convince institutions and established powers to commit to necessary funding and take regulatory and legal measures needed for transformational change. This would be facilitated if coalitions of change makers have been built, including at the international and global level.

It is in this way that true transformative approaches can take shape and improve, increase, protect, or save the livelihoods of people around the world. Billions of individuals are affected: the poor but also the richer classes; in the developing world but also in the developed. It is in the self-interest of both major and minor players to take action and lead the way. There is plenty to be done and many places to start. Coalitions of interested stakeholders should come together to start this process. Others will catch up and the momentum will grow.

## Notes

1. See more at www.gavi.org.
2. WISE (the World Innovation Summit for Education) offers a wealth of good practices across the developing world (see www.wise-qatar.org). Such experiences cover many fields: efficient ways to provide places for poor children in primary and secondary schools, the provision of minimal education to migrants and displaced people, the mobilisation of schools to solve local community issues and develop vital skills, etc.
3. See www.rockefellerfoundation.org/our-work/current-work/digital-jobs-africa/impact-sourcing for more details on the initiative.
4. The name is inspired by a pioneering initiative of a computerized teaching system developed in the 1960s at the Illinois University, and entitled "Programmed Logic for Automatic Teaching Operations" (Plato). The concept and tool were further refined by the Control Data Corporation, and tested in the US and South Africa. The latest incarnation appeared online in 2004 (Source: Wikipedia, accessed 22 January 2015).
5. See www.lasselehtinen.net/content/view/149/100/lang,en.
6. For an interesting discussion on the idea of a basic income for all, see the following article in The New York Times: http://economix.blogs.nytimes.com/2013/12/10/rethinking-the-idea-of-a-basic-income-for-all.
7. See http://treasury.worldbank.org/cmd/htm/WorldBankGreenBonds.html for the World Bank's Green Bonds, for example.
8. M-Pesa (M for mobile, pesa for money in Swahili) was launched in Kenya and Tanzania in 2007 by Vodafone for Safaricom and Vodacom, the largest mobile network operators in the two countries (Saylor, 2012).
9. See www.100resilientcities.org.

# *References*


Anderson, C. (2012), *Makers: The New Industrial Revolution*, Pearson, 2012.

Attali, J. (ed.) (2014), *Pour une Économie Positive*, La Documentation Française, Paris.

Chen, H., et al. (2013), "Exploring China's transboundary water treaty practice through the prism of the UN Watercourses Convention", in *Water International, Special Issue: The 1997 UN Watercourses Convention – What Relevance in the 21st Century?* Vol. 38, Issue 2, 2013, Taylor and Francis, Oxfordshire, www.tandfonline.com/doi/abs/10.1080/02508060.2013.782134#.VMde1nCsX3o.

Clark C. (2012), "How to keep markets safe in the era of high-speed trading", *Essays on Issues*, The Federal Reserve Bank of Chicago, Chicago, October 2012, No. 303. www.chicagofed.org/digital_assets/publications/chicago_fed_letter/2012/cfloctober2012_303.pdf.

DARPA (n.d.), Defense Advanced Research Projects Agency website, www.darpa.mil (accessed 21 January 2015).

Evenett S., (2014), *The Global Trade Disorder: The 16th GTA Report*, Centre for Economic Policy Research, London, www.globaltradealert.org/16th_GTA_report.

Feenstra, R.C. (2003), *Advanced International Trade Theory and Evidence*, Princeton University Press, New Jersey, http://press.princeton.edu/titles/7608.html.

Friedman, Milton (2002), *Capitalism and Freedom: Fortieth Anniversary Edition*, University of Chicago Press, Chicago, pp. 192-194, http://press.uchicago.edu/ucp/books/book/chicago/C/bo3613452.html.

G20 (2014), *G20 Plan to Facilitate Remittance Flows*, G20, September 2014, www.g20.org/sites/default/files/g20_resources/library/g20_plan_facilitate_remittance_flows.pdf.

The Global Commission on the Economy and Climate (2014), *Better Growth Better Climate: The New Climate Economy Report - Synthesis Report,* New Climate Economy, Washington DC, http://static.newclimateeconomy.report/wp-content/uploads/2014/08/NCE_GlobalReport.pdf.

Grueber, M. et al. (2014), 2014 Global R&D Funding Forecast, Battelle R&D Magazine, December 2013, Colombus OH, www.battelle.org/docs/tpp/ 2014_global_rd_funding_forecast.pdf.

Iati, R. (10 July 2009), "The real story of trading software espionage", Information Week website, www.wallstreetandtech.com/trading-technology/the-real-story-of-trading-software-espionage/a/d-id/1262125?.

IFC (2013), *The Power of Partnerships*: *Annual Report 2013*, International Finance Corporation, The World Bank Group, Washington DC, www.ifc.org/wps/wcm/connect/d020aa004112357a8975fffe5679ec46/AR2013_Full_Report.pdf?MOD=AJPERES.

infoDev (2013), *Crowdfunding's Potential for the Developing World*, Information for Development Program, The World Bank, Washington DC, www.infodev.org/infodev-files/wb_crowdfundingreport-v12.pdf.

IOSC (2011), *Regulatory Issues Raised by the Impact of Technological Changes on Market Integrity and Efficiency - Consultation Report*, International Organization of Securities Commissions, Madrid, www.iosco.org/library/pubdocs/pdf/IOSCOPD354.pdf.

Lietaer, B. (2001), *The Future of Money: Creating New Wealth, Work, and a Wiser World*, Random House, London, http://library.uniteddiversity.coop/Money_and_Economics/The_Future_of_Money-Bernard_Lietaer.pdf.

Lin, T. (2014), *The New Financial Industry*, 65 Alabama Law Review 567, Temple University Legal Studies Research Paper No. 2014-11, Philadelphia PA, http://papers.ssrn.com/sol3/papers.cfm?abstract_id=2417988.

Le Nouvel Observateur (2014), "L'Autre Économie", *Le Nouvel Observateur*, Hors-série Société n°2 - 03/14.

Norton (2011), "Norton Cybercrime Report", Norton website, http://uk.norton.com/cybercrimereport (accessed 22 January 2015).

OECD (2015), *All on Board: Making Inclusive Growth Happen*, OECD Publishing, Paris, http://dx.doi.org/10.1787/9789264218512-en

OECD (2014), *Megatrends: Policies for a Shifting World,* Global Strategy Group, discussion notes for the second meeting of the OECD Global Strategy Group on 25-26 November 2014, OECD Publishing, Paris.

OECD (2013a), *Action Plan on Base Erosion and Profit Shifting*, OECD Publishing, Paris, http://dx.doi.org/10.1787/9789264202719-en.

OECD (2013b), *Green Growth in Cities*, OECD Green Growth Studies, OECD Publishing, Paris, http://dx.doi.org/10.1787/9789264195325-en.

OECD (2012a), *Systemic Financial Risk*, OECD Publishing, Paris, http://dx.doi.org/10.1787/9789264167711-en.

OECD (2012b), *Better Skills, Better Jobs, Better Lives: A Strategic Approach to Skills Policies*, OECD Publishing, Paris, http://dx.doi.org/10.1787/9789264177338-en.

OECD (2011a), *Future Global Shocks: Improving Risk Governance*, OECD Publishing, Paris, http://dx.doi.org/10.1787/9789264114586-en.

OECD (2011b), *Learning for Jobs: Pointers for Policy Development*, OECD Reviews of Vocational Education and Training, OECD, Paris, www.oecd.org/edu/skills-beyond-school/LearningForJobsPointersfor%20PolicyDevelopment.pdf.

OECD and World Bank (2014), *Making Innovation Policy Work: Learning from Experimentation*, OECD Publishing, Paris, http://dx.doi.org/10.1787/9789264185739-en.

Prahalad, C.K. (2006), *The Fortune at the Bottom of the Pyramid*, Prentice Hall, Upper Saddle River, New Jersey, http://books.google.fr/books/about/The_fortune_at_the_bottom_of_the_pyramid.html?id=R5ePu1awfloC.

The Rockefeller Foundation (2014), *Securing Livelihoods: Visions of a Better Future,* The Rockefeller Foundation, www.visionariesunbound.com/static/pdf/EIU-Rockefeller_Livelihoods report_Dec 2014.pdf.

Rockefeller Foundation and USAID (n.d.), Global Resilience Partnership website, www.globalresiliencepartnership.org.

Saylor, M. (2012), *The Mobile Wave: How Mobile Intelligence Will Change Everything*, Perseus Books/Vanguard Press, London, p. 304, http://michael.com/the-mobile-wave.

Slater, R. (2008), *Cash Transfers, Social Protection and Poverty Reduction (Draft)*, working paper, Overseas Development Institute (ODI), London, www.odi.org/publications/2738-cash-transfers-social-protection-poverty-reduction.

United Nations Conference on Environment and Development (1992), *United Nations Framework Convention on Climate Change (UNFCCC),* Rio de Janeiro, 3-14 June 1992, http://unfccc.int/resource/docs/convkp/conveng.pdf.

UNDP (2014), *The 2014 Human Development Report – Sustaining Human Progress:Reducing Vulnerabilities and Building Resilience*, Human Development Report Office, United Nations Development Programme, New York, http://hdr.undp.org/sites/default/files/hdr14-report-en-1.pdf.

UNECE (1992), *Convention on the Protection and Use of Transboundary Watercourses and International Lakes (Water Convention)*, United Nations Economic Commission for Europe, Helsinki, 17 March 1992, www.unece.org/fileadmin/DAM/env/documents/2013/wat/ECE_MP.WAT_41.pdf.

UNESCO (2007), *Finland Regional Preparatory Workshop on Inclusive Education, Eastern and South Eastern Europe*, UNESCO International Bureau of Education, Sinaia, Romania, 14-16 June 2007, www.ibe.unesco.org/fileadmin/user_upload/Inclusive_Education/Reports/sinaia_07/finland_inclusion_07.pdf.

UN General Assembly (1997), *United Nations Convention on the Law of the Non-navigational Uses of International Watercourses*, resolution 51/229 of 21 May 1997, www.internationalwaterlaw.org/documents/intldocs/watercourse_conv.html.

Van Atta, R. (2008), *Fifty Years of Innovation and Discovery*, Defence Advanced Research Projects Agency, Darlington VA, www.darpa.mil/WorkArea/DownloadAsset.aspx?id=2553.

Wolf, M. (2014), *The Shifts and the Shocks: What We've Learned – and Have Still to Learn – from the Financial Crisis,* Penguin Press, New York.

World Bank (2014), *World Development Report 2015: Mind, Society, and Behavior*, The World Bank Group, Washington DC, www.worldbank.org/content/dam/Worldbank/Publications/WDR/WDR 2015/WDR-2015-Full-Report.pdf.

Wouters, P. (2014), *Keeping Peace: China's Upstream Dilema*, China Water Risk, Hong Kong, http://chinawaterrisk.org/resources/analysis-reviews/keeping-peace-chinas-upstream-dilema.

# ORGANISATION FOR ECONOMIC CO-OPERATION AND DEVELOPMENT

The OECD is a unique forum where governments work together to address the economic, social and environmental challenges of globalisation. The OECD is also at the forefront of efforts to understand and to help governments respond to new developments and concerns, such as corporate governance, the information economy and the challenges of an ageing population. The Organisation provides a setting where governments can compare policy experiences, seek answers to common problems, identify good practice and work to co-ordinate domestic and international policies.

The OECD member countries are: Australia, Austria, Belgium, Canada, Chile, the Czech Republic, Denmark, Estonia, Finland, France, Germany, Greece, Hungary, Iceland, Ireland, Israel, Italy, Japan, Korea, Luxembourg, Mexico, the Netherlands, New Zealand, Norway, Poland, Portugal, the Slovak Republic, Slovenia, Spain, Sweden, Switzerland, Turkey, the United Kingdom and the United States. The European Commission takes part in the work of the OECD.

OECD Publishing disseminates widely the results of the Organisation's statistics gathering and research on economic, social and environmental issues, as well as the conventions, guidelines and standards agreed by its members.

# OECD DEVELOPMENT CENTRE

The OECD Development Centre was established in 1962 as an independent platform for knowledge sharing and policy dialogue between OECD member countries and developing economies, allowing these countries to interact on an equal footing. Today, 26 OECD countries and 21 non-OECD countries are members of the Centre. The Centre draws attention to emerging systemic issues likely to have an impact on global development and more specific development challenges faced by today's developing and emerging economies. It uses evidence-based analysis and strategic partnerships to help countries formulate innovative policy solutions to the global challenges of development.

For more information on the Centre and its members, please see *www.oecd.org/dev.*

OECD PUBLISHING, 2, rue André-Pascal, 75775 PARIS CEDEX 16
(41 2015 03 1 P) ISBN 978-92-64-23174-0 – 2015-05

www.ingramcontent.com/pod-product-compliance
Lightning Source LLC
Chambersburg PA
CBHW061216240926
51846CB00006B/1243
*9789264231740*